Scholarship Boy

SCHOLARSHIP BOY

A Personal History of the Mid-Twentieth Century

◆

J.F.C. Harrison

Rivers Oram Press
LONDON

First published in 1995 by
Rivers Oram Press
144 Hemingford Road, London N1 1DE

Published in the USA by Paul and Company
Post Office Box 442, Concord, MA 01742

Set in 11/13 Bembo by
Slater McCarthy Ronson, Southport
and printed in Great Britain by
T.J. Press (Padstow) Ltd, Padstow, Cornwall
This edition copyright © J.F.C. Harrison, 1995

British Library Cataloguing in Publication Data
A catalogue record for this book is available from
the British Library

ISBN 1–85489–072–7

For John, Thomas, James and Victoria

Contents

Acknowledgments

In a book as subjective as this one, it would be invidious to implicate others even by association. Nevertheless several people have helped to jog my memory, notably my sister Eileen Pickersgill about our childhood, Ted Ward about schooldays, and Joseph Henri Rey and René Rey about events in Mauritius. Christopher Tongue and Adrian Henstock patiently answered my queries concerning family and local history; and Jack Ravensdale recalled our days together in Cambridge. The manuscript was read in whole or in part by Malcolm Chase, Roy and Gwen Shaw, Tom Caldwell and Richard Harrison, and I have profited greatly from their comments. Many of the experiences recorded here have been shared, and all discussed with my wife Margaret. The conventional thanks for help and encouragement would be totally inadequate to express my debt to the loved one with whom I have shared every aspect of life for the past fifty years. Without her these things would not have been possible.

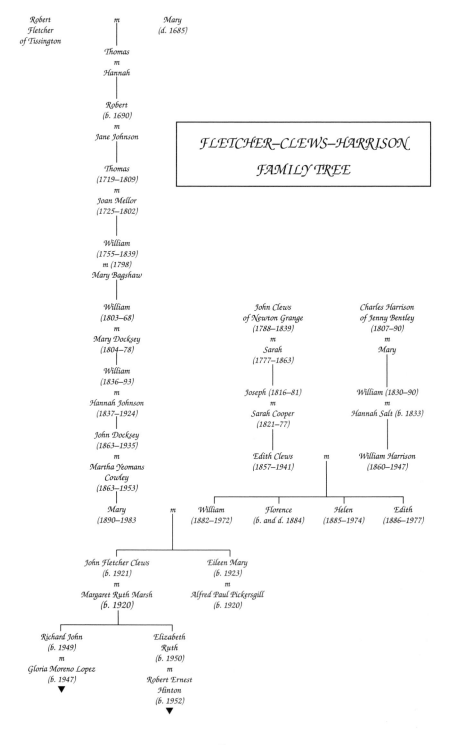

Robert
Fletcher
of Tissington
m
Mary
(d. 1685)

Thomas
m
Hannah

Robert
(b. 1690)
m
Jane Johnson

Thomas
(1719–1809)
m
Joan Mellor
(1725–1802)

William
(1755–1839)
m (1798)
Mary Bagshaw

**FLETCHER–CLEWS–HARRISON
FAMILY TREE**

William
(1803–68)
m
Mary Docksey
(1804–78)

John Clews
of Newton Grange
(1788–1839)
m
Sarah
(1777–1863)

Charles Harrison
of Jenny Bentley
(1807–90)
m
Mary

William
(1836–93)
m
Hannah Johnson
(1837–1924)

Joseph (1816–81)
m
Sarah Cooper
(1821–77)

William (1830–90)
m
Hannah Salt (b. 1833)

John Docksey
(1863–1935)
m
Martha Yeomans
Cowley
(1863–1953)

Edith Clews
(1857–1941)
m
William Harrison
(1860–1947)

Mary
(1890–1983
m
William
(1882–1972)
Florence
(b. and d. 1884)
Helen
(1885–1974)
Edith
(1886–1977)

John Fletcher Clews
(b. 1921)
m
Margaret Ruth Marsh
(b. 1920)

Eileen Mary
(b. 1923)
m
Alfred Paul Pickersgill
(b. 1920)

Richard John
(b. 1949)
m
Gloria Moreno Lopez
(b. 1947)
▼

Elizabeth
Ruth
(b. 1950)
m
Robert Ernest
Hinton
(b. 1952)
▼

Introduction

———◄◆►———

THIS BOOK IS a footnote to history. For several years I have been interested in the history of ordinary people, as distinct from the rulers and
decision-makers of our society. My desire has been to do justice to some
of the people, including my sort of people, who have been left out of history. I count myself among the lucky ones from the largely inarticulate
ranks of respectable, lower middle-class England. The lower middle-class
has hitherto attracted little attention from historians. Unlike the working
class, whose history has been enthusiastically recovered by several generations of labour and socialist historians, the lower-middle classes still await
a devoted chronicler. The lives and values of non-proletarians have lacked
romantic appeal and have been dismissed as reactionary, philistine and boring. The warmth, toughness, and revolutionary potential attributed to the
working classes has been absent from the class immediately above them, it
is alleged; and instead we have only mediocrity and snobbishness. In my
youth I shared this view; and these memoirs may be seen as the odyssey of
my escape from what I perceived as the constraints of a narrow and limiting background. The escape route was education, which provided a ladder of opportunity for upward social and economic mobility.

The process of social change is difficult to assess while it is still going
on, for we cannot see clearly the ultimate outcome. But we can now see
how well the middle-class way of life was attuned to the aspirations of
ordinary people. Lower middle-class society between the wars was male-
dominated, excessively class conscious, and culturally starved. But its
emphasis on security, respectability, family and home provided modest
material happiness for millions, and a base from which a few people like
me might move outwards. My friend and colleague, the late Edward
Thompson, in *The Making of the English Working Class*, expressed his desire

1

to rescue the people about whom he was writing from 'the enormous condescension of posterity'. Perhaps the time has come to rescue the lower-middle classes from the enormous condescension of intellectuals and literati.

A discovery common to authors is that all the best titles for books have already been taken. But if I had my choice I think I would adopt that of an old Newcastle Chartist who called his autobiography *Memoirs of a Social Atom*. However my book is not primarily an autobiography but a series of vignettes linked together and put in context by the chronology of my life. The result is a mosaic or collage of memories, portraits and anecdotes. In this way I have tried to satisfy a desire to write about the social history of my own times while avoiding the self-centredness of the autobiographical form. Although a good deal about myself is inevitably revealed, my overriding consciousness is of the representative nature of my life, of the extent to which my individual development has been part of a general social process.

Part I
PLACES AND PEOPLE

◆

MEMORY IS closely associated with the sense of place. When we recall our buried memories they do not appear in a vacuum but in some particular place which we see in our mind's eye. Early childhood comes back to us through the house in which we lived, the schoolroom where we spent long, hot afternoons, the street in which we played at weekends and on summer evenings. Houses are particularly evocative. They determine our day-to-day living conditions and surround us with a certain colour, atmosphere, and quality. Our journey through life may be charted as much by the houses we have lived in as by schools we have attended and the jobs we have done. When I think of elderly relations I always see them either in their own homes or on a visit to our house. It is in specific rooms that I hear their speculations to my parents of how I remind them of Uncle So-and-So or some remote cousin.

Houses of course are full of things. Most of us have a need to attach ourselves to certain objects: a favourite armchair, a carved oak chest, a reading lamp by the side of the bed, little ornaments on the mantelpiece. We see and touch them every day. Their familiarity is reassuring; their tie with habit is comforting; and we remember them as contributions to happiness. To other people these things are boring. But for most of us life is made up of simple pleasures; and what appears to an outsider to be trivial may for us be indispensable. It was an axiom of Sherlock Holmes that the little things are infinitely the most important. The chapters in this part suggest that it was not exalted feelings but the sentiments that flow from the little things of home which for me were dominant.

In addition to the sense of place and things there is the sense of time. Memory does not proceed evenly. After the episodes of childhood and youth comes a period of forgetfulness. Middle age is vague in some parts, vivid in others. A long jump brings us to the present. Unless one has kept a diary over the years (which I have not), it is not possible to construct a steady narrative, allotting equal space to all the years, even if this were desirable. Time in the memory is measured by its intensity rather than duration: the years between the ages of ten and twenty seem as long as those between thirty and sixty.

Chapters 1, 2, and 5 are about my childhood and schooldays in Leicester between 1921 and 1939. My grandparents and family history appear in chapters 3 and 4. Student days at Cambridge follow in chapter 6; and my first twenty years are rounded off in chapter 7 with a wartime romance and engagement.

♦ 1 ♦

Linton Street

———◄◆►———

THE TRAIN from London approached Leicester station; past the cemetery on the right, then a view of Welford Road, the 'reccy' (recreation ground) and the prison before being enveloped in a deep, brick-lined cutting. Within minutes we were in the tunnel under London Road, standing in the corridor ready to get off. Then the platform glided past and the train jerked to a halt. I stepped down from the carriage and joined the other passengers making their way to the steep flight of steps marked 'Way Out'. This was 'Leicester London Road', four long, straight platforms beneath a high glass roof, light, clean, roomy, and with waiting rooms and offices in red, Midland brick. It had none of the grandeur of the curving platforms of York, nor the subterranean gloom and chaos of Birmingham New Street. It was in fact symbolic of the town: a pleasant, prosperous, comfortable, ordinary sort of place, based on hosiery, boots and shoes, and some engineering. If one did not expect life in Leicester to hit the high spots, neither were there fears of the worst effects of urban squalor and decay. This was the town made familiar to the outside world in the early novels of C.P. Snow and William Cooper, though the provincial society which they described was broader and more sophisticated than mine. The station was familiar. It was where my father came every day to work in the parcels office and where we always left when visiting Derby or going on holiday. In the 1920s and 1930s Leicester had boasted two rival stations: the Great Central (LNER), perched high above the oldest part of the town near the river; and Belgrave Road, a little-used terminus of the Great Northern line to the eastern counties. Now only London Road, formerly the LMS, remained. It seemed to have altered little as I went through the ticket barrier, crossed the booking hall, and went into the brown and brick coloured forecourt where the taxis were parked.

London Road was as wide as I had remembered it but the hill, up which I had toiled so many times on foot and on my bicycle, was little more than a gentle rise to Victoria Park. But the trams were missing. I had come to revisit the scenes of my childhood sixty years earlier, and began walking up London Road. It was a strange feeling: the names of the streets were the same and brought back memories of journeys to school, and expeditions 'down town', but the people and the names over the shops were completely unknown to me. I felt a bit like Rip Van Winkle. At the entrance to the park I turned left down Evington Road, still missing the rattling and clanking of the trams. My destination was Linton Street, but I thought I would take a look at Medway Street School first. So I wandered up St Stephen's Road, as I had done many hundreds of times between the ages of five and eleven years old.

There it stood: a typical red-brick, two-storeyed board school (the sign 'Medway Street Board School' was still on the wall), with a central hall and surrounding classrooms, tarmac playground, and separate entrances for boys and girls. Its forbidding presence was softened only by the large-leafed plane trees along St Stephen's Road. I cannot say that I was unhappy there, but neither do I remember a particular enthusiasm for any aspect of it. In the infant class I recall the dark green walls splattered with pictures of animals and alphabets. The windows were set high up, presumably so that we should not be distracted by gazing outside during lessons. We sat in pairs at little desks which had fixed seats, no back, and holes for the inkwells. From the blackboard we copied our pothooks and learned to write. I remember we were taught to knit, boys as well as girls, using thick needles and string—the problem was what to do with the results; but a solution was found by sewing the six-inch squares together to make dusters for the blackboard. 'Nature study' was encouraged and we grew plants and bulbs on the window sills. A favourite specimen was the hyacinth which was perched in the top of a tall jar so that one could see how the leaves and flowers were balanced by the roots which struggled down towards the water in the bottom of the jar. Good work and/or behaviour was rewarded by the privilege of helping as a 'monitor'. There were ink monitors (filling up the inkwells), chalk monitors (ensuring that there was always a piece of chalk on the teacher's desk), book monitors (storing the books in a cupboard), and no doubt others.

After the first three years our education became more purposive. From Standard III (ages 8–9) we were streamed according to ability, and an annual written report was prepared. The boys (though not, I think, the girls) were henceforth addressed by their surnames only. Great emphasis was placed on English: reading, writing, spelling, composition, grammar, literature were all taught and assessed as separate subjects. Arithmetic ('sums') was taught daily; and there was provision for geography, history, drawing, needlework (for the girls), handwork, science, and 'general knowledge'.

In our eleventh year (Standard V) we were thoroughly coached (or crammed?) for the 'scholarship exam', which determined whether we should go to the grammar or senior school. I was in the 'A' stream and near the top of the class of those who were considered to be possible grammar school entrants. We were pressured to learn lists of words and tested on their correct spelling. Every morning we had 'mental arithmetic'. The teacher would put on the board a sum which we had to do in our heads. This was not one of my strong points, and I would sit there hoping that she would not pounce on me. Since there were some fifty-two of us in the class, the odds were at least even that one might escape. But sooner or later my turn would come.

Two teachers only stand out in my memory. The first was 'Daddy' Garner, the headmaster, whom we saw every morning at assembly. Standing on a dais, he would greet us with 'Good morning, children' to which we replied 'Good morning, Sir'. We then sang a hymn, accompanied on the piano by one of the teachers, and afterwards closed our eyes while the headmaster offered a short prayer. He then read out the notices, and sometimes gave a short talk while we sat cross-legged on the floor. He was reputed to have a cane; and the ultimate punishment was to be 'sent to Mr Garner'. The other teacher was named Hallam, and also nicknamed 'Daddy'. He was a breezy, knock-about, no-nonsense sort of man who taught the 'B' class. The usual punishment for talking or not paying attention was to be made to stay in after school. But Daddy Hallam had an alternative in the form of a short cane which he kept prominently on his desk. Culprits were given the choice of a cut on the hand with the cane or staying in after school; 'Stick or stay?' he would demand briskly. I think most children elected to stay.

Children for the most part accept the world as they find it, and judging by my reports it would seem that I had few problems with my school work. However, I was dimly aware that there were alternatives. In the street parallel to ours (Rowsley Street) and backing on to the bottom of our yard, was a private school kept by two sisters, the Misses Grimley. This I now realise was a private venture day school for lower middle-class children whose parents could afford modest fees and who, for various reasons, did not wish their children to go to the state school. From our bedroom windows we could see the school, but the only thing we knew about it was that Miss Grimley mowed the grass at night after we had gone to bed, and this kept us awake. The school seemed to us very small, so small as to be hardly a school at all. We knew none of the children who attended it and assumed that they must be snobbish. In reality it was a curious historical relic; one of the last in a long tradition of dame schools that had lingered on, despite the 1875 Education Act which had been designed to kill them off.

These recollections did not occupy me very long. I retraced my steps back to Evington Road and continued on my way, still haunted by the absence of the trams (what a grinding and squeaking they had made as they negotiated the right-angle bend into East Park Road). The newsagents and sweet shops were still much as before, but the names above them were Indian. The women wore saris below their coats and anoraks, and the children seemed quiet and well-behaved. It would be an exaggeration to say that this added an exotic touch; at the most it modified the outward signs of a typical English, lower middle-class district. How the neighbourhood had changed at a deeper level I had no means of knowing.

A few minutes later I was in Linton Street, standing outside Number 25. It was one of those small, red-brick terraced houses put up for the artisan and lower-middle classes of Edwardian England, part of the development of the Highfields district as urban Leicester spilled out into the surrounding countryside towards the village of Evington. I looked up at the front bedroom window. The original sash windows had been replaced by single-pane, louvred 'improvements', and the stone sills and lintels painted white. In that front bedroom I was born at five o'clock on Monday morning, 28 February 1921. By all accounts I was not handsome, being long and thin and looking rather like a raw rabbit. A year later I had been fattened into a replica of the balloon-like child in the advertisements for 'Cow and Gate' baby food. But by the time I was five I had reverted to my original skinny proportions, beyond which I failed to develop at any time during the next sixty years. Home confinements were at that time usual, and a full-time nurse was engaged to look after me and my mother, who remained in bed for about two weeks. Her sister Elsie came to help with the housework. A fire was lit in the bedroom grate. This was a rare occurrence in our bedrooms, which otherwise completely unheated but which we were assured was very healthy, like open windows and fresh air.

My parents had come to Linton Street after my father was demobbed. They were married in 1915 and this was their first real home together. Both came from a rural background, with which they maintained close links, but they regarded the transition to town life as emancipation, and a

8

move in the direction of social betterment. The village of Fenny Bentley was 'home' for them both, and they were married in Fenny Bentley church. Their families had lived in the same part of Derbyshire for several generations and were well known to each other. For my father (born in 1882), as for so many young men from the villages of late nineteenth century rural England, work on the railway was the means of escape. For him it offered white-collar status, reasonable remuneration, and security. After attending the village school in Fenny Bentley he went on to Ashbourne Grammar School, leaving at fourteen to join the LNWR. He spent the next few years working as a booking office clerk in Selly Oak (Birmingham) and Coventry before being posted to Leicester. During this period he lived in lodgings and returned to Fenny Bentley at weekends. I have no idea what he did, apart from work, or what his interests were (except that he used to say that he bred white mice which won prizes at shows) during these years. I always think of him as similar to one of the young men in an H.G. Wells or Arnold Bennett novel. His meetings with and courtship of my mother came about through his regular visits to Fenny Bentley. She always joked that she fell in love with him when she saw what a fine figure of a man he was on his bicycle, presumably cycling from Ashbourne to Bentley. Mary Fletcher was born in 1890 in the neighbouring village of Tissington, where the family had been farmers since at least the seventeenth century and probably earlier. In 1896 her father, John Docksey Fletcher, decided to give up farming and the family went to live in Buxton, where he obtained employment as a gardener in the public gardens. They lived in a rented house at number 38 West Street. My mother was therefore brought up in the town, which she always preferred to the country. She went to the Girls' High School and stayed on as a pupil-teacher during 1907–8, thus becoming a qualified, uncertificated teacher. As a result of this training she always prided herself on her 'correct' English. She was adept at parsing and her letters were always rather formal, perhaps stilted, in the manner of a school essay. Her handwriting was round and straight up, with all the letters fully formed—unlike my father's hand which was sloping and had flourishes suggesting copperplate models. She taught in Buxton and later in Leicester. In 1911 her father, having decided to leave Buxton, moved to Halfway House, a small-holding between Ashbourne and Fenny Bentley, which he bought from a cousin. My mother now also came home at weekends, and thus began the romance.

There is no doubt that they were very much in love and remained so for the fifty-seven years they were together. My father worshipped my mother. She was his ideal of womanhood and he always deferred to her.

The only occasions on which he ever lost his temper with me (for he was normally the most patient and even-tempered of men) were when I was rude to her or disobeyed her. He had a romantic, not to say exaggerated view of women, with whom I suspect he had had little to do during his bachelor days. He never really got over his good fortune in persuading my mother to marry him, and indeed to the Harrison family she probably seemed quite a catch. She completely ruled him while pretending that his role was that of the dominant male. From the beginning of their life together she insisted on calling him Billy, though he had always been (and remained) Willie to his family and Bill to his mates. She decided what he should wear, and when he should change his underclothes. His mild, self-effacing, easy-going nature was a perfect foil for her assertive, directing intelligence. As time went on his lack of drive and ambition was frustrating for her. He preferred to dig his allotment rather than take on the responsibilities of churchwarden, which my mother would have loved him to do. We thought of her qualities as those of a schoolmistress; in reality they sprang from her temperament.

Their wedding photograph shows the groom in morning coat, pin-stripe trousers, and sporting a waxed moustache. The bride wears a long, white satin dress, veil and chaplet, and carries a large bouquet of lilies. A year later the costume has changed completely. L/Cpl. Harrison now poses in khaki beside his beloved who sits on the arm of a chair, looking intently from beneath a large-brimmed hat worn at a rakish angle. A few months after their marriage my father was called up and posted to the Royal Engineers. Being a railwayman he was assigned to the ROD (Railway Operating Division); and after a period at Longmoor Camp in Hampshire he went to France in September 1916. He spent the next two and a half years in north west France, was promoted to sergeant, and was fortunate enough to avoid the trenches. During this time my mother struggled to control classes of seventy senior pupils in St Margaret's School, Leicester—an experience which she later recalled with horror. By 1919, when they were together again, they were more than ready to settle down—and their love nest was Number 25.

The house, which opened directly onto the street, had two living rooms and a kitchen or scullery downstairs and three bedrooms above. It had no bathroom or inside toilet. There was a small entrance passage, dignified by the name of hall, which made the house superior to those in which the front door opened straight into the living room, but inferior to those which had a few feet of garden between the front door and the pavement. The stairs ran up between the two living rooms and were always dark as there was only a little indirect light from the landing. This was a rather frightening place for young children; so at night a small oil lamp on a bracket was kept burning at the top of the stairs. The kitchen and the small back bedroom above it were built out at right angles to the main row of the terrace, making an 'L' shape which enclosed two sides of the yard. Like all the families in Linton Street we lived almost exclusively in the back room. The front room was never called the parlour (unlike the seldom-used sitting room at Halfway House, my grandparents' farmhouse near Ashbourne) but was in fact used, like the classic Victorian parlour, only on special occasions. It was furnished with the most prized family possessions: an upright piano, a small settee, china ornaments, and various watercolours which my parents had either bought or been given at the time of their wedding, including a large picture in a heavy gilt frame of the Ponte Vecchio in Florence. The other pictures were still lifes (bowls of fruit) or landscapes (sunsets) and sea scenes of the Edwardian genre, all in plain, gilt frames. The room was always cold; which was a blessing in disguise, as it meant that my daily, half-hour piano practice was reduced to twenty minutes, my fingers having been reduced to complete numbness. Apart from my purgatory at the piano the room was used only when we had visitors, usually on Sunday afternoons, and that infrequently. It was a kind of mausoleum of family respectability.

The living room by contrast was a cosy place, with a coal fire. In it we ate, played, did our homework, and had baths on Saturday evenings. Later my mother decided that it would be more genteel to eat elsewhere, and so the kitchen was converted into a sort of breakfast room with a table and stools. But it remained basically a scullery, with a brown slopstone rather than a sink, and a built-in copper in the corner. The kitchen was a step lower than the living room, and contained the back door which opened onto the yard. Beyond the kitchen was a row of three outbuildings: a wash house, with the wash tub, dolly, tin bath, and a heavy iron-framed mangle; the toilet; and the coal house. There was also a shed, made by placing a piece of corrugated iron roofing between the end of the coal house and the bottom wall of the yard. It had an earth floor and was used to store garden tools, nails, and general outside clobber. Much the most memorable of these small buildings was, of course, the lavatory. Although it was a water closet, with a long chain to pull and a funnel-shaped, glazed, earthenware pan, it was designed like an old earth privy. The fixed wooden seat was scrubbed white, the floor was brick, and the walls were unplastered. Here I spent many happy hours (well, parts of hours) reading the bits of torn-up newspaper which served as toilet paper. Later, in my first year at the grammar school when we 'did' woodwork, the first exercise was to make an open box-like object for which the only conceivable use was as a repository for such paper. My masterpiece was henceforth nailed to the wall and we wondered how we could have been so uncivilised as not to have had such a convenience before. There was no bolt on the lavatory door and it was, therefore, a convention that it should be fully closed only when someone was inside. The seat was the right height for adult use; but when children were seated on the throne their feet dangled above the floor.

The yard was mostly paved with blue stable bricks, apart from a small grass plot with a border of London pride. A fatsia (caster oil plant) struggled in one corner, a privet bush in another, and a climbing rose along the bottom wall. The dustbin stood opposite the back door; and the waste water from the sink gurgled into an open drain beneath the kitchen window. Access to the yard from the street was through a tunnel, called the entry, which served each of the two houses on either side. There were doors at both ends of this passage, and in it we kept our bikes, remembering always to remove them before the dustbin men came on Tuesday mornings. The entry tunnel was also useful for drying washing on wet days.

In the house the only heating was by coal fires. There was no hot water system, only a cold tap, and water was heated by kettle on the fire or gas cooker (the 'stove'). The house had virtually no cupboards, storage in the kitchen for instance being on open shelves. The only closet was the 'glory hole' under the stairs, opening out of the back living room. This dearth of storage space meant that upstairs each bedroom was crowded with a large wardrobe, in addition to the bedstead, dressing table, wash stand, clothes horse and chairs. A chamber pot (a 'po' as we called it) was kept under each bed and emptied every morning when the beds were made. Small bedside mats slipped about on the cold and shiny lino. The cold of the bedrooms was mitigated in winter by the use of stone hot water bottles, which were ritually filled every night. The lighting was by gas. But since it was deemed too troublesome and expensive to have to light all the upstairs rooms every night, we went to bed with candles, which gave relatively little light and cast long and frightening shadows. In the morning we shivered into our underclothes and took it in turns to wash in the kitchen: my father first, then we children, and (much later, after we had all gone out) my mother.

Life in these surroundings was relatively uneventful, or so it seems now. Not many of the myriad sights and sounds and smells of childhood remain; and those that do are disconcertingly separated from each other by huge gaps and stillnesses. Nevertheless certain images emerge to give a child's view of some aspects of life in the 1920s. There were, for instance, the regular callers at the house. First in importance was Mrs Marston, who called on Monday mornings to collect the rent. She was the widow of the builder who had built the houses around 1906. 'It's Mrs Marston', I would call, as I opened the front door to a severe-looking woman who looked down on me through a pair of pince-nez; whereupon my mother would come forward with the rent book and the 7s 6d. in half crowns. Mrs Marston wore large, pendulous ear rings and carried a small gladstone bag. She initialled the rent book and put the money in the bag. After passing the time of day she moved on to the next house, where the business was repeated. The money for the rent was kept in a drawer of the sideboard, for my mother's method of management was to put the housekeeping money in several little tin boxes each allocated for a specific purpose. Every second Thursday (for he was paid fortnightly) my father would empty his pay packet onto the table and mother would put it away in the boxes, leaving a small sum for my father's tobacco, tram fares and pocket money.

Much more interesting was the daily arrival of Mr Flower, the milk-man. As we heard him calling 'milko' in the street, I would be sent out with a jug and the milk book to join the other children and housewives who gathered round the horse and two-wheeled float. The combined odour of horse and milk was very strong. Standing on the float, which tipped alarmingly when he jumped up alongside the churn, Mr Flower ladled the milk out in quart, pint and half-pint measures, while the horse snuffled and shook its head in a feed bag. There were smaller measures for the cream. The milk book had a hole in the cover through which the cus-tomer's name could be read; and on Saturday mornings Mr Flower came to the back door to collect the money for the week's milk. He was then in a good mood and chatted with my mother while adding up the account.

Unlike the milkman who came every weekday, the coalman's round was weekly. He too called his wares in the street and the customers responded by coming out to him. But there the similarity ended. No one queried the quality or type of milk for sale; but it was crucial to know what sort of coal was available since it varied much in price and quality from week to week. With coal being the sole means of heating, customers were keen to get the best deal. Good coal burned steadily with a mini-mum of smoke and left little ash; 'dirty' or inferior coal did none of these things. So the coalman was always asked what he had 'on' today, and whether it was in big lumps, or nuts, or slack. The types of coal had strange-sounding names. Some of it came I think from the Baggeridge colliery near Dudley. Having received an order for say, three bags, the coalman and his mate would each hoist a hundredweight sack onto his back and carry it at a trot down the entry, through the yard, and throw it over his head into the coal house. They then picked up the empty sacks and stored them in a pile on the end of the lorry. To us children it was all very exciting: the blackened faces of the men, their rough clothes, leather back-harness, and huge boots; the crash of the coal as it hit the coalhouse floor, creating a dense, black cloud of dust; the inspection of the load sometime later when the dust had settled and all was quiet again. When father came home in the evening he would go and inspect it and pronounce a verdict: 'a bit bigger than that last lot', 'looks a bit mucky', or (worst of all) 'it's naught but slack'.

Even dirtier, but fortunately less frequent than the coalman, was the visit of the sweep. Daily coal fires deposited considerable quantities of soot in the chimney, causing problems of draught and fire hazard. A chimney on fire was quite a spectacle and sometimes required the fire brigade to put it out—though some people, it was rumoured, deliberately set their chimneys alight once a month to get rid of the soot and avoid the cost of a sweep. But for law-abiding citizens it was the custom to have the chimney swept at least once a year, usually in the spring so as to coincide with the annual major operation known as spring-cleaning, when all rooms in the house were given an extra-thorough clean. Preparations for the sweep were made the night before: carpets rolled back, mantleshelf cleared, and the furniture covered with dust sheets. The next morning the sweep appeared, pushing his brushes, rods and sacks in a handcart. He already had a black face and smelt strongly of soot. Throwing his bundle of apparatus on the floor, he got to work. He put an open bag in the hearth and covered the fireplace with a heavy cloth, wedged into position with a couple of rods. Inside the centre of the cloth was a circular brush about eighteen inches in diameter, the shaft protruding through a hole in the cloth. Onto this shaft he screwed the first rod and pushed it upwards, repeating the process until the brush reached the top of the chimney. The rods were about five feet long and were made of cane, with brass fittings at either end. As the brush got higher and higher it became increasingly harder to move, and the sweep had to push strongly on his rods. A rattling sound could be heard as the brush went up; soot came falling down into the fireplace; and some of it escaped round the edges of the cloth into the room. When there was no more resistance to his pushing the sweep knew that the brush was clear of the chimney; after a few twirls he then pulled in down again, unscrewing the rods one by one and laying them on the floor. He wrapped the brush in the cloth and took it outside with the rods. The bag of soot was next removed, and finally he brushed any remaining into a pile and shovelled it into another bag. He left the soot in the yard for my father who treasured it as a fertiliser and anti-slug treatment for his allotment. Mother was relieved to pay him and see him go, leaving her to cope with the thin layer of soot which covered everything in the sitting room. During the performance we children stood in the street, watching for the brush to pop out of the chimney. When it did so we let out a yell and ran indoors to announce the fact. There was much talk among neighbours as to which sweep made least mess; but in all cases the results were much the same. In the 1930s an improved method of chimney sweeping, using vacuum and suction devices and sealing the fireplace with tape was much advertised. Indeed, one firm went so far as to dress their men in white coats. This cost more than the old type of sweep, but was felt to be worth the extra, so traumatic was the effect of his visit on a careful housekeeper.

Next door, in the house that shared our entry, lived Mr Abbey, a widower and retired railway official. He had been station master at a small station in Bedfordshire and now lived alone, spending most of his time either reading the paper or doing odd jobs about the house. In the evening he went out regularly to his local, returning about 10 o'clock and apart from this he did not seem to have any contacts or hobbies. My mother was sorry for him as she felt he was rather helpless at looking after himself after his wife died. So it was arranged that he should share dinner with us, and every day at 12.30 I would take round a plate of hot food. 'Dinner, Mr Abbey', I would call as I entered his house through the back door and knocked on the sitting room door. He would be sitting at the table, apparently reading the paper, but in fact probably dozing quietly. The table was always covered with layers of newspaper in place of a table cloth, and he tore off one each day as it became soiled. Once a week he would pin on a fresh supply with drawing pins. He always wore navy blue trousers and sat in his shirt sleeves and waistcoat, with an Albert watch chain and large metal pocket watch. When he went out he put on a jacket (also of navy blue serge, rather like a railwayman's uniform) and a black bowler hat. His dress was different from my father's or anyone else I knew. On his upper lip he had a thick moustache which dipped in the cup when he drank his tea. He would then put his finger across his lip and suck his moustache dry—much to my fascination and my mother's disgust. After putting down the plate I would hurry back home for my own dinner, remembering to collect the clean plate from yesterday's meal.

Mr Abbey was quite a handyman. Amongst other skills he always repaired his own boots. He bought the soles and heels from Woolworth's (his favourite shop) and cobbled them on with the aid of a shoe anvil and hammer. He was also adept at soldering and taught me how to make a steam engine out of a cocoa tin. I loved going to see him: unlike in our house, it didn't matter if you made a mess, and he was always willing to answer endless questions. He talked mysteriously about the Duke of Bedford; and a root of rhubarb in the corner of his yard impressed my father in that it was alleged to be of superior quality ('champagne rhubarb') 'from the Duke of Bedford's estate'.

My mother was quite a good cook; though like so many of her generation, was inclined to over-emphasise the need to eat a proportion of fat meat with the lean. Her speciality was puddings: baked sponge puddings with Bird's custard; steamed suet puddings with golden syrup poured over them; treacle tarts; and the currant pudding, Spotted Dick. For breakfast we usually had fried bread or, as a special treat, Derbyshire oat cakes. There was also a cereal called Force whose packet read 'High o'er the fence leaps Sunny Jim; Force is the food that raises him'. At teatime we had to eat a certain amount of bread and butter in order to 'earn' a piece of cake. Meal times were the occasions when we had to remember to take our vitamins to ward off coughs, colds, and diseases. We tried a succession of preventive medicines: Virol, Scott's Emulsion, cod liver oil and malt, and our bedtime cup of Ovaltine. There were no alcoholic drinks in the house, apart from a little bottle of brandy for medicinal purposes. I never tasted beer until I went to Cambridge, and spirits only after I became an army officer.

The weekly rhythm of the home reached a zenith on Saturdays with bath night, and descended to its nadir on Mondays which was wash day. As there was no piped hot water system and indeed no bathroom in the house, bathing became a family ritual. Before bed time the zinc bath was brought in from the washhouse and put on the hearth rug in front of the sitting room fire. It was then filled with kettles of hot water and we took it in turns to sit in it and wash ourselves thoroughly, including our hair. Eileen, my sister, would be first, and while she was being wrapped in a towel and dried I would take my turn. We then had our cup of Ovaltine and were packed off to bed. When we were safely out of the way my parents bathed themselves, or so we believed, for of course we never actually saw them doing so. The greatest modesty prevailed in the home and I don't remember that I ever saw my parents undressed. Indeed, on the very rare occasions that my mother and father wore bathing costumes at the seaside I was embarrassed. Bath night involved a good deal of upset and organisation: the boiling and carrying the hot water from the kitchen; the towels warmed on the fender round the fire; the brisk rubbing of our heads to make sure we didn't catch cold; the warm drink and biscuit; and finally (long after we were in bed and asleep) the ladling out of the dirty water and the carrying of the bath outside. The next day, Sunday, we all put on clean underclothes, a week being the usual time for their wear.

Wash day began on Sunday evening with the filling of the 'copper' and the laying of the fire underneath it. The laundry boiler was built into a corner of the kitchen, with its own fireplace and chimney. Since the boiler did not have a tap over it for filling, nor a spigot for emptying it, the cold water was carried from the sink and the dirty water ladled out later. First thing on Monday morning father lit the boiler fire, the clothes having been put in to soak overnight. By the time he had gone to work and we children had set out for school the copper was boiling merrily, the kitchen was full of steam, and there was a strong smell of bubbling soap suds. The heavy work of getting the clothes out of the boiler was done with a stout stick; they were next taken to the wash house to be 'dollied' in a tub, and finally rinsed and mangled. They were then pegged out to dry on a line in the yard. Sheets were of cotton or linen, underwear usually of wool, so that handling the wet washing was heavy, tiring work. A wet day made the business even more onerous, and in addition the entry and house were festooned with drying garments. Naturally there was little time for cooking on Monday mornings; and so we came home at midday to the most unappetising dinner of the week. This was usually bubble and squeak, consisting of the remains of the Sunday joint and left-over potatoes and greens, all fried together in a pan, followed by rice pudding or hasty pudding (which was simply flour and water). Any complaints or long faces were met with the rejoinder that we were lucky to get anything at all on wash day. There was a general air of take-it-or-leave-it, the kitchen walls were running with condensed steam, and the sitting room fire was barricaded off by drying or airing clothes. Monday evening was no more comfortable, because then mother was completely preoccupied with piles of ironing.

Our playground was the street, which was quite safe to play in. No one in Linton Street owned a car and none was parked there. The only vehicles were those of visiting tradesmen like the milkman or coalman. On fine evenings, at weekends and during the holidays we children played on the pavement. On wet days we had to improvise games in the entry or in the shed. My special friend was a boy of my own age, Jack Smedley, who lived a few doors away. The Smedleys and Harrisons were friends and neighbours, and we sometimes went on summer holidays together at Skegness or Cromer. Harold Smedley was a short, cheerful, dapper little man, who was manager of a sewing machine shop (Wilcox and Gibbs) in the town; his wife, Ida, was a tall, refined, aristocratic-looking woman who was more reserved and 'proper' than her husband. There were not many other children of our age in the street, but we usually enlisted the services of my sister, Eileen, and her friend, Barbara Hill, who lived in the house opposite. Tick, cowboys and indians, soldiers, hide and seek, trains, and various ball games were our usual staple. Skipping and hopscotch were only for girls. My greatest joy was our trolley, made simply from a plank of wood and two pairs of pram wheels. There was room for two of us to sit on it, one behind the other, the driver steering with a rope tied to the front wheels. Its main limitation was that it had no means of power other than pushing by a third person, except when going downhill. Linton Street was completely flat; but Osmaston Road, at the end of our street, was hilly; so it was there that we had to go. Once round the corner and we were off, until the pavement ended at the next intersection, and we had then desperately to stop the brakeless trolley before it tipped us into the road. I spent many happy hours in the shed or the backyard hammering and sawing pieces of wood to add refinements to the skeleton-like trolley, which in our more imaginative games served as a racing car or a tram or train. Later came the bicycle, but by then I had largely passed the stage of playing on the pavement.

At the opposite end of Linton Street was Evington Road, our main local shopping area. Mr Hopkins and his wife ran the butcher's shop, assisted by their daughter, Mabel. Most of their business was in the mornings, and the afternoons were spent swilling out the shop with buckets of water, after which they sprinkled the floor with sawdust. There was also a pork butcher's on the opposite side of the road, notable for the pig's head in the centre of the window. It had a tomato in its mouth and was beautifully pink and fresh-looking. Martin Elgood's was the bicycle shop where we bought our puncture outfits and replacement brake blocks. In his window was a magnificent Raleigh 'roadster', black and shiny, with a Sturmey-Archer 3-speed gear; also a Hercules which was cheaper, though at £3 19s:6d. it might as well have been £1000. A little higher up was Mr Barker, the chemist. He not only dispensed medicines but also gave advice on minor ailments. Only when we were ill enough to be in bed would the doctor be called in. My father was 'on the panel' which meant that his medical costs were met through his contribution to the National Deposit Friendly Society; but this coverage did not extend to the family. Doctor's bills were a cause of much anxiety. Unpaid bills were one of the hazards of the medical profession before the coming of the National Health Service; but it was a mark of respectability among the lower-middle classes that doctors' bills should be paid, despite the hardship entailed. My parents were immensely deferential to the doctor, who was regarded as an oracle of wisdom. Before his arrival my mother was at great pains to tidy the house (even more than usual), put out little towels for him, and straighten the bed clothes. His manner was pleasant, reassuring, though authoritarian, reflecting his public school background. There was no thought of ever questioning his competence in any medical matter: in such things he was God. Nevertheless on grounds of cost unorthodox healers might be consulted. Thus my father went to an alternative practitioner in the town who professed to be able to treat cataracts by the application of some substance that looked (according to my father) like mud. The effects were negligible.

The shops I have mentioned were not without their rivals. Customers however were very loyal. We would never think of deserting Mr Hopkins for the Home and Colonial, nor Mrs Hill's little grocery shop for Worthington's, the chain grocers, even though her butter was probably not as fresh. It was a point of pride with my mother always to give us butter rather than margarine which she regarded as irredeemably working class. This problem of class association arose again in connection with the Coop. The variety and convenience of our local branch of the Leicester Industrial Cooperative Society, as it was grandiloquently called, made it sensible to shop there. But for my mother the coops had too many proletarian associations for her to feel entirely comfortable in the store. Nevertheless if we bought our groceries there regularly throughout the year the 'divi' could amount to £5, which was as much as my father's weekly wage. She therefore pocketed her distaste and we became members of the Society. For years I remembered our coop number which you had to give the assistant when he wrote out a little ticket recording the purchase. The shop had a fascinating system of overhead wires running from each counter to a central cashier. When the money was put into a little cannister and a cord was pulled it shot along the wire to the cashier, who opened it and then shot it back to the counter with the change. I could imagine nothing more delightful than being a coop employee and playing with the system all day.

Trying to assess our life in Linton Street with the benefit of hindsight I see how secure, and relatively untroubled, we were. We knew nothing of the hardships of unemployment, the trials of looking after aged grandparents, or prolonged and disabling illness. Money was in short supply and there was little opportunity of getting any extra. Married women like my mother were not encouraged or expected to take jobs outside the home. But she was an excellent manager; and since she was a skilful seamstress she undertook small sewing jobs for neighbours which brought in a little pocket money. Her 'ladies' were always taken into the front room for a 'fitting'. My father was a steady and reliable breadwinner, who never went to the pub and who had few luxuries beyond his pipe. He supported my mother in her striving for respectability, though he was quite free from the usual innocent snobberies of the lower-middle class.

These things came back to me as I stood outside Number 25. I now noticed that the road was no longer granite sets but tarmac, and there were several cars parked in it. A number of the houses had been tarted up, with new front doors, double glazing, painted sills and doors on the entries, though there were no lilac doors or carriage lamps. Television aerials and telephone lines were also in evidence. As I stood there dreaming, a little boy came out of Number 25. He eyed me suspiciously.

'I used to live here. I was born here,' I said. He looked at me blankly, uncomprehending.

'No,' he replied, 'it is my house. I live here.'

✦ 2 ✦

Evensong at St Philip's

————◄◆►————

Angels of Jesus, Angels of light
Singing to welcome the pilgrims of the night!

A S THE singing reached the end of the first verse, one of the choirmen who acted as crucifer quietly slipped out of his seat at the end of the back row of the choir stalls and walked slowly into the sanctuary. He took the plain wooden cross which had been leant against the wall in the corner after the procession at the beginning of the evening service and raised it high. Facing the middle of the altar for the moment, he turned round and walked slowly down the middle of the chancel. When he came to the chancel steps he stopped; whereupon the choirboys (decani on the vicar's side, cantoris on the curate's) filed out, two by two, and formed up behind him. The smallest and most junior boys went first, followed in order of seniority by the remainder, the two head choristers (distinguished by a bronze medal on a red band round their necks) last. All wore red cassocks, white surplices and white neck ruffs but this was a recent innovation, and was regarded by some members of the congregation as popish when compared with the purple cassocks and Eton collars once worn. At full strength there were twenty-four choirboys, twelve on each side; but usually several were missing. This was just as well, since the front stalls could comfortably accommodate only ten each side.

The refrain of Frederick William Faber's popular hymn had been sung fortissimo. But now the organist pushed in the stops and the second verse began softly. With books held high and heads back, the choirboys sang:

Onward we go, for still we hear them singing,
Come, weary souls, for Jesus bids you come.

21

The congregation joined in lustily, for this type of Victorian devotion was still appreciated. Chas, the cross-bearer (the word crucifer was avoided) moved forward slowly down the two steps into the central aisle of the nave. He held the cross high and pressed against his nose to keep it vertical. Chas (I do not know why he was called that rather than Charles) was a tall man in his early twenties with fair hair and a thin, Ronald Coleman moustache. He was the only son of doting parents who were much inclined to spoil him. He had some occupation in an office, but was generally thought to be supported by his father who was 'something in hosiery', so my mother said. The young ladies in the congregation doubtless included him in their dreams, perhaps in their prayers.

After the boys came the women choristers, wearing purple gowns and mortarboards with tassels. The older ones stared straight ahead and were rather prim and proper. But the younger women, whose mortarboards were pinned at a rakish angle and who made no attempt to cover up their bright dresses beneath their gowns, sang with gay abandon as they looked round for their friends in the congregation. The men, basses and tenors, came next, the older ones shambling out of the choir stalls, the younger men looking seriously at their books. Most wore cassocks too short for them, and their long surplices had a rather grey and crumpled look. Lastly the two clergymen left their stalls; first the curate, a man in his late twenties, in cassock, surplice and B.A. hood lined with white rabbit fur; then the vicar, similarly dressed, but with a Cambridge M.A. hood of black and white silk.

The vicar—the Reverend G.P. Winter—was a small, roundish, comfortable man with large tortoiseshell glasses. He looked, and was, friendly and solid, a person you could trust, with firm but not high falutin' ideas. When smoking a pipe he reminded one of the advertisement for 'Parson's Pleasure' tobacco. His first name was George; but no one in our family ever referred to such an authority-figure so familiarly. He was always Mr Winter. After some years he was made a canon of Leicester Cathedral, no one quite knew what this meant and it did not appear to affect his parish duties or his dress, but was felt to be an honour which enhanced his standing as a clergyman. His innovations were always towards more ceremonies (one could hardly say ritual) and beautification of the building. St Philip's remained a middle-of-the-road, sometimes evangelical church—no candles on the altar, and no figure on the plainest of wooden crosses. Mrs Winter was a tallish, craggy-looking woman who dressed always in tweeds and sensible shoes. She chaired the Mothers' Union meetings (of which my mother was a devoted member) and with her southern accent and authoritarian manner provided appropriate female leadership in the parish.

In our household, religion and the church were closely identified with the social life which flourished at St Philip's.

The mother church in Evington Village was a mile-and-a-half away, and St Peter's in the Highfields district almost equidistant. About ten years before the First World War a tin mission church had been erected on the site, and this was used as a hall after the new St Philip's was built. The tin tabernacle burned down one night in 1925 and was reduced to a heap of blackened, corrugated iron sheets, amongst which the local children rummaged happily, collecting dozens of bolts and washers. Plans for an additional hall, (the 'small hall') were soon drawn up and the cost was met by endless fund-raising occasions. By the 1930s the parish halls were in use every weekday night for the various guilds, dramatic society, badminton club, cricket club, cubs, brownies, scouts, guides, whist-drives, dances, bring-and-buys, jumble sales—over all of which the vicar kept a watchful eye, and the curate had a more direct involvement (indeed, a curate's poor preaching performance could always be overlooked if he were popular with the 'young folks' or had some talent as an entertainer).

Evensong on Sunday was the climax of the St Philip's week. The attendance was larger than on Sunday mornings, when many of the women were busy cooking the Sunday roast and the men were doing odd jobs around the house or allotment. There was a feeling of unhurriedness on Sunday evenings—and no great eagerness to think of tomorrow, which meant school, washday and the workaday world. So the mood was benign and relaxed. As evening service drew to a close the sentiments of the hymn seemed somehow appropriate:

> Far, far away, like bells at evening pealing,
> The voice of Jesus sounds o'er land and sea.

The choir was now halfway down the church aisle. The vicar liked a long choir procession. It created an impressive atmosphere of colour and ritual without raising any awkward liturgical questions. Not that the church building was particularly adapted for liturgy, being a large barn-like structure of red brick in late Arts-and-Crafts Gothic style. The massive arches springing from floor to central roof and the absence of a chancel arch gave a great sense of openness, which was in no way interrupted by the light oak pews and fittings. There were no side chapels, no dark areas with dim sanctuary lights, no sense of mystery, no feeling of awe. All was open at a glance, like a rather elegant meeting house. By the time the vicar had left his stall the head of the procession had reached the bottom (that is, the west end) of the church. Chas turned slowly to the right, past the table on which were piles of the parish magazine and diocesan pamphlets, towards the north aisle. Here he had to lower the cross, for the aisles were no more than passages which ran along the sides of the nave, of use only for access to the pews.

St Philip's was proud of its choir. For several years the choirmaster was the curate, the Reverend H.O. Newman (known as Noggs). When he left to become rector of a rural parish in Leicestershire ('Most unsuitable for a bachelor,' said the ladies of the congregation), his place was taken by a schoolmaster named Cox who was also the organist. Coxie was not such a disciplinarian as Noggs, and in any case he could not watch the boys so closely during service when he was tucked away behind the organ. For the boys the choir functioned as a youth group. It was like a small and exclusive club, with its own culture and rituals, and was a rival or alternative to the cubs and scouts. Choirboy life was strictly hierarchical. At the bottom were the probationers; at the top the two, head choirboys, who were also usually the soloists. As my voice did not break until I was nearly fourteen I was head boy for quite a long time. In the choir vestry all was chaos and confusion until the service began. After a short prayer there was a hurried exodus into the side aisle, with much shoving and jostling to get into correct place in the procession. But like actors going on stage, all appeared in church (as my mother put it), 'as if butter wouldn't melt in their mouths'. Choir practice was held twice a week and on Monday and Friday evenings we played round the church until it was time to go in for practice. Afterwards there was the walk home, dawdling in the summer, hastening along in winter from gas lamp to gas lamp up Evington Road. On Sundays there were two services: matins at 11 o'clock and evensong at 6.30 pm. Most of us also attended Sunday school in the afternoon. At Monday evening practice the boys sat in the front two rows of pews in the nave while Coxie conducted from a piano. On Fridays, when the adults were with us, we sat in the choir stalls. For many weeks before Christmas we rehearsed the earlier sections of the *Messiah* preparatory to a recital in December. Throughout Lent we struggled with the *Dream of Gerontius*, *Olivet to Calvary*, *Stainer's Crucifixion*, and similar compositions. There were also new settings for the canticles from time to time, and occasionally we were drilled in particularly difficult chants for the psalms. It was assumed that hymn tunes were sufficiently well known to need no rehearsal. We always sang from scores, though I cannot remember that we were ever taught to read music. Not that it mattered much, as the well-known settings were soon learned by heart. 'Lord, now lettest thou thy servant depart in peace'; the lovely sounds of the *Nunc Dimittis* still echo round my head, and the crashing triumph of the *Magnificat* haunts me. But it was not all plain sailing.

'My soul doth magnify the Lord...' we began

'No, no, no, you blockheads', interrupted Coxie; 'not Lard, but Looord. Now try it again.' Off we would go.

However, two bars further on there was another rapping of the baton, and we came to a stop once more.

'How do you think you can sing with your heads on your chests?' the choirmaster exploded: 'Hold your music sheets high up and open your mouths wide....'

We would finally make it to the end, remembering always to sing Israel as Iz-rye-el in the last verse.

The choirmaster kept a register and there was a notional payment for each attendance. This however was not paid until the end of one's time in the choir (that is, when one's voice broke) and usually amounted to perhaps £3 or £4. In addition the boys were paid 2s 6d. for a wedding. There was a fairly steady demand during the summer for choristers to sing at weddings. But from our point of view they were often hurried affairs, as unless they were on a Saturday they had to be fitted into the lunch hour and necessitated a mad rush back to school by 2 o'clock. My mother, who loved weddings, was always most envious that from the choir stalls one had a close-up view of the bride, and never failed to ask me afterwards about details of the bride's dress and whether or not she was nervous. Another welcome cash benefit was from carol singing at Christmas. The choir went the rounds of the parish on Christmas Eve, and half the money collected went to charity and half to the choirboys.

The procession had by this time come to a halt. There were still two more verses to go:

Rest comes at length; though life be long and dreary,
The day must dawn, and darksome night be past;

The choir sang steadily on until the last verse was reached. But now we were on the home stretch, the end was in sight, and we were ready to roar down the straight. Coxie pulled out all the stops, and we burst into the final refrain:

Angels of Jesus, Angels of light,
Singing to welcome the pilgrims of the night!

When the music ended the congregation all knelt down. The pilgrims shuffled quickly up the aisle and disappeared into the vestry. Before the last choirmen had got there the congregation were standing up and filing out of the pews. In the vestry pandemonium broke out. After an hour and a half of controlled good behaviour the pent-up energy of twenty boys was suddenly let loose. Scuffling, punching, chattering, they tore off their cassocks and surplices and made for the door—and freedom. Another Sunday was over; another week would soon begin; and the cycle of St Philip's would repeat itself.

• 3 •

Halfway House

———◆———

FROM THE MISTS of my early childhood there emerges a picture of Halfway House, the home of my maternal grandparents. I am lying in bed in a low-ceilinged, whitewashed room, the window is low, almost on the floor. There is a dark settle against one wall, and beneath its seat are wooden, orange boxes containing seed potatoes. The bedroom is at the end of a corridor and I listen for my mother's footsteps as she comes to kiss me goodnight. Afterwards I hear the clack of the wooden latch as she closes the door, and I lie staring at the whitewashed beams of the ceiling. It is summer and still quite light, and the curtains do not darken the room completely. In the distance an engine whistles. It is the 7.30 a.m. milk train leaving Ashbourne station.

In the 1920s and 1930s we always spent part of our holidays at Halfway House. My father would bring us on the train on a Saturday. As he had to continue working during the week he used to return to Leicester on Sunday evening, leaving my mother, my sister and me with the grandparents. Halfway House was a modest redbrick farm house, built around 1780 and later enlarged. It had a parlour, which was never used; a sitting room which was occasionally used, for visitors and on Sunday afternoons; and a large kitchen, with cooking range, which was used all the time. The front door, which opened out of the hall, was also seldom used because the path from the road led directly through the yard to the kitchen door. There was also a large, whitewashed, stone-flagged larder, with long shelves and earthenware jars. It was neither a gracious nor convenient house; and to a child the long unlighted corridors, upstairs and downstairs connecting the front and back rooms, were rather frightening. But the kitchen was always warm and cheerful. Halfway House had been in the Fletcher family since 1815; but my grandfather had lived there only

27

since 1911 when he had bought it from his uncle, Francis Bagshaw Fletcher.

The holding consisted of two fields, about six acres in all, together with the usual stable, barn, cow shed, pig sty, chicken run, and (most intriguing to us children) an earth privy with a two-hole seat at the bottom of the garden. I think when my grandparents first moved there they kept a cow or two; but by the time we visited them the fields were let to a neighbouring farmer. The property bordered the main Ashbourne to Buxton Road and sloped down to the Bentley Brook. It was described in legal documents as situated in Offcote and Underwood in the parish of Ashbourne, but the area was more usually called Sandy Brook. This part of Derbyshire is more akin to George Eliot's Loamshire (Staffordshire) than to her Stonyshire (Derbyshire). It is *Adam Bede* country. Her uncle's cottage was at Ellastone, about five miles south-west of Ashbourne. Yet Stonyshire is not far away: the entrance to Dovedale lies two miles to the north, and the moors and stone walls begin at Tissington. Halfway House was so named because it was halfway between Ashbourne and Fenny Bentley. My grandparents regarded themselves as part of the Fenny Bentley community, and are buried in the churchyard there. But for all their shopping and business transactions they had to go to Ashbourne, the market town.

Ashbourne in the 1930s seemed a sleepy place which came to life once a week for the open-air market and cattle market. An annual riot known as Shrovetide football put the town briefly in the news when the local lads fought each other in the mud of the Henmore stream, as they had, it was claimed, 'from time immemorial'. The one architectural glory of Ashbourne was, and is, the parish church, with its graceful fourteenth-century tower and spire and great perpendicular windows. On a quiet Sunday evening its bells could be heard at Halfway House. In the guide books the church is always referred to as the 'Pride of the Peak' and we are reminded that it was the bells of Ashbourne church which inspired the long-forgotten Irish poet, Tom Moore, when he was living in a cottage at Mayfield:

> Those evening bells! Those evening bells!
> How many a tale their music tells
> Of youth and home and that sweet time
> When last I heard their soothing chime.

And so on, for two more stanzas. As a boy I found these verses rather appealing; but that was before I had learned that one was expected to be critical of Victorian sentimentality. Near the church was the gabled

Elizabethan grammar school which my father attended; and in the market place was Barnes's, the ironmongers, managed by Uncle Willie, my mother's brother. For a romantically inclined schoolboy Ashbourne was not without possibilities. In 1745 Bonnie Prince Charlie and his wild Highlanders had marched into the town and spent a night at Ashbourne Hall before continuing their ill-fated march south to Derby. King James was proclaimed in the market place. What might not one's ancestors have been doing and thinking in such stirring times? More prosaic are the recorded memories of Dr Johnson's connection with the town. His friend Dr John Taylor lived in the old, brick house facing the grammar school and here Johnson visited him in the summer when he (Taylor) could be spared from his pluralist duties as rector of Market Bosworth in Leicestershire, rector of St Margaret's at Westminster and prebendary of Westminster Abbey. Boswell characterised Taylor as a typical squarson (squire cum parson) and Johnson regretted that 'as it is said in the *Apocrypha*, "his talk is of bullocks"'. More relevantly for us, Boswell in 1779 mentioned as friends of Taylor and Johnson 'Mrs and Miss Fletcher—the first an ugly widow, the second a fat, old maid, both good cheerful women'. These two were apparently members of the family of Fletcher at Thorpe, and the Reverend Thomas Fletcher and Mr Joseph Fletcher were under-masters at Ashbourne Grammar School in the 1770s. I liked to think that these Fletchers were another branch of our family. They may well have been. But fifty years later I realise that the evidence is not without certain weaknesses.

I have never been entirely clear why my grandfather Fletcher gave up farming in Tissington and eventually went to live at Halfway House. It never occurred to me to ask him: in any case he was a most unapproachable figure for a child—austere, taciturn, intimidating. The explanation in the family was that his eyesight failed him and he feared he was going blind. At Halfway House he could not see well enough to read the newspaper, and Granny had to read the main items to him. But he was perfectly able to perform outside jobs, and walked to Ashbourne regularly each morning to collect the newspaper and do bits of shopping. A more likely reason for his leaving Tissington when he was only thirty-three years old is that he just could not make a living in the hard times that afflicted English agriculture in the 1890s. So he decided to sell up and move to Buxton where he worked as a gardener in the public gardens.

After some fifteen years there he retired to Halfway House and lived modestly on income from investments. He occupied himself with pottering about the place, clipping the roadside hedge (in which he took great pride), digging the garden, cleaning out ditches, and mending fences. As

Maternal grandparents: *John Docksey Fletcher (1863–1935), farmer.*
Photograph taken about the time of his marriage in 1888

Granny Fletcher (née Martha Yeomans Cowley, 1863–1953),
as I remember her in the 1930s

a mole-catcher he was something of an expert, and he also had considerable skill in catching rabbits by means of snares. He had a peculiar sense of humour which was completely lost on children. His favourite stories were usually about how he had been mistaken for a tramp or a lunatic, which considering his penchant for wearing an old army tunic and talking to himself were quite credible. As a boy he had not attended the village school but was sent away to a school somewhere near Leek. In his sixties he developed a cancerous tumour on his head and had to go weekly to Derby Infirmary for, what was then, experimental treatment. He told us that 'they put a box of radium on my head', which we found difficult to comprehend. But we knew that there must be something strange because from then on he always wore a skull cap, even in the house. He died in 1935.

In contrast, Granny Fletcher was a completely sympathetic character. A buxom, motherly little figure, she bustled about and gave us small jobs to do. The favourite task was helping to feed the hens and collect the eggs, which had to be done in the morning and again at night.

Granny Fletcher was born Martha Yeomans Cowley and came from Breadsall, a village about three miles from Derby. The Cowleys were an old family of small farmers who had been in Breadsall since Elizabethan times. A genealogical tree compiled from the parish registers by a former rector of Breadsall shows baptisms of Cowleys from 1602 and a Thomas Cowley who was churchwarden in 1621 and 1639. Martha, or Patty as she was usually called, was the last of seventeen children, her father being sixty-one years old when she was born in 1863. He was married twice and had eleven children by his first wife and six children by the second. Granny probably met my grandfather when she was staying with an aunt or uncle in the neighbourhood, as was quite common in large families. They were married in 1888, both aged twenty-five, and lived in Tissington. According to family legend, strongly denied by Granny when teased about it, they managed to fall into the village pond at Tissington while courting. In my recollections of her at Halfway House she always seemed to be wearing an apron, and often a hat. Her hair was white with yellowish streaks, and drawn back into a bun. She seemed to us children to have strange tastes, such as a liking for cold rice pudding, which was stored in basins in the larder, or dry arrowroot biscuits which were kept in a china biscuit barrel on the sideboard in the sitting room. The culinary delights of Halfway House for me were the Derbyshire oatcake which we had fried for breakfast, and the very tasty dripping which we spread on our bread for supper. As a farmer's wife she had a very necessary preoccupation with the danger of foxes. She told of unbelievably daring raids by these crafty animals and every evening at dusk we had to go round the chicken run to make sure that the hens were all safely inside and not perching in the trees. One of her favourite songs, which she sang in a quavering old woman's voice, was:

John, John, John, the grey goose is gone, and the fox is off to his den—O.

The ballad went on for several verses, but I particularly liked the ending in which the fox went back to his little ones who shared in the feast:

The fox and his wife, without any strife,
Said they never ate a better goose in all their life:
They did very well without fork or knife,
And the little ones picked the bones—O!
Bones—O! Bones—O!

Granny Fletcher had quite a repertory of old songs and rhymes, including reminiscences of the mummers who came round to the house at Christmas time when she lived in Breadsall and Tissington. She could repeat lines from the play:

In come I, Saint George,
The man of courage bold;

And the equally forthright announcement by his enemy, Bold Slasher:

In come I, the Turkish Knight.
Come from the Turkish land to fight.

While we were small, Halfway House was just a place where we could play happily but, as I grew older, I became aware of how different life in the countryside was from our lives in Leicester. My mother hated the dirt and mess of farm life. It was not that she was ashamed of her roots, though I think she found bucolic manners at times embarrassing, and took care to avoid any broad Derbyshire speech, but that she had simply grown accustomed to urban conveniences and ways of thinking that were alien to rural life. Historically my parents were part of that last exodus from the villages and farms to the towns of England which had begun with the Industrial Revolution and continued throughout the nineteenth century, the so-called flight from the land. Inevitably, between my grandparents and parents, there developed to some extent a gulf: it was not a gulf of social class, but of town and country.

Granny Fletcher was a mine of information and I think she was secretly rather pleased that her eldest grandson, who had been named after his grandfather, John Fletcher, should show an interest in his forbears. She was only too happy to talk about the past as she remembered it, and I was only too happy to listen. Sometimes it would be about the weekly trip from Tissington to Ashbourne market in the 1890s, when the village housewives travelled in the carrier's cart but had to walk the last mile up-hill on the return journey because the horse could not pull the cart laden with both provisions and passengers. Or she would explain the economy of cheesemaking to a young townsman who had never thought what happened to gallons of milk produced daily before the invention of modern transport and processing plants. Without knowing it I was introduced to the delights of what, in the 1970s, became known as oral history. But I was too young to realise the importance of asking the right questions and recording the answers, so that what remains is only a part of something that could have been far richer. One day she produced a box of old documents, mostly eighteenth-century deeds and some old notebooks and wills but there were also photograph albums and loose *cartes de visite*. Although at first I had some difficulty in deciphering the legal script on the parchment indentures, I was now squarely launched into the stuff of history. Like Molière's character who discovered that he had been speaking prose without knowing it, I was soon engaged in historical research.

It was quickly apparent that in this piece of family history all roads led back to Tissington. It was there that the physical memorials of the Fletchers were to be found: the grey-stone seventeenth-century farmhouse near the church, the tombstones in the churchyard, the entries in the parish registers. Tissington is one of the most secluded and beautiful villages in Derbyshire. It lies half a mile from the main Buxton road, at the end of a splendid avenue of lime trees which looks as though it must be the approach to a private residence, and which perhaps for that reason inhibits visitors. The triangular green is faced by stone cottages and the Jacobean manor house, Tissington Hall, home of the Fitzherbert family for more than four-hundred years. The tiny church with a sturdy, Norman tower, standing on a low bank above the road, is crowded with Fitzherbert monuments and outside, beneath the sycamores and yews, lie buried generations of farming families.

To the outside world Tissington is known chiefly for its well-dressings held on Holy Thursday (Ascension Day). The five wells from which the village derived its water supply are decorated with flowers and blessed by the priest in a religious ceremony. Crowds of people come from all around to participate and admire the work of those who have spent days making the elaborate mosaics and biblical scenes out of flowers, moss and leaves pressed into beds of moist, salted clay set in frames. The decorations are left round the wells until the following Sunday, after which Tissington reverts to its customary quietude. Our family albums are liberally sprinkled with postcards of the well-dressings in various years of the late-nineteenth and early-twentieth centuries, for not only the Fletchers but the Harrisons also were Tissingtonians, and uncles, aunts, cousins and friends were closely associated with the festival.

Tissington was historically a 'close', as distinct from an 'open' parish, that is to say it was dominated by the local squire, in this case the reigning Fitzherbert baronet. In an open parish, such as that described in Flora Thompson's *Lark Rise*, the land was divided between many smallholders and cottagers, and was not under the control of a squire or small group of farmers. Tissington was also a nucleated village. The older farm houses were in the centre, separate from their land which was scattered in parcels around the village as it had been in medieval times. This was the case with the Fletchers' farm and was felt to be a great inconvenience. Some farms however, such as Shaw's Farm, Broadclose, Tissington Wood Farm, Sharplow, or Newton Grange, were sited on their land and these probably dated from the enclosures of the late-eighteenth and early nineteenth centuries. Farmers either owned their own land (in which case they were usually called yeomen) or rented it from the Fitzherberts, and sometimes combined both modes.

There was no difficulty in my getting permission to search the parish registers which in those days were still kept in the church, though the vicar was somewhat curious about this schoolboy who was happy to spend his holidays poring over the old volumes in the vestry. Parishes were ordered to keep a record of baptisms, marriages and burials in 1538 but most parish registers date from the late-sixteenth or early seventeenth centuries. The Tissington registers begin in 1658, and the earliest Fletcher entries are for the burial of Jane Fletcher in 1667 and her husband, Richard, in 1671. Robert Fletcher was 'buried in woollen according to Parlmt. Act—Mar. 3rd. 1679'. This was in accordance with the 1678 Act for the encouragement of the woollen industry.

After abstracting all the relevant entries it was a comparatively simple matter to construct a family tree, checking the dates where necessary against tombstones, documents, and family legend. Little could be gleaned about the seventeenth-century Fletchers who had lived through the upsets of the Civil War, when Colonel Fitzherbert had garrisoned Tissington Hall for the king in December 1643 but abandoned it the following February after a skirmish with the parliamentarians at Blore Heath. It is probable that the Fletcher family owned some land at that time: William

The Fletcher farmhouse, Tissington, Derbyshire

My father's two unmarried sisters, Edith (1886–1977) and Helen (1885–1974)

Their cottages, Fenny Bentley, Derbyshire

Fletcher is described in a document dated 1712 as 'late of Tissington, yeoman'. But the exact amount and whereabouts of the holding, apart from the house near the church, is not known.

From the eighteenth century it is possible to trace the fortunes of the family more precisely. Thomas Fletcher, born in 1719, was brought up as a butcher, like his father, Robert, before him. In 1752 Thomas married Joan Mellor, the daughter of a yeoman farmer at Thorpe. The marriage settlement included a dowry of £140 and various 'household effects', among which was a small, silver teaspoon engraved with the initials JM which was passed to me many years ago. Thomas and his wife lived in a house rented from his uncle, George Ensor, and the latter, having no children, left all his land and property to his nephew who thus became the owner of two houses and three additional closes of land known as Highway Flatts (7 acres), Greenway Ditch (5 acres) and Bentley Fields (4 acres). With this increased wealth Thomas was able to give up butchering and start farming. In 1752 he was described as 'butcher'; after 1770 'yeoman', and in the probate copy of his will 'gentleman'. In 1795 he purchased part of the Newton Grange estate known as the Mootlow, containing about 46 acres. This Newton Grange estate was sold by auction on 'Saturday the 6th Day of June, 1796 at the Black-Moor's-Head in Ashbourne' and Thomas bought lot number four for the sum of £1281 10s. The land was not very fertile—chiefly moorland—but was suitable for pasturing sheep and perhaps a few cows.

The years in which Thomas was farming (1770–1800) were times of prosperity for farmers, especially after the outbreak of the long war with France in 1793, when agricultural prices rose rapidly. The patriotism of some of the villagers of Tissington was doubtless stimulated by economic benefit when, according to the *Derby Mercury* of 3 May 1798, they raised a subscription for the government as proof of their loyalty to the king and an earnest that they would exert themselves to the utmost in the defence of their country. Among the subscribers was Thomas Fletcher who gave £2 2s. The rise in prices is well brought out by comparing Thomas's account book with that of his son William (1755–1839). One of the chief sources of income was the sale of cheeses which were made daily from the milk and which were stored in large cheese attics at the top of the house. An entry for 8 January 1778 reads:

> Mr Evans's Man [the cheese buyer] weighed 395 cheeses at
> 32 shillings per cwt.

A similar entry on 10 March 1819 reads:

Mr Simpson weighed 83 cwt of cheese at £2s.0d. per cwt.

But in spite of this rise in the cost of food, wages remained the same. The yearly wage for a farm labourer varied between £8.8s. and £12.12s., and even then much of the wage was paid in kind. The following is a typical extract from William's account book for one of his labourers:

Thomas Allsop. 1822. Old Christmas

	£	:	s	:	d
Half a load of meal			15	:	0
Smock frock for Billy			4	:	4
Rent	1	:	17	:	0
Gave Fanny	1	:	0	:	0
For coals and a pig	2	:	0	:	0
Fanny at Midsummer	1	:	0	:	0
July 25th	1	:	0	:	0
Rent	1	:	15	:	0
Cash	12	:	11	:	4

These vellum-bound account books were also used for general memoranda: births and deaths, receipts, notes on the weather:

One ounce of Gunpowder in one Quart of milk for a Beast that is swelled

and

For a cold
a large cup of Linseed
two pennyw'th of stick Liquorice
a quarter of sun-raisins.

Put them into two quarts of soft water.
Let them simmer over a fire.
Add a quarter of brown sugar-cake pounded, a large spoonful
of old rum, a large spoonful of wine-vinegar or lemon juice.
The rum and vinegar are best put to it when you take it.
Drink half a pint at going to bed, and then a little when the
cough comes.

Thomas records:

July 18th 1794. Finished the Hay.
Aug 26th. Began to cut the corn at the Moor.

And his son, William, notes:

The year 1816 was a late Harvest; we did not cut any of our corn before
the 10th of October, and did not get it till the end of November, and a
great quantity was then not got in nor cut.

To which my grandfather added later:

> After an interval of 70 yrs the above mentioned W. Fletcher's great grand-
> son makes another memorandum. The winter of 1886 was an unusually
> severe one.

Both Thomas and William served their time as churchwarden at
Tissington and traces of their parochial duties lie scattered throughout
their notebooks and other documents. Thomas noted his disbursements in
1791:

		£	:	s	:	d
May 14th.	Charges to Visitation at Derby			2	:	0
	Fees					4
	A Form of Prayer			2	:	0
Bread and wine at Whit Sunday				3	:	6
June 16	Cleaning the church			1	:	6
Sept. 27	Bread and wine			3	:	6
Oct.13	Visitation at Derby			2	:	4
	washing and mending surplice			1	:	6
Bread and wine at Christmas				3	:	6
Bread and wine for Good Friday and Easter				7	:	0½

There were also duties in connection with the Poor Law and William
Ensor's charity for the apprenticing of poor children from Tissington.

Thomas retired from farming when his son William married Mary
Bagshaw in 1798. The Bagshaws were farmers from Newton Grange, and
a Thomas Bagshaw was churchwarden of Tissington in 1760. Mary inherited a number of household effects, including an oak dower chest made
for her parents, Anthony and Mary (née Beresford) Bagshaw on their marriage in December 1760. William and Mary Fletcher lived first at Alsop
Hall, but after the death of Thomas in 1809 they moved into the Fletcher
house in Tissington. This was a pattern repeated several times in the nineteenth century, when the eldest son had to set up home on another farm
in the parish before moving later in life into the family house on the death
or retirement of his father. In 1815 William purchased Halfway House,
and with the land he had inherited from his father in 1809 was in an altogether comfortable position. He had five children and left all his land and
property to his son William, and to each of his daughters a legacy of £100
in cash.

This William Fletcher (1803–68) in 1832 married Mary Docksey,
whose family were tenant farmers at Sharplow. On his marriage William's
father set him up at Shaws Farm, ready stocked as a wedding present. The
Shaws was a 260-acre holding rented from the Fitzherberts, and William

lived there as a gentleman farmer. He kept sixty milking cows, made two cheeses per day, and employed two housemaids. Groceries were purchased from Manchester twice a year. Candles, beer and the like were all made at home. Tangible evidence of this prosperity remains in the silver cutlery, silver tankard and elegant furniture handed down to later generations. In the 1842 Tissington Tithe Award, showing owners and occupiers of land, William appears as the occupier of other pieces of land in the parish in addition to the Shaws farm. He also owned the house and land in Tissington inherited from his father and land outside the parish.

The fifty years between 1830 and 1880 were a golden age for English farmers, to which my grandparents' generation looked back nostalgically. Decline set in from the mid-1870s and the period of High Farming came to an end. But, in the case of the Fletchers the decline set in earlier because William Fletcher dissipated his fortune. By the late 1850s he was living a wild, drunken and extravagant existence. At times he would go away for days on end, taking his labourers with him, on a drinking spree; though when sober he was a most pleasant and kind little man. When I first heard this story I was inclined to think it was exaggerated. But the documentary evidence in the form of mortgages on the property is conclusive. For instance, Halfway House was mortgaged for £750 in a series of borrowings on eight separate occasions between 1855 and 1857. William Fletcher's behaviour was attributed by Granny Fletcher to his 'not very suitable marriage' (whatever that meant) to Mary Docksey and to the blow suffered in July 1846 when three of his six children died within a few days of each other. The mute evidence of their little tombstone in Tissington churchyard records the death of Mary, John and Martha from 'sore throat fever'. They were aged 11, 8, and 2 years respectively.

On William's death in 1868 his property, heavily burdened with debt, was divided between his two surviving sons. Halfway House, some land at Waterfall in Staffordshire, and two cottages in Tissington went to Francis Bagshaw Fletcher (1841–1928), who became a chemist and had a business in Retford until he retired in 1897. The eldest son, William (1836–93), inherited the old house in Tissington, together with the Mootlow and Greenway Ditch, Highway Flatts and Bentley Fields. As a young man he worked with his uncle Tunnicliffe (married to his aunt, Anne Fletcher), who was a tanner at Earl Sterndale. Later William became a farmer and lived at the house in Tissington until his death in 1893.

The history of the Fletchers is typical of the quarter of a million or so farmers of Victorian England. First, they were remarkably stable, being rooted in the same village for 300 years—indeed, perhaps as long as the Fitzherberts at Tissington Hall. Second, they inter-married with similar families from the surrounding area—the Ensors, Johnsons, Bagshaws, Buxtons, Alsops, Hands, Whieldons, Beresfords, Mellors, Harrisons. With each succeeding marriage, a fresh rivulet flowed into the family stream, and each rivulet was itself the product of the same process, thus creating an extensive cousinage and intricate family relationships. Third, their rise and decline over four or five generations is clearly charted. From the late-eighteenth century they prospered steadily, buying more land and living well—in marked contrast to their labourers whose lot remained hard. But with the onset of the agricultural depression in the last quarter of the nineteenth century the struggle to make a living from the lands at Tissington was too hard; and in 1905 they were sold to the Fitzherberts.

At this point a decisive break with several centuries of the past was made. The context of family history was now decisively changed. Although my grandfather returned to Halfway House, which remained in the family until 1935, he was no longer an active farmer. His children were not farmers nor did they marry farmers like their ancestors. His two daughters, Mary (my mother) and Elsie, married clerks and went to live in Midland towns; his son, Willie, became an ironmonger in Ashbourne. However, the break with the past was not sudden or complete. Not everyone of my parents' generation left the land, and uncles, aunts and cousins several times removed continued to live in the Ashbourne region. We sometimes forget that we all have four grandparents and sixteen great-great-grandparents, so that our roots are widely spread. My genealogical excursions extended only a limited way into this maze of local history. The challenge to explore further remains.

♦ 4 ♦

The Aunts

————◆————

IN THE 1950s, on our way from York to the Midlands, we usually called in to see my aunts who lived in Fenny Bentley. Strung out along the Ashbourne to Buxton Road, the village consisted of a succession of cottages of red brick or grey, Derbyshire stone. A trout stream, the Bentley Brook, flowed through the village and down the side of the road on its way to join the River Dove two miles away at Sandy Brook. The village had no manor house or substantial farm houses except for 'Cherry Orchard', the imposing, fifteenth-century fortified house of the Beresford family, then occupied as a farm by the Websters, who were cousins of my father. The church, heavily restored in the nineteenth century, had a fine, early-sixteenth century chancel screen and some curious, marble table-tombs of medieval Beresfords. Grandparents and great-grandparents, on both sides of the family, lie buried in the churchyard.

My father's two unmarried sisters, Helen (Aunt Nellie) and Edith (Aunt Edie), lived in adjoining cottages on the main road. Although they took some of their meals together, each was jealous of her independence so they lived side-by-side in these tiny cottages, popping in and out of one another's adjacent front door like the antique figures in a cuckoo clock. Before 'visiting' next door they usually put on a hat, secured by a long hat pin. When we visited them we had to be very careful not to spend more time in one cottage than the other. On hearing the car draw up they would come out to welcome us, declaring in strong Derbyshire accents, 'My, how the children have grown'; how pleased they were to get my letter telling them we were coming, and how Willie (my father) had told them this and that in his last letter. We always crowded into Edie's cottage first, mainly I think because it was also the post office and so she (Edie) had 'to keep an eye on things'. Later we split up and took it in turns to visit Nellie next door.

Each cottage had two rooms up and two down, though the room on the left of the door in Edie's cottage was divided, making a narrow vestibule which served as the post office. The floors were of tile, covered only with a rag rug in front of the hearth. The door, as in most cottages, was usually left open in summer to admit light and air, but also to indicate that the post office was open. On the walls several decades of wallpaper formed a thick skin which covered up the blemishes in the plaster (or lack of it). The ceilings and beams were heavily encrusted with layers of whitewash, renewed annually at spring-cleaning time. In a corner of the sitting room a door with a wooden latch concealed the steep, twisting stairs which opened directly into the bedroom above. The paintwork was green and brown. Both cottages exuded an air of scrubbing and hard polishing.

The cottages were extremely primitive. Almost the only modern conveniences they had were a cold-water tap and an electric light downstairs. When 'the electric' had come to the village in the 1930s it had been considered an unnecessary luxury to extend it to the bedrooms. Earlier when, as children, my sister and I visited them in the 1920s and 1930s all the water was fetched from the village pump across the road and stored in pails, and lighting was by oil lamps. There was no proper kitchen, only a slopstone set in a kind of extended larder. Heating and cooking were by means of an old-fashioned coal-fired range in the living room: one side of the fire had an oven and the other a boiler from which the water had to be ladled since there was no tap. In hot weather, when a fire was insufferable in the tiny room, a two-burner paraffin stove was used instead. To go to the lavatory one had to go out of the front door, round the end of the cottage, up a flight of steps into the garden, to a bucket-type closet housed in a little brick shed. It was scrubbed scrupulously clean and smelt abominably. The cottages, wedged in between the road and the garden, which was at a higher level, had only a front door, as the back wall was built up against the earth. The garden was a glorious mixture of flowers (Michaelmas daisies, marigolds, primroses) and vegetables (mostly potatoes, cabbage and rhubarb), apple trees, and infrequently mown grass. In one corner, bordering a lane, was the stables, used as a bicycle and garden and washing shed and, when my grandfather was alive, as a home for his ferrets.

Into this cottage world, so different from my own upbringing in Leicester, the two sisters seemed to fit perfectly. They could have come straight out of Flora Thompson's *Lark Rise*, and there were even shades of Mrs Gaskell's *Cranford*. Everything about them harmonised, from their long, tweedy skirts, woollen stockings and flat-heeled shoes to their shrewd country women's comments on what they heard on the wireless.

They had an unrivalled knowledge of the village and its inhabitants which extended to the neighbouring villages of Tissington, Parwich, Bradbourne, Balidon, Thorpe, Mapleton, Mayfield; and even more explicitly to the farms of relations and friends: Bassett Wood, The Ashes, Brookwood, Broad Close, Bank Top, The Firs, Cherry Orchard, Newton Grange. There was not a family whose comings and goings were unknown, nor whose past fortunes and antecedents were not remembered. Every field and outlying farmhouse, every footpath and ditch were familiar. They knew where mushrooms could be gathered in the early morning, where the violets, primroses and cowslips grew in profusion, and how to cut across the fields to Thorpe at night with a telegram. These things were the residue of their childhood, reinforced later by the exigencies of running the post office. Nellie and my father were born while the family lived at The Green Farm in Tissington. My grandfather described himself at that time as butcher and cattle dealer; but sometime thereafter he moved to Fenny Bentley where he became postmaster. He probably inherited this position from his grandfather, Charles Harrison, who died in 1890 and who had been appointed postmaster at Fenny Bentley in 1860. Edie was born (1886) in Bentley and the three children spent their childhood there in the 1890s, attending the village school across the road from the cottages. In due course Nellie and my father escaped from the village but Edie was destined to remain there, for over eighty years.

Like so many unmarried women of their generation it was the lot of both sisters to spend their lives looking after their parents and aged relatives. Of the inner and earlier life of the aunts one knew little. Why they remained unmarried is not clear. In later life they both had female friends to whom they were much attached: Nellie to Florrie Gilman, a firm, masculine-looking spinster who was the school mistress at Fenny Bentley; and Edie to Ada Wright, a girlhood friend who later married and ran a boarding house at Harpur Hill, near Buxton.

Although my grandfather was nominally the postmaster at Fenny Bentley, many of the duties were undertaken by Edie. She conducted all the office work and shared the letter delivery. In the days before telephones became plentiful there was the additional burden of telegrams, which had to be delivered immediately. This could entail a journey of several miles across wet fields, as the territory to be covered included Thorpe which had no post office of its own. From October 1941 Edie was appointed sub-postmistress in her own right and continued as such for the next twenty-two years. On her retirement in 1963 there was a suggestion that her name might be put forward for an award (BEM) but she vetoed the idea vehemently. In old age she would reminisce about events at the turn of the century: the building of the Ashbourne to Buxton railway line and the huts that were built for the construction gangs to live in; how she used to be asked to write letters home for illiterate Irish labourers and gypsies who came to work in the harvest fields; and how during Queen Victoria's last illness she used to deliver telegrams to R.W. Hanbury, President of the Board of Agriculture and a member of the Cabinet who was staying at Ilam Hall.

Life with her parents could not have been without its tensions for Edie. Her father was a thick-set, bull-necked man who was not an enthusiast for hard work. He was probably a rather rough individual, though to us as children he seemed a stout, jolly character who produced nuts and sweets from his waistcoat pockets and who smelt strongly of tobacco, sweat and Sloan's liniment. He would take us to see his ferrets, which he fed with raw meat and which, he assured us, would 'take y' finger off' if you didn't look out. His talk was of strange and fascinating things about which we knew nothing: gypsies whom he had met at Ashbourne cattle market; charms and cures for his lumbago; dogs and horses he had once possessed. In the cottage he always sat on a wooden armchair in the corner to the left of the fireplace, with his shotgun propped up against the wall and the dog lying at his feet. When we visited there was not room for us all to sit round the table for dinner, so he remained in his corner chair and ate his plateful with a red handkerchief spread out across his paunch as a serviette. Although it was many years since he had been a butcher he retained his expertise with knives and always carved the joint (a special treat for our visit) after a display of sharpening on the steel which hung from a nail above his chair. He was reputed to have been rather 'wild' in his youth, whatever that meant. He was just twenty-one when he married in 1881. His bride, Edith Clews, was three years older; and their first child, my father, was born nine months after the wedding. The Clews of Newton Grange were an old farming family and more prosperous than the Harrisons, and the match bears some signs of a runaway romance. Three more children were born during the next four years, though one (Florence) survived only five days, leaving my father and his two sisters to be brought up in the cottage in Bentley. As a breadwinner William Harrison must have been something of a disappointment to his young wife. It soon became apparent that she was not destined, as she might reasonably have hoped, to become the wife of a hard-working village butcher or farmer, but the spouse of a cottager who served as the village postmaster. To eke out this steady but modest income my grandfather turned his hand to any rural pursuit that would bring in a few pounds, such as coal dealing. He would order a truck of coal to be delivered to Bentley railway sidings and then employ a carter to deliver loads to the local farmers. The coal business and early morning letter delivery were by no means an onerous means of livelihood, which suited him down to the ground, since his tastes were somewhat above his station. He was an excellent shot and as a young man had joined a local troop of the Derbyshire Yeomanry. He loved nothing better than to take his dog and gun and enjoy an hour or two of rabbiting.

By contrast my grandmother was refined and sweet-natured. In her sixties, when I remember her, she was already severely crippled by arthritis and could only hobble round the house. She normally sat in a wicker armchair beneath the grandfather clock whence she superintended Edie's cooking and undertook such tasks as shelling peas or mixing batter in a bowl. Nowadays she would have been diagnosed as needing a hip-joint replacement; but no such alleviation was available in her time. Her hair was drawn back from her forehead and she seemed always to wear a white apron over her dress.

My grandfather was essentially an out-of-doors man. He seemed ungainly and out of place in the tiny cottage and, when banished to his corner, he would light up his pipe from the fire, using spills of folded paper. From time to time he would spit in the fire, which gave great offence to Edie and my grandmother. He resented being marginalised in a family gathering and would begin to tell us some story about his doings or acquaintances, whereupon my grandmother would reprove him: 'Give o'er, Will, they don't want to hear such things'. We would of course have loved to hear such things, but they were not deemed respectable enough for the occasion, when in any case the centre of attention was my father, who was the apple of his mother's eye and much looked up to by his sisters. In their eyes he was everything that my grandfather was not; successful, courteous, attentive—and at a distance.

For most of her life Edie lived in the post office cottage. Until the death of her mother in 1941 and her father in 1947 she did not have a home of her own. Only when she was in her sixties did she enjoy freedom and independence. Nor for most of her life did she have much income, though presumably either her father or the post office made her some allowance for her services. In the 1940s, after she was appointed sub-post mistress, her monthly pay was £16 9s 5d., or nearly £200 per year. Amazingly, she did not spend it all but managed to save some of it. From time to time, according to her notebook, she had to subsidise the post office business out of her own money. The post office provided both a means of livelihood and an unrivalled social focus. People coming to buy stamps, draw money, or make telephone calls (there was no outside booth) inevitably stopped for a few minutes to pass the time of day and exchange news and gossip. The postman delivering mail by van every morning and collecting it from the postbox each evening passed on news from Ashbourne and carried out small errands. Summer visitors, usually staying at the Coach and Horses public house, dropped in to buy postcards of the village and were the subject of endless speculation and comment. They were shrewdly assessed by their clothes and accents. Some were approved of as being ladylike and gentlemanly; others were judged to be too loud and coarse. All of them expected to be informed about anything they wished to know about the village; and they were not disappointed

Edie was also quite well informed about national and world events, especially when they had some connection with a friend or someone whom the friend knew about. She read the local weekly newspaper regularly, though she never bought a copy, preferring to borrow from a neighbour and to pass it on when done with. She also read books. The travelling county library service, which brought books to the villages, provided her with a fortnightly supply of novels, biography, and general literature. Her selection was based on recommendations from people she talked to. She wrote the titles in her note book and then requested them from the county library. In the 1950s they ranged from Nicholas Monserratt's *The Cruel Sea* and Dodie Smith's *I Capture the Castle* to John Buchan's *Oliver Cromwell*, Eric Williams's *The Wooden Horse* and Gracie Fields's autobiography, *Sing As We Go*.

Nevertheless, Edie was at heart a countrywoman and her interests were intensely local. She had a strong sense of history, but it was family and local events that shaped her perceptions. She measured time by generations, using the succession of rectors at Fenny Bentley or baronets at Tissington Hall as bench marks: 'that would be while old Sir William was still alive', or 'that was before Mr Baggaly came'. Her ideas of what was right and proper were firm, and she had a strong streak of obstinacy. For instance, in 1937 a new rector, the Reverend Morgan Williams, was appointed. She soon came to disapprove of what she regarded as his authoritarian ways in changing things at the church and the rectory. All her life hitherto she had been a regular worshipper and supporter of church activities. After quarrelling with him she declared that she 'would never set foot in his church again'—nor did she. For many years thereafter (in fact until the next incumbent arrived), she ceased to attend Bentley church and noted, with some satisfaction, how the congregation dwindled to a handful of parishioners. Again, there was the case of the grandfather clock, which stood in a corner by the fireplace. Although it kept good time the striking mechanism did not function properly, so that the clock struck the hours incorrectly. For years Edie put up with this disconcerting habit; yet it could have been remedied quite easily by a small adjustment, as I discovered years later when I inherited the clock.

In some ways the aunts were surprisingly literate. Their grounding in the three Rs at the village school had been sound; and the experiences of the post office ensured that Edie continued in a clerkly rhythm. Partly because of this she lived a very ordered life, with a daily, weekly and annual routine which varied very little through the years. She had to be up in good time to receive the post and begin her letter delivery. She had to clean the cottage and do the washing for herself and her parents. The cooking was done mainly by my grandmother I think, though Edie certainly had to bake the bread. This was done once a week. The dough, having been kneaded, was left to rise in a large earthenware bowl and covered with a damp tea towel. It was then put into tins and popped in the oven while the fire was banked up. Some time later Edie would take out a tin, smartly tap the crisp top of the loaf to see if it was 'done' and, if it were, tap the bottom of the hot tin to release the loaf. The new bread, smelling appetising and yeasty, was taken into the scullery to cool off. It was generally believed that new bread caused indigestion and so the loaves were not eaten for several days, by which time they had become solid if not stale. This also allowed the bread to be cut much more finely than otherwise, making possible those wafer-thin slices of bread and butter so admired by my mother, who always thought that thick bread (like eating cheese) showed a lack of gentility.

The great break for Edie and the highlight of her year was the annual two-week holiday. This was usually taken in North Wales (Llandudno), Scotland or Devonshire (Ilfracombe). Nellie's holidays were similar though she was more adventurous and in 1931 went to Switzerland. The sisters did not go together but each with her special friend, Edie with Ada Wright and Nellie with Florrie Gilman. Accommodation was in boarding houses and the days were spent on trips by boat and charabanc to neighbouring beauty spots. A steady stream of picture postcards flowed back to the relatives with reassuring messages about the weather and the food. These were kept and treasured in cardboard photograph albums, alongside photos of uncles, aunts and cousins, forming a visual residuum of memorabilia. Neither of the sisters had a camera of her own and perhaps for that reason valued the postcards and snaps sent to them.

The aunts were part of that majority of the population left out of history: ordinary people who have left few written records in which they described their thoughts and feelings and the events in which they were involved. Their history has to be sought elsewhere, in the record or memory of their conversations (oral history), in the occasional reference in a newspaper, in odd documents like birth and death certificates and copies of wills, manuscript entries on the fly-leaves of prayer books and bibles, and in the things they left behind them. A piece of jewellery, a grandfather clock, a chest of drawers, may seem unlikely witnesses. But if the right questions are asked they may no longer remain mute. A family photograph album in its original, untidied state, may be made to yield much more than pictures of yesterday's fashions. It is a palimpsest on which is recorded (or not recorded) the social and individual habits and assumptions of successive generations. From the earliest *cartes de visite* of grandfather and grandmother Clews, born respectively in 1816 and 1821, to photographs of my parents in their garden at Leicester during the Second World War, the layers of family history can be peeled off. The aunts were part of this history and felt themselves to be so.

Another and somewhat wider world than that of Fenny Bentley was open to Nellie. She had left the village as a girl of fifteen to live with an aunt and uncle. Samuel Clews had married a cousin, Florence Clews and they had no children. He was a successful dairy farmer at The Elms farm, Littleover, near Derby, and treated Nellie like a daughter. She became a dairy maid and in June 1906 was awarded first prize in buttermaking at the Royal Agricultural Show at Derby; and on a further trial of all the winners of first prizes was 'awarded the highest prize the Royal Society can bestow, viz. the Champion Buttermaking Prize for All England', according to the local parish magazine. Uncle Sam (a rather jolly man, with a pointed beard) prospered during the First World War to such an extent that he was able to retire shortly after, having sold his farm at a good price for building land. He bought a tall, detached Victorian villa standing on the main Burton road in Littleover. It was named South Yarra by its former owner, an Australian, and was notable for the enormously long, tiled passage or hallway which ran from the front door through the length of the house to the back sitting room. In the front sitting room were hung large, engraved portraits of Gladstone and Disraeli, one on either side of the fireplace. It seemed to me later, when I had discovered who these Victorian arch-rivals were, that it demonstrated a remarkable degree of political impartiality or canniness to display both the Liberal and Conservative champions together.

When we visited Uncle Sam and Aunt Florrie, which we could easily do by train from Leicester, in the 1930s, the house was lit by gas. Even after the Second World War on one occasion when we stayed there for the night, we had to go to bed in the dark because the bedrooms were

Edwardian: *Harrison family group, taken in the garden, Fenny Bentley, c. 1913. Standing: Edith, William (my father, 1882–1972), Helen Sitting: Granny (née Edith Clews, 1857–1941) and Grandfather (William, 1860–1947)*

1930s: *Studio portrait, Leicester, c. 1930, Father, Mother, Eileen and me*

The move from terrace house to semi-detached was a change of both lifestyle and status. Linton Street, Leicester: (above, left) Outside Number 25, c. 1925 (above, right) In the backyard, 1921 (below) The choirboy

still lit by old-fashioned gas burners which were no longer safe. As Aunt Florrie explained, the absence of lights during the war saved the expense of having to put up blackout material; and after the war she didn't need lights because there was a street light outside the front bedroom window. Her careful if not miserly ways were sometimes carried to extremes, as in the case of the damson stones. South Yarra had a large garden and an orchard plentifully supplied with damson trees, whose sour little fruits were dutifully collected and made into jam. One afternoon at tea time we were presented with a pile of damson stones, skimmed from the boiling jam earlier, and which we were instructed to suck with our bread and butter instead of spreading it with jam.

Habits of carefulness and frugality were deeply ingrained. But in the case of Nellie they were also combined with a dash of adventure and daring. She was a stockily-built woman, like her father, with big hands and hairs on her face. Unlike Edie, who was at times morose and narrow-minded, Nellie had a mischievous smile and was altogether more open. Because she lived at Littleover, which after the First World War became absorbed as a suburb of Derby, she was regarded as sophisticated and emancipated in a way that the Fenny Bentleyites could never be. She was a favourite of Uncle Sam who I think helped her financially from time to time. Certainly she managed to save money, which she invested in a small rentable house in Derby. She also fancied herself as a speculator in stocks and shares which she occasionally bought on the advice of her bank manager. After the death of Aunt Florrie in 1947, Nellie returned to Bentley and when the cottages were offered for sale to the tenants she bought them. There had originally been three cottages, all belonging to the Fitzherbert estate, but two of them were converted into one, and in that she lived, side by side with Edie in the post office cottage next door.

In old age they decided that they would take advantage of an offer from the county council to rehouse them in one of several new cottages which the council had built in what was now called Ashes Lane. Edie, as a life-long inhabitant of the village and a non-property owner, was apparently eligible for one of the new cottages, the post office being condemned as sub-standard in matters of sanitation and amenities. So Nellie sold the cottages, which were bought as a second home by a solicitor from Derby, and the two old ladies moved into their new accommodation. They now had a bathroom, a kitchen with a cooker, a hot-water supply, and a garden with a path leading to the front door. No longer did the lorries thunder past, no longer did they have to use a bucket closet and chamber pots. But neither did people drop in so frequently to pass the time of day. Old habits died hard: Edie insisted on keeping the door open even when it was cold outside. Nellie died first, in 1974, and Edie three years later. They were 89 and 90 respectively.

The aunts had a strong sense of place. When I think of them it is always in relation to the village. Edie's world was in Fenny Bentley, Ashbourne, and the neighbouring villages. Even Nellie, who had left the village, was not very far away: it is only thirteen miles from Ashbourne to Derby. At any rate that is how it seemed to me as I listened to the talk in Bentley and Littleover. The townsman's imagined ideal of a village postmistress, according to Flora Thompson, was that she should wear a white apron and speak the dialect. For one townsman at least no imagination was necessary.

✦ 5 ✦

Semi-Detached

---◆---

I<small>N</small> 1936 <small>A GREAT</small> change came into our lives. We moved to a new house, all our very own. It had long been my mother's dream to have a truly modern home in one of the newly-developing suburbs, but the means of achieving this were unavailable. My father's earnings were not considered (at any rate by my parents) adequate for them to take advantage of such credit facilities as were offered. The family had neither the capital for a down payment on the purchase of a house nor the means of servicing a mortgage if one were obtainable. But in 1935 grandfather Fletcher, my mother's father died. He had been suffering from a cancer on his head for several years and latterly had gone to live with his daughter Elsie and her husband, Frederick Cartwright, who ran a greengrocer's shop in Derby. Halfway House, grandfather's smallholding near Ashbourne, was sold, and money was made available to his three children. With mother's share of this inheritance my parents were able to go ahead with plans for a new home.

My mother, as always, had very definite ideas of what she wanted. The area selected was Evington Parks, where a tangle of new roads had been laid out and semis were sprouting up like mushrooms. This location had the advantage of being handy for the same shops that we used when we lived in Linton Street and was also within the parish of St Philip's, so that all our social relationships remained uninterrupted. There was also a direct bus service into the centre of Leicester. The move would, therefore, have all the excitement of a decisive break, a new start, while retaining old friendships and church loyalties. My mother had set her heart on having a house with a 'through' room instead of the usual separate sitting and dining rooms. None of the houses my parents were shown had this feature so they approached a small builder named Ellis to see if he would be interested. He and his brother were working bricklayers who had an option on several plots of land and they agreed to build a pair of semis to my mother's specifications. The price was £650. Another £50 or so was spent on laying out the front garden and paving at the back, making about £700 in all.

Number 15 Byway Road was a classic 1930s semi. Downstairs it had a small breakfast room and a scullery with sink and cooker in addition to the relatively large sitting room ('the lounge'). Upstairs there were three bedrooms, none of which was very big and one which was little more than a boxroom, together with a bathroom and separate lavatory. Outside was another loo and a coal house. Heating was by coal fire. A garage on the side of the house was barely large enough for an Austin Seven; but that hardly mattered since we did not have a car. It made an excellent tool shed and store place, and during the war was turned into an air-raid shelter. Only by comparison with the terrace house in Linton Street can the conveniences of 15 Byway Road be appreciated. A bathroom and indoor lavatory, a front door that no longer opened directly onto the street, a garden with a lawn and flower beds—these were things which transformed the quality of family life. And there were other delights which gladdened the heart of the 1930s generation: a bay window looking onto the front garden, the leaded lights in the front door, the gleaming white tiles and chromium taps in the bathroom. Even the address was socially superior for we now lived in a road, not a street.

In the new home my parents' roles were sharply demarcated: broadly, the house and everything in it were mother's preserve, and the garden was left to my father. She happily spent her mornings washing, dusting, polishing, vacuum cleaning. These were the days when vacuum-cleaner salesmen on the doorstep used all their persuasive powers to make a sale, with payment by instalments ('on the never-never') if necessary. A favourite ploy was to demonstrate the efficiency of the machine by scattering dirt on the best carpet, much to the alarm of its owner, and then showing how quickly the mess could be cleaned up. My mother was curiously susceptible to this form of pressure, despite her initial caution and suspicion. 'It beats as it sweeps as it cleans' proclaimed the Hoover ads. And sure enough it was soon doing that at Number 15. The acquisition of labour-saving gadgets and electrical appliances in the home, of which the Hoover in place of the old carpet-sweeper was a good example, marked a steady trend toward that 'Ideal Home' which inspired my mother. Yet it was not until many years later that there was a telephone, a television or even a wireless in Number 15. Coal fires still made a lot of work; but they, along with washing up or peeling potatoes and cleaning the shoes, were one of the few jobs inside the house allocated to my father.

Not everything from Linton Street fitted into the new home; but most of the furnishings had to be accommodated since there was not enough money to replace them. The large oak dining table and chairs had to be squeezed into the small breakfast room. The living room, although larger than anything we had enjoyed previously, was soon filled by a massive three-piece suite. It was the fashion that everything had to 'match': cutlery, linen, tea sets, furniture; and my mother was much occupied that this should be so. She schemed and saved and economised until she could afford the latest object on which she had set her heart. To say that she was houseproud would have been the understatement of the year. The happiest time of her life was the quarter century she spent at Byway Road. She had a circle of friends based on the church and was active in the Mothers' Union, the Guild, and (later) the Old Folks' Club (the 'Evergreens'). In the afternoons she would 'go shopping', which meant a bus trip downtown to visit Adderleys, her favourite department store. I don't think she spent much, except on shoes, for which she had a weakness—all the more remarkable in that she hated walking anywhere. The experience was always the same. She would come home and announce that she had been lucky enough to find a pair which fitted her (for she had very narrow feet) and which were fashionable and would 'go' with her latest outfit. However, within a short time she would discover that they were uncomfortable, whereupon they were consigned, still in their box, to the wardrobe where they joined others in the same condition. She belonged to the generation who in their youth had always worn hats; and it may have been that when millinery fell out of fashion, as it did after the First World War, attention was switched to other accessories like shoes and handbags. Millinery had, like school teaching, provided a respectable job for many women before 1914. Mother's sister Elsie was a milliner; and so too was Margaret (my wife's) grandmother, Phoebe Hemmings. Hat consciousness was high among mother's generation, nurturing a secret longing which could never be fully realised once the great days of the hat had gone.

Space in the living room was further attenuated by the piano which survived the move from Linton Street to inflict continuing trials of my spirit. The instrument was a black upright with brass, candle sconces, though these were later removed. Playing the piano was an accomplishment by which my parents set some store. Mother had acquired the art, at least to the level of playing the hymns at school assembly or plonking out favourite tunes from the First World War such as *There's a Long, Long Trail*

A'winding, Let the Great Big World Keep on Turning 'Round, Oh, Oh, Antonio and, of course, *Tipperary*. But I never heard her play any 'pieces' nor did she practice regularly, if at all. The piano itself, which was very expensive, had been a status symbol and was also a useful form of entertainment before the coming of the radio. But by the time we arrived at Byway Road these functions had been largely displaced. It now served only as an instrument of refined, though unintended, torture for JFCH. Every day I was supposed to sit down at the thing and practice for half-an-hour, beginning with scales and finishing with the week's 'piece', which had some such title as *Rustle of Spring* or *Selections from Chopin*. Who Chopin was I had no idea, nor did I care much. How I envied my sister Eileen who was spared all this in exchange for attending a ballet class once a week on Saturday mornings. The piano lessons had begun long before the move. At first I had gone to a Miss Stacey, a kindly spinster who gave reassuring reports of my musical progress; but after I went to the grammar school I qualified for free tuition under an enlightened scheme of the LEA and was sent to a Mr Cox. This was the same Coxie who was also organist and choirmaster at St Philip's Church. He was supposed to teach me the theory as well as the practice of music. For two years I wrestled with harmony and tones and fifths, but made little headway. When the scholarship came to an end so did my classes with Coxie, and my career as a pianist withal. Looking back I now see that what was wrong was that I never progressed from the mechanics of operating the instrument to an appreciation of music. The emphasis was on playing the piano rather than the fun of making music. After a time, when neither I nor my mother used it, the piano was got rid of, and the sitting room gained more space.

Life in the semi also brought many boons for my father. He now had a real garden instead of merely an allotment. True it was a long, thin strip running down from the back of the house; but it provided him with an occupation that absorbed nearly all his free time. At weekends and on summer evenings he would methodically mow the lawn and weed the flower beds. Three, or four, apple trees at the bottom of the plot exercised his horticultural skills to the full since they obstinately refused to bear much fruit and regularly suffered from blight of one sort or another. His greatest successes were his roses and 'chrysanths'. He concentrated on producing fine individual plants rather than planning their overall effect. The size and perfection of a bloom was more important to him than how it related to the garden as a whole. His knowledge of gardening was entirely empirical. When we gave him a book on gardening for a birthday present it remained largely unread, and if he had a problem he would instinctively ask a friend's advice, not look it up in the book. He spent comparatively little money on the garden, always raising his plants from seed or exchanging plants with a fellow-gardener. The days of instant gardening and garden centres were still far in the future. Like a true countryman he could never get away from the idea that a garden should be productive and not solely ornamental. Unlike rooms in the house, which had to have money spent on them, the garden should at least be self-sustaining. He realised that this could never really be so at Byway Road, but a few token rows of lettuce, beans, peas, and carrots testified to this sentiment. The joys of our suburban garden however were savoured most sweetly on a sunny afternoon, sitting in a deckchair on the concrete slabs outside the french window which we designated the terrace or patio.

In other directions too life at Byway Road changed for my father. After nearly forty years of working as a booking clerk and then in the parcels office, he was given an outside job as a 'commercial representative' for the LMS. We knew very little about what he did at work. He seldom talked about it. On the rare occasions I called for him at the London Road parcels office he seemed quite a different person. The office with its rough wooden floor, high desks, ledgers and parcels stacked in piles, smelled strongly of milk, paraffin and disinfectant. I hardly recognised my father who was wearing an old jacket (which he kept there) and sleeve protectors, with a pencil stuck behind his ear. The office was run on a shift system, with father working 'early turn' (6 am to 2 pm) one week and 'late turn' (2 pm to 10 pm) the next. All this was now behind him. As a goods agent he spent his time visiting firms in the city, soliciting business and investigating complaints. He was free from office routines and restrictions, he could make up his own day's work, and had a printed visiting card with his name on it. I do not know whether his job was on a higher grade than his previous one. It certainly made him happier. But in any case he was the most uncomplaining of men and it took very little to make him happy, since he was quite without ambition and never expressed frustration.

For me semi-detached life coincided with my progress through grammar school. This again was a process which had begun before the move to Byway Road but which there developed most memorably. After I passed the scholarship examination in 1932 my parents were faced with a difficult decision of which school to choose, for Leicester was blessed with four boys' grammar schools and their opposite girls' numbers. The oldest, largest and most prestigious was the Wyggeston School. There was also Alderman Newton's, an eighteenth-century greencoat foundation; the City Boys' School; and the Gateway School. Like everyone else in a similar position we knew virtually nothing about any of these schools; and so the choice had to be based on rumour, gossip and general impressions. The 'Wiggie' was ruled out as being too expensive and la-de-da; Alderman Newton's was thought to be a bit lax and raffish; nothing was known about the Gateway, which was one of a new breed of technical grammar schools. That left the City Boys' School. As it turned out, this was a lucky choice. The school had recently acquired a new and progressive headmaster, an Oxford graduate in his forties, who was keen to turn this rather easy-going, and not very distinguished, Victorian institution into a first-rate academic establishment. His name, appropriately enough for a schoolmaster yet somewhat unfairly I always thought, was Crammer. The success of the school was to be measured by the examination results, the size of the sixth form, and the number of pupils who went on to university, especially to Oxford and Cambridge. By these criteria the City Boys' School was within a few years a shining light in the city's educational firmament.

The school photograph of 1933, at the end of my first year, tells all. Taken outside the main building in Humberstone Gate, the picture stretches across three feet of black-and-white print. *A Schooldays' Souvenir*, reads the label on the cardboard cylinder encasing it: 'Please keep clean and return to school next day if not required or 1s 6d. if kept', adding hopefully, 'Further copies can be obtained'. The school photograph was a welcome event as we missed a period of lessons to sit for it. We were arranged in a huge semi-circle and had to sit still while the camera, mounted on a tripod, traversed from left to right. The first row, sitting cross-legged on the ground, in black blazers, short grey trousers and long stockings, are the first formers: 1A, the scholarship boys; 1C the fee payers; and 1B a mixture of both. Behind them, some sitting and most standing (the back rows on benches) is the rest of the school, everyone wearing the black and gold striped tie, black blazer or jacket, and grey trousers. Sitting right in the centre is the headmaster, flanked by the staff and prefects. All the staff wear gowns except the woodwork, music and games masters who did not have degrees. Two women, the school secretary and the art teacher are placed next to the head. Four-hundred boys' faces gaze intently at the camera. Sixty years later I can remember almost none of them.

With the staff it is different, for they made an indelible impression on me. In retrospect I see that the school was held together by a core of about ten experienced teachers, men in their fifties, each with his own unmistakable style. They never had any discipline problems; one look was enough to subdue, even terrorise unruly spirits; and they were capable of drawing out the best in willing pupils. A chemistry lesson from 'Bull'

Smith was something not likely to be forgotten. At the beginning of the lesson, as we all sat round the laboratory benches on tall stools, Bull would come round to each of us, returning our homework which had entailed writing up the experiment we had carried out the previous week. 'We inserted a lighted TAPPER, it burnt with a blue flame, eh Harrison?' he said, bringing down the exercise book on my defenceless head. 'And where is the Duke of Thurnby this week?' he would enquire, referring to one of the absent county pupils who came from an outlying village. A geography lesson with 'Jos' Carter was liable to be mostly about his bronchial complaints: 'It's all down here', he would say, drawing a bony hand down his scrawny neck. We shivered with horror at his agonies. On more cheerful days he would enthral us with stories of his vacation travels to foreign parts, illustrating for instance the poverty in India by telling us of the gratitude of a poor man when he gave him a tiny square of chocolate. We were much impressed; in fact I almost wept. Then there was 'Carps' (Carpenter), who was able to transform the drudgery of 'sums' into something called mathematics which, he hinted, was an arcane science to which we might one day aspire. In rare moments of relaxation he would expand upon his home town of Guildford, to which he retreated in the holidays, and where he said he had known two brothers who had kept a bicycle shop, and one of them had gone on to become the greatest motor manufacturer in the country—a story strangely reminiscent of the Nuffield saga. I do not remember how this had any connection with mathematics; but it confirmed our impression that 'Carps' must be an important man. The classics master, whose name I think was Cooper, affected a weariness with the modern world, so remote from the glories of Greece and Rome. Rebuking a boy who was wearing cycle clips in class, he drawled, 'Boy, take those bracelets off your legs'. Later, in the 1930s the old guard was supplemented by younger men not long out of the university. Latin was replaced by German as the second language, and societies and clubs of all kinds proliferated. Elocution lessons were also introduced; and—even more daring—were taught by a beautiful young woman named Miss O'Driscoll. Badly as this slight counter-weight to our flat, Midland accents was needed, the experiment alas, was soon discontinued, mainly I suspect because Miss O'Driscoll's lovely red hair and attractive figure was just too disrupting for our coarse, all-male community. However, the good-looking junior physics master was not slow in dating her. After a few years he gave up teaching to become a barrister.

The City Boys' School was a very different place from Medway Street Elementary School. For one thing it was much further away, being in the centre of the town. I had to cycle there, or on very wet days go on the bus. More importantly the atmosphere was entirely different. One now had a desk of one's own in which to keep text books which were supplied by the school and had to be covered in brown paper at the beginning of each year. We belonged to forms, not classes; and we were taught not by plain teachers but by masters in black gowns. A superior body of young men called prefects, who seemed to be neither mere pupils like us nor yet masters, and who wore a gold tassel on their cap and a silver, wyvern badge (the crest of the City Boys' coat-of-arms) in their button hole, ordered us about. It is obvious from my school reports that I was one of those for whom the grammar school was tailor-made. The system was competitive: monthly and termly examinations, form positions, and detailed reports on every subject. The three-form entry was streamed, with the top and bottom of each form changing places periodically. From the start I was always in the top three and often first in English, History and Geography. After school there were rehearsals for the school plays—*Twelfth Night*, *A Midsummer Night's Dream*, *The Rivals*—in which I usually had to take a girl's part. There was also the debating society for which the family always assumed I must be a natural: 'Oh, John can always talk the hind leg off a donkey'.

Apart from the school play, which we rehearsed during the winter months, the main events in the school year were sports day and prize giving. Not being very interested in games, I never won any medals for athletics or colours for soccer or cricket. But at prize giving I always managed at least one award and sometimes 'went up' twice to shake hands with the distinguished visitor who had been persuaded to grace the occasion: Sir Frederick Marquis (later Lord Woolton, war-time Minister of Food), Harold Laski (Professor at the LSE), or Harold Nicolson (at that time MP for West Leicester). Prize giving was held in the De Montfort Hall, the main civic concert centre, as the school hall was not large enough to hold the whole school plus parents. 'Presented by the Governors to J.F.C. Harrison, Form IIIA, for History, 1935' reads the bookplate inside my copy of H.G. Wells's *The Outline of History*. The stories of R.L. Stevenson, Wilkie Collins, and Conan Doyle were other favourites for prizes. Later, in the sixth form, I used the occasion to acquire books which I knew I should need for the Cambridge History Tripos. Finally we were all presented with a copy of the bible (revised version), signed by the headmaster.

An altogether more sinister affair was the 'Great Sex Lecture' which as fifth formers we had to attend. It was not called that officially but wrapped up in some euphemism such as 'preparation for life' or 'the duties of adulthood'. We had to take home a sealed letter to our parents, requesting their assent to our attendance, the whole thing surrounded by mystery and rumour. There were stories of boys fainting and having to be carried out of the lecture, of unimaginable horrors to be revealed to us, and all by an unknown visitor called Dr Weeks, who apparently went round schools in Leicester and elsewhere delivering this annual homily. The lecture was given in the hall where, unusually, the doors were closed and the windows shaded. The Head introduced Weeks, and we listened excitedly and expectantly as he (Weeks) propounded his views on sexual conduct. Most of the lecture passed me by. I simply could not understand what he was talking about. I suppose he was warning us against masturbation; he did not mention homosexuality or prostitution, at least in any form recognisable by fifteen-year-old schoolboys. He spoke with passion about the glories of womanhood and threatened to thrash any chap who 'touched' his daughter. I felt deeply embarrassed. Somehow he managed to make us feel guilty and ashamed, though I am sure most of us were as innocent as new-born lambs, with no more than the usual curiosity about sexy pictures and dirty jokes. We left the hall disappointed and baffled. No one had fainted; no one had been named for unknown offences. I now see that this was Crammer's, or the LEA's, response to the (then progressive) demand for some form of sex education in schools. But the over-heated atmosphere and religiously emotional tones in which the lecture was delivered largely defeated its purpose. Much better was the talk on reproduction we were given in the newly-introduced subject of biology.

It was about this time that my interest in history began. I went through the usual collecting phases, beginning with stamps and moving on to swords and pistols; then it was coins, antique objects, and finally books. There was no special reason for spending my pocket money on two old, brass candlesticks in Ashbourne, or Roman coins which I took down to be identified in Leicester Museum on Saturday mornings. But the thrill of acquiring my first really old book has never left me. It was a battered copy of Baxter's *The Saints' Everlasting Rest*, dated 1657. I found it on a bookstall in Leicester Corn Exchange and the price was 2s 6d. No matter that I found it totally unreadable: the cracked leather binding, the worm holes in some parts, and its musty smell, endeared it to me. I loved it simply because it was old, nearly three-hundred years old. I cannot pretend that remembering *The Saints' Everlasting Rest* has the effect on me that Proust's famous eating of the madeleine cake had in recalling his childhood memories. But his point that the past may be hidden beyond the reach of the intellect in some unsuspected material object is well taken. My historical awareness was greatly stimulated by an illustrated, weekly publication entitled *The Story of the Nation* to which we subscribed at home and which was later bound into two volumes. I also made good use of the public library. From my grandparents, especially Granny Fletcher, I listened to stories about times past, although I only asked her the important questions many years later when it was too late. Even so, I became aware of a world of ancestors about whom I knew nothing, but with whom I was mysteriously linked. Before my eyes floated pictures of my grandparents when young, and their parents and grandparents. The quest for historical identity was awakened within me. With Granny Fletcher's assistance, and the opportunity to go through the parish registers at Tissington, I managed to put together a family tree and short history of the Fletchers, for which I was awarded a bronze medal under the Sir Jonathan North Endowment Scheme of the LEA. This was in 1938 and stood me in good stead when I went to the university a year later.

The inter-war semi has never been highly regarded in intellectual circles. For Orwell, Priestley and leftish writers generally it stood for petty bourgeois mediocrity. Yet for millions of ordinary people it was a great step forward. Number 15 was one of some three-million new houses built by private enterprise in England and Wales between the wars (another million were built by local authorities). As a form of popular housing the semi was infinitely superior to the Le Corbusier-inspired tower blocks. It was an ideal family house and it allowed for individual tastes and preferences. Pride of possession was fostered and an Englishman's semi-detached house was indeed his castle. And this castle was available to many more Englishmen (and women) than ever before. The most modest semis could be bought for as little as £350. The Harrison family adventure into semi-detached suburbia was thus hardly unique. In fact as one surveyed the confusing tangle of 'way' roads (Byway, Highway, Ridgeway, Trueway, and others) sprawling across what had been green fields towards Evington, one was conscious of being part of a vast, social migration.

The critique of semi-detached England however was not primarily as a type of housing, but as a form of lower middle-class culture. Both the strengths and limitations of that culture were apparent at Number 15. We were, for instance, typically inward-looking, not unfriendly but we kept ourselves to ourselves. Although my mother spoke to the neighbours on either side, usually across the fence when hanging out the washing, she would never have dreamed of popping in and out of their houses for a friendly chat or cup of tea. Very rarely, and only on some special pretext, did we ever cross the threshold of another house in the road. For several years we referred to 'the people opposite' without any idea of their name or occupation. They kept a car, from which we assumed that they must be better off than us. Then one day my mother came back from town with the news that she had seen the woman opposite serving behind a fruit-and-vegetable stall in the market and that their name was Ratcliffe. So that pigeon-holed them nicely: 'fairly coarse people who were making a lot of money'. In later years we progressed as far as passing the time of day with them; though I do not think my mother ever bought anything from their stall. Social life in Evington Parks was not organised on a neighbourhood basis: there were no corner shops, no pubs, no street life. Community spirit was virtually non-existent, though wartime exigencies temporarily softened this a little. People preferred to develop such social relationships as they needed through means other than the accident of propinquity. The fellowship of a church or chapel, friendly clubs for tennis, golf, bowls, or the intimacy of a game of bridge were the most favoured agencies. In our case St Philip's Church was the place where we felt we belonged. The 1930s was the time when regular cinema-going developed. Leicester had its share of the five-thousand picture palaces in Britain: the Odeon, Gaumont-British, and ABC; and long queues stood outside them on Saturday evenings. But we never went to the pictures every week as many did. As children we could not afford to go; and our parents were simply uninterested in films. Nor did we go in for that other popular 1930s recreation, ball-room dancing; though my mother was convinced that this was a social accomplishment that I ought to acquire, and so paid for me to have lessons. Alas, my long legs and general gaucherie proved invincible, and the dancing lessons ended the same way as the piano lessons.

Political or international events in the outside world did not make much impact on us before the outbreak of war in September 1939. The family had been shielded from the great scourge of unemployment by the security of my father's job as a railwayman; and his earnings remained steady yet modest enough for me to qualify for any free educational advantages that were going. Politics were not a subject of much interest to my parents. My father as a young man had voted Liberal, but later switched to Labour. He belonged to a trade union, the Railway Clerks' Association, but did not play any active role in the branch. Years later, when I tried to question him about the 1926 General Strike, I gained the impression that he simply did what everyone else did, which meant not going to work for several days; but he retained no very definite views about the struggle. My mother, by inclination of course, voted Conservative since she assumed that that was what all the best (that is, socially superior) people did. It always remained a puzzle to her why I, who had all the advantages of a higher education, should later be a socialist. Enlightenment on political matters came mainly from the *Daily Mail*,

*Unexciting as it now seems, the semi was a brilliant
design success for the realisation of lower middle-class ideals. Byway Road:
Number 15*

The delights of a garden. Wartime relaxation at Number 15

Holidays: *An annual holiday of a week or fortnight, usually at the seaside, was an eagerly awaited event among the lower middle-classes. (above) On the sands at Cromer, 1920s (below) Braving the elements at Shanklin, Isle of Wight, 1930*

though my father was more interested in the sports pages, especially football and boxing. Greater interest was shown in the evening paper, the *Leicester Mercury*, which was delivered about teatime. Father read this through thoroughly, including the small ads. Unlike the war in Abyssinia or Hitler's reoccupation of the Rhineland, a murder in Oadby or someone from the Belgrave Road area convicted of petty theft was within the bounds of imaginative comprehension. There was always the thrill of seeing the name of someone we knew or had heard about 'in the paper', even if it was only a list of mourners at a funeral or the organisers of a church outing. The newspaper and an occasional women's magazine were the only reading matter in the house. Habits of reading were strictly utilitarian: 'Is John doing anything?', 'No, only reading a book'—a telling response from one who had been a schoolteacher. In the 1950s my mother decided that it would be an improvement to have some shelves fitted in the sitting room, on which she could put various ornaments. However, when they were up she felt that bookshelves would look better with some books on them, so I was commissioned to buy a yard of books from a bookseller friend, choosing them for their bindings, not their content. An assortment of titles from Gene Stratton Porter to Scott and Dickens was soon in place; and to my great surprise some of them were actually read. I do not think my father ever went into the public library, nor did my mother while they lived in Leicester. The genteel thing to do was to borrow books from Boots' Library, but this cost money which we could ill afford. Fiction from the public library tended to be well-used and sometimes the books were a bit grubby. Moreover there was no branch library in our part of the town, and my mother imagined that the main, public library was frequented by people with whom she did not wish to associate, such as snuffly old men and people off the streets. Later, in retirement at Gosport, she was quite happy to read 'a nice book' from the local public library. People of my parents' generation and in their class did not in the 1930s think of social services, apart from schooling, as intended for them. The Welfare State was still only in scaffolding; the lower-middle classes had not perceived that there might be substantial benefits for them, as well as for the working class, from that source. Their thought was along the lines of individual, not social provision: one paid to borrow books from Boots' Library rather than look to a municipal service.

Our middle-class status was nowhere more fully asserted than in the matter of holidays. Father was allowed a fortnight's holiday with pay each year, and that at a time when only a minority of wage earners was entitled to a week's paid holiday annually. Moreover, as a railwayman he was allowed several free passes for himself and his family to go anywhere in the

British Isles, and an unlimited number of PTs (privilege tickets) at a reduced rate. My parents made full use of these concessions to arrange seaside holidays during July and August in places as remote from Leicester as possible. Not for us the usual East-Midlander's trip to Skeggie or Cromer, though we did go there when we were small. Instead we went to Dunoon, Paignton, Shanklin, Ilfracome, and Jersey. The decision where to go this year (always different from last) was the subject of much discussion. I cannot remember that we ever looked at glossy brochures tempting us with the allures of particular resorts. Rather we were guided by what So-and-So at work, or Mrs Whatshername in the church social guild, said about their holidays the previous year. To a considerable extent the place was determined by the availability of a 'good' landlady. We always stayed in boarding houses, sometimes buying our own food to be cooked by the landlady but latterly leaving the catering entirely to her. The 'digs' were always something of a gamble. How far were they actually from the sea? '10 mins from sea front' might turn out to be true only for champion sprinters. 'Rooms with sea view' might mean they were attics. Would the beds be comfortable and not sagging in the middle and most important of all, would the house measure up to our exacting standards of cleanliness? What sort of person was the landlady: generous and homely, or rigid and grasping? What would the other guests, if any, be like? These questions and many more exercised us greatly. Experience made us wary, but there was no way of finding out until we arrived. As the day of departure approached the intensity of preparations grew. A large, black trunk with a rounded top had to be carefully packed with all our newly-laundered clothes. This was collected by a railway van and taken to the station, where my father made sure that it was safely despatched to our holiday address. It would then be waiting for us when we arrived. 'Luggage in advance' was one of the services offered by the railway company when one purchased a ticket. After the digs and the landlady the most important aspect of the holiday was the weather; but about that we could, of course, do nothing. Where to go and what to do on rainy days were the great unresolved problems of the English seaside holiday.

Number 15 was a symbol as much as a habitation, though we would not have expressed our feelings about it in quite that way. The voices that I hear from that time are those of the 1930s lower-middle class, part of that vast section of the population ignored by historians as too uninteresting to warrant serious attention. It is true that the voices are about the small things of daily living, and are nearer to the novels of Barbara Pym than of Jane Austen. Yet for those who would probe the subtleties of

English class formation and social attitudes there is a wealth of information to be mined. Consider for instance the matter of social mobility. On the surface the move from Linton Street to Byway Road was a clear example of upward social mobility. But if we look at the means by which it was achieved the case appears somewhat different. The purchase of Number 15 was with inherited money, not savings out of income. The wealth was already in the family in the form of grandfather Fletcher's land and property, and some of it (my mother's share) had simply been transferred to her on his death. From this point of view Number 15 represented a shift from rural to urban property within the family. The farmer's daughter became a suburban housewife; but whether this was upward social mobility is arguable. For my father, who did not inherit anything from his parents, the progression from the cottage in Fenny Bentley via Linton Street to Byway Road was perhaps greater than for my mother.

Life in Byway Road, and before that in Linton Street, did not conform entirely to the stereotypes of the inter-war years to which we have become accustomed. It was the age of the motor car, we are told; but we still lived in the railway age—as did a majority of the population. It was the age of mass communication; but we did not have a wireless until the war years. We were not conscious of living in the age of Art Deco, though now I recognise several of the designs on our tea sets and lamp shades in the fashionable Art Deco shops in Brighton. The symbolism of T.S. Eliot's *The Waste Land* or Aldous Huxley's *Brave New World*, which writers have used to typify the mood of the times, had little relevance to our condition. We had never heard of the Bloomsbury Group; nor had we any knowledge of cocktails and the culture of roadhouses. We knew little of the England on the dole, and were aware of hunger marches only through the newspapers. Our contact with country life was maintained through my parents' rural roots and our regular holidays at Halfway House; but the Derbyshire we knew was not the countryside of the popular Batsford books of English country life.

If it is true, as has been alleged, that we perceive the world once and for all in childhood and adolescence, Byway Road was for me a formative influence. Behind me was the period of pencil boxes and the *Modern Boy*. My bicycle was now a full-size Raleigh, with three-speed gear and butterfly handlebars, on which I explored the lanes and villages of Leicestershire. From about the age of ten or eleven years I had been much attracted to the novels of Sir Walter Scott—*Ivanhoe, Kenilworth, Peveril of the Peak*—but now my taste changed, under the influence I think of the books we were given to read at school. These were the usual English classics: R.L. Stevenson, Dickens, Joseph Conrad. I cannot put an exact date on this change. Indeed, in my memories of Number 15 time is to some extent suspended, and the house is like an opaque globe in which people and events float around together. Only when I look at snaps in the photograph album can I focus on exact times. Later, the momentous events of my departure for Cambridge and the onset of the War sharpen the memory; but before that the fragments of life at Byway Road coalesce into a generalised picture of untroubled existence. I am sure that in reality, life was not without its minor traumas. However, the fact that I can remember nothing about them suggests that for a child growing up in the 1930s there were many worse places than a semi.

◆ 6 ◆

The Label

———◄◆►———

IT HAPPENED towards the end of March 1939. About the middle of the morning there was a knock at the front door. When I opened it there stood a post office messenger boy in his blue uniform and leather pouch. 'Telegram for Harrison', he announced, and stood waiting to see if there was a reply. I tore open the little buff envelope and glanced at the message. 'No reply', I said, and shut the door. I read again the words on the strips of ticker tape stuck on the telegram form: 'AWARDED EXHIBITION SELWYN COLLEGE STOP LETTER FOLLOWING'. The effect was one of enormous relief, and at the same time, tremendous anticipation. Nothing else mattered: I was going to Cambridge. It was no longer a lovely but distant dream: it was going to be a reality. Everyone congratulated me. At school I was a hero. The Headmaster announced the news at morning assembly. Masters came up to me in the corridor and said 'Well done, Harrison'. My name appeared in the local newspaper; and my mother took good care that all her friends at St Philip's were well aware of what a clever son she had. I now see that the telegram marked a turning point in my life and was much more than the marking of a stage in my natural development, the ending of schooldays and the beginning of university life. Cambridge put a label on me which said 'this man is one of ours, and we are the elite'. No matter that this was largely untrue: in England a Cambridge 'First' was hard social and intellectual currency. For me Cambridge opened doors. It admitted me to the ranks of the privileged.

These thoughts were of course far from the mind of the schoolboy who opened the telegram on that March morning a half-century ago. At that time the exhibition represented the culmination of two years' intensive school work. After passing the School Certificate examination at matriculation level in 1937, the decision was made that I should stay on into the sixth form and try to get to university. Since my parents could not possibly afford to pay for me I had to rely on winning a scholarship. There were two ways of doing this. The first was to pass the Higher School Certificate examination at a sufficiently high level to be awarded a state scholarship from the Department of Education. The second was to sit for an open scholarship at Oxford or Cambridge. The two methods were not mutually exclusive, but in practice they determined the degree of specialisation one undertook in the sixth form. With the encouragement of the Head and the history master I opted for the second, and more prestigious, course. In my first year in the sixth I took history, English and geography; and in the second year concentrated solely on history. This was a gamble, and I realised that I was putting all my eggs in one basket; for if I failed to get an open scholarship my chances of a state scholarship were very slim indeed, given my inadequate preparation for the HSC. When I raised this fear with the Head he told me not to worry, and assured me that 'we can always get you into Leicester' if all else failed.

The great adventure began in December 1938 when I went up to Cambridge to sit the open scholarship examination at Jesus College. Curiously it never occurred to me to think of going to Oxford, mainly I suppose because the masters who taught me were Cambridge men. The examinations were held after the end of term, so that accommodation was available in college. I had never been away from home by myself except when staying with the family, and the experience was thrilling and yet a bit daunting. We (the candidates) stayed for three nights in rooms in the college. We dined in hall, and between the examinations were free to roam around Cambridge, familiarising ourselves with the colleges and wandering in and out of the bookshops. I was absolutely bowled over by the whole thing: it seemed to be a perfect form of existence. We had to take three, three-hour papers: English history, European history, and a general paper. I had been well coached for all these and had no difficulty in selecting questions which I thought I could answer. Nor did the interview with one of the dons, Bernard Manning, faze me, because again I had been well prepared in what to expect. I came away feeling confident that I had answered the questions to the best of my ability, but much less confident that I was the equal of some of the other candidates who seemed far ahead of me. In the event I did not gain an award. The letter to the Head said that I was up to exhibition standard but regretfully they did not have enough exhibitions for all the deserving candidates. This was hard to make out. Was I really up to standard or were they just letting me down lightly?

However, all was not lost. It was possible to try a second time, as a small number of colleges held their examinations later, in March. I entered my name for the group which included St Catherine's and Selwyn; and this time I was lucky enough to be offered one of the ten scholarships and exhibitions at Selwyn, being in fact top of the history candidates. The basis for the award was that I was regarded as having a chance of a First class in the Historical Tripos. The selectors had decided that I had a touch of that magical 'whiff of alpha', so much prized at Cambridge. Not all scholars and exhibitioners in fact fulfilled this promise, and some undergraduates who had not won awards nevertheless got Firsts. The system was, to say the least, somewhat hit and miss.

The months between the news of the exhibition and going up in October 1939 were busy ones. First, I had to pass the Previous Examination in Latin, as an elementary knowledge of that language was still required for matriculation at Cambridge. I knew no Latin, having studied German as the second language at school. So the Head arranged an intensive course for me. Having crammed myself with ablative absolutes and mastered the use of *quominus* ('by the which not the less than'), I managed to satisfy the college in this respect by the required deadline of June.

There was, however, a second hurdle: finance. A fair amount has been written in recent years about the phenomenon of the working-class scholarship boy, and in most of these accounts one is left to conclude that having won a scholarship to university there were no more money problems. This was not so, and my own case is instructive in this respect. The *Cambridge University Handbook* suggested that a minimum of £210–£220 per annum was necessary to cover the cost of fees, accommodation, and general living costs during the three terms of the academic year from October to June. Selwyn College, founded in 1882, after the abolition of religious tests in the university, and mindful of the straitened circumstances of some of the sons of Anglican clergymen for whom it was intended, advised that by the exercise of habits of frugality the cost could be reduced to £195 per annum. So that was my target, which I had to reach if I was actually to go to Cambridge. The exhibition was worth £40; and on the strength of that the Local Education Authority made me a grant of £50. I got another £30 from the Sir Jonathan North Endowment Scheme as I had won one of their bronze medals the previous year. That still left me a long way short of £195. I therefore applied to the LEA for a loan, and they agreed to lend me £60 at 4 per cent per annum, repayable during the first four years after graduation. I was also required to take out a life insurance policy, the premiums for which were added to the loan. I now had £180 for my first year, still £15 short. At this stage I discovered the existence of various educational trusts whose policy was to provide just such top-up sums. I applied to several of them. They were mostly City livery companies or seventeenth-century charitable foundations for apprenticeships whose funds were now directed into broader, educational channels. One of these, the Thomas Wall Trust, gave me the necessary £15. My first year was thus taken care of, and I was assured that once I was at Cambridge other means of support would become available. This was indeed so; and in May 1940, after a competitive examination, I was awarded a Goldsmiths' Company exhibition of £100 per annum for the remainder of my degree course. I was now financially secure and did not have to think of borrowing any more money from the LEA. As a postscript, repayment of my £60 loan was made in 1946–7 after I got my first job; though the LEA wrote to me in 1942 while I was in the army in Africa saying that I might like to consider repaying the loan out of my officer's pay—an invitation that I declined. The scholarships were the first money I ever had so I now had to open a bank account, write cheques, and manage my own finances.

My preparations for Cambridge preoccupied the family throughout the summer of 1939, and my happiness continued, despite the darkening international situation. The college sent a list of all the items we should require: sheets, towels, table linen, crockery, cutlery, as well as instructions about laundry, bicycles and trunks. My mother delighted in supervising the collection of all these things, which until then I had never even thought about. She rummaged in cupboards for articles which could be spared. She mended and darned and fussed in her practical way. Should I need a hearth rug? Would there be a reading lamp provided? Did I have enough shirts and underclothes to allow me to send my washing home each week? It was borne in on me that university life involved more than reading interesting books, but even the most tedious details only seemed to enhance the attractiveness of the anticipated Eden.

There was, however, one threat to my idyll. The cloud on the international horizon had now grown into a mighty storm. On Sunday, 3 September, the Prime Minister, Neville Chamberlain, announced over the wireless that the British ultimatum to Germany had expired and we were now at war. Under the National Service (Armed Forces) Act all men between eighteen and forty-one years were made liable for conscription. It looked as if my immediate destination would be the army, not Cambridge. Then, to my immense relief, it was decided that students could defer their call-up and stay at the university until they were twenty.

My plans and preparations for Cambridge continued as before. In the meantime I helped to put 15 Byway Road onto a war footing. For weeks the newspapers had been full of talk about ARP (Air Raid Precautions), evacuation of schoolchildren, and what to do in the event of a gas attack. There were pictures of trenches being dug in the parks and advice on how to improvise a bomb shelter under the stairs or beneath the kitchen table. We built a barrier of sandbags and wooden boxes filled with earth to protect the breakfast-room window, as this seemed to be the safest place to shelter during an air raid. Later my father had a concrete shelter built in the garage. We covered the windows with strips of sticky tape to minimise the shattering effects of blast. My mother had the Herculean task of making black-out curtains for all the windows in the house. We practised putting on our civilian-issue gas masks, but the result was so uncomfortable they were quickly put back in their little brown boxes. On the first night of the war in our fortified semi we awaited the onslaught of the Nazi hordes. But nothing happened. The period of the 'phoney war' or 'bore war' had begun and lasted until April 1940.

The glorious summer weather continued throughout September, and early in October I went up to Cambridge for my first Michaelmas term. Already I was familiar with Cambridge jargon and with the Cambridge intellectual year which was divided into Michaelmas, Lent and Easter terms. Cambridge amply fulfilled my expectations. At first I shared rooms in Selwyn with another boy from the City Boys' School who was also reading history. I was persuaded to do this on the grounds of cheapness. The rooms had recently been 'modernised', by which was meant redecoration and the installation of a washbasin in the bedroom and an electric fire in the keeping room. But the arrangement was not satisfactory as our living and studying habits did not coincide, and the following term I moved into a set of rooms on my own. I loved those rooms. They were far from grand. Indeed, when I visited friends in Trinity or St John's and saw their large and antique rooms I realised how humble the Selwyn accommodation was. But that did not matter. My rooms were the place I could call my own. My name was painted at the foot of the staircase, and when I wanted to be left alone to read there was a double door for 'sporting the oak'. The keeping (or living) room had a Gothic window overlooking the bicycle sheds. A square, deal table and wooden office chair of the type known as a captain's chair, together with a rather dilapidated easy chair, pretty well filled the room. A gas fire had recently been installed in place of the antiquated grate. This was a great improvement over the coal fire which went out if left for more than two hours and which was devoid of any means of relighting until the next morning. Round the mantelpiece was a leather fringe, fixed with brass studs. The table was covered with a dark red cloth, also with a fringe. Two shelves for books filled in the alcove by the side of the chimney breast. The general effect was reminiscent of a study in a Victorian rectory. A door opened into the bedroom, which was furnished with a narrow iron bed, wash-stand, towel rail, and painted, deal chest of drawers. Most of the furniture in the rooms was provided by the college, supplemented by odds-and-ends inherited or purchased from the previous occupant.

Life in this sanctum was made to depend upon the ministrations of a college servant known as a gyp. He would arrive every morning about 7.30 with a cup of weak tea, most of which he had managed to slop into the saucer. 'Morning, Sir', he would announce as he drew back the bedroom curtains. I looked up blearily while he went back to bring in a jug of hot water for shaving and washing—performed somewhat perfunctorily during the winter months in the unheated bedroom. The baths were a long way off, in the basement, and necessitated a special trip, armed with towel, soap and dressing gown. In rooms which had a coal fire the gyp cleared out the ashes, relaid the fire, and brought up a scuttle of coal. He busied himself during the morning with general cleaning duties, and did the washing-up if one had lunch or tea in rooms. In the evening he acted as a waiter in hall. Each gyp looked after his own 'gentlemen', on whom he relied for a generous tip at the end of term, as the colleges were notoriously mean in the payment of their servants. I had had no experience of this sort of thing. It was a system which seemed to me to generate a mixture of subservience and insolence on the one side and arrogance and superiority on the other.

Breakfast was provided in hall, usually limp toast, cornflakes, undercooked, fatty bacon, or soggy sausages. Lunch I ate in my rooms, mainly bread and cheese or something cheap and filling which I had discovered in the town, such as nut cutlets. Dinner in hall was a requirement for all undergraduates. Summoned by the loud clanging of a bell, each evening we rushed across the court, struggling into our short, black gowns as we went. Inside the heavily panelled hall, beneath the portraits of benefactors and former Masters of the college, we stood either side of three, long tables, while the Master and fellows filed into High Table at the far end of the room. A college servant handed the wooden plaque on which was written the long, Latin grace to the scholar whose turn it was to read it. '*Benedic domine...*', he began. The moment he finished ('...*dominum nostrum.*') a great clatter and roar broke out as the benches were scraped back and we flopped down on them, everyone talking at once. The gyps, attired in short, not very clean, white coats, rushed forward with the first course, usually bowls of some sort of soup, into which they invariably managed to stick a dirty thumb. This was followed by meat-and-two-veg., and rounded off with a token sweet of ice cream or piece of fruit. We waited impatiently until the High Table—whose menu was superior to ours—retired, and then went back to our rooms or to the Junior Common Room to read the daily paper. Alternatively we hurried into town for a meeting or a visit to the 'flicks'.

Cambridge had its own lore and language which undergraduates absorbed within a remarkably short time. By the end of my first term, which only lasted eight weeks, I felt as if I had lived in Cambridge for years. Like all generations of youth we had our own style of manners and dress. A tweed jacket with leather, elbow patches, flannel 'bags', open-necked shirt, and long, college scarf, were *de rigueur*. I had a college blazer and tie, but never wore them in Cambridge. They were to please my mother and impress people at home. We went everywhere on bicycles. Their bells tinkled continually as undergraduates, gowns flying out behind them, pedalled furiously down Sidgwick Avenue and along King's Parade to get to lectures on time. Every college gateway and lecture theatre was jammed with basketed bikes. Undergraduates were required to be in college by 11 o'clock at night, after which time the gates were locked and entrance could be made only by ringing for the porter. Persistent lateness was grounds for disciplinary action by the Dean. To avoid being 'gated' (that is, disciplined) the bolder spirits tried to climb in. This involved scaling the college walls and negotiating the iron spikes on the top. All colleges were full of stories about such escapades, but I was never tempted. Even more daring were those members of the fraternity devoted to climbing the roofs of college buildings at night and leaving evidences of their prowess, such as a chamberpot on the top of a pinnacle, for all to see the next morning. There was even an illustrated book on sale in Heffer's bookshop entitled *The Night Climbers of Cambridge*.

The porter's lodge was a central institution in college life. Situated immediately inside the main gateway, it was manned day and night by him or one of his assistants. The porter wore a dark-blue suit and bowler hat, and sat behind a window through which he could see everyone going in or out of the college. The lodge was the centre of communication and general information on college matters. All letters were delivered there and collected from pigeon holes. If you wanted to get in touch with someone in the college you left a note for him in the lodge; if you wanted to know whether Mr So-and-So was in his rooms you asked the porter, who would tell you whether or not he had seen him come in, or go out—a useful service before the spread of telephones. The porter knew everyone by name and always called you 'Sir'. He was always referred to by his surname alone, which in my day was Hignell, thus occasioning the unkind clerihew:

> The swollen head of Higger
> Has grown much bigger
> Than ever it ought'a
> Since he became Head Porter

Higger was nevertheless a fount of wisdom on all non-academic, college matters, and had to be generously tipped at the end of each term. Whenever you went in or out of college you looked in at the lodge out of habit just to see 'if there were anything' for you. At the beginning and end of term the space outside the lodge was piled high with trunks (either delivered or to be collected by the railway company) as undergraduates sent their clothes and books to and from home each term. Lugging these heavy trunks to and from the rooms was a task not welcomed by the gyps.

Soon after my arrival I found a note in my pigeon hole from George Burr Perrett, the History tutor, to the effect that Mr Perrett would be pleased to see Mr JFCH in his rooms at 5 pm on such and such a day. I duly presented myself, in my undergraduate gown, and was joined by another exhibitioner who had received an identical note, and who was henceforth to be my tutorial partner. The weekly tutorial or 'supervision', lasting about an hour, supplemented by attendance at lectures and reading in the library, was the hallowed pattern of instruction at Cambridge. That first meeting with Perrett set the tone for all our subsequent supervisions. We sat down, one on either side of the fireplace, while GBP leaned against the mantelpiece or paced up and down the room which was cold and had a faded, unlived-in air about it. Later I realised that this was because GBP was a married fellow who lived out of college and only used his rooms in the evenings for supervisions; but these things were hidden from me at that first meeting. I don't know what I had expected a Cambridge history don to be like, but Perrett struck me as very unusual indeed. He was a stocky, well-built man in his fifties, with sandy coloured hair and moustache, and dressed in a tweed Norfolk jacket, thick woollen stockings and heavy, brown boots. He looked, and smelt, like a farmer. On his nose was a pair of *pince-nez* glasses, and he slobbered continuously over a loosely-rolled, foul-smelling cigarette. I had never before seen anyone roll their own cigarettes and was fascinated by GBP's performance, which was repeated several times during every tutorial. Taking a cigarette paper between thick, clumsy fingers, he would extract several strands of coarse tobacco from his pouch and lay them along the paper. He then rolled the paper into a rough tube, licked it heartily with much spit, stuck it in his mouth, and lit it. A flame leapt up from the end of the tube but quickly subsided as he sucked noisily on the other end. Everything about him seemed to be earthy and practical and he gave the impression of having just come in from a day's shooting. I never heard anyone refer to him as 'squire', but it would have been quite appropriate. He was a thousand miles from the aesthetic scholar in his ivory tower.

The supervision centred on the essay which we wrote for him each week. It had to be handed in the day before and when we arrived he had usually just finished reading it and writing a few remarks in red ink at the end. He also gave it a grade, using the arcane Cambridge system of Greek letters and pluses and minuses. Thus one was quite likely to get an alpha-/beta plus (A-/B+) or a beta plus plus (B++). For very good work (that is, first-class quality) one had to get an alpha of some sort. The intention was to indicate whether the essay was of first-, second- (II i or II ii) or even (heaven forbid) third-class quality. Most of the week's work had gone into preparing the essay and the supervision provided the opportunity for asking questions and seeking clarification about it. Unfortunately most of the tutorial was spent in talking about other things which had nothing to do with the subject of the essay nor with history at all. GBP, in addition to being college tutor in history, was also at this time the college bursar, and we had to sit and listen to all his bursarial tribulations of the week, which were many and varied. With the war had come shortages of all kinds: food was rationed, staff left and could not be replaced, blackout had to be provided for all buildings, and bureaucracy grew rapidly in such a fertile environment. Poor GBP had to cope with all of this. It was understandable that he wished to pour out his troubles and frustrations. So for the first half of our precious, weekly hour we had to sympathise with his difficulties in finding potatoes and carrots in sufficient quantity for our dinners in hall, or agree with his robust rejection of the demands of government officialdom. All too soon came knocks on the door, indicating that the next tutees had arrived and our time was up. Handing us back our papers, he hurriedly gave us a title for the next week's essay: 'Read So-and-So, and have a look at the essay by Such-and-Such. Oh, and don't forget that article by Dr Bloggs in the *EHR*....'

GBP was no great scholar. He lectured on Tudor and Stuart constitutional history, but he did not write books or publish learned articles. I doubt whether anyone outside Cambridge had ever heard of him, though presumably to gain a fellowship he must have shown promise as a young man. He was a very good history tutor in that he knew the Tripos examination system inside-out and geared his teaching to getting his men through. He was not above giving us tips about form: 'You ought to attend Mr So-and-So's lectures this term as he's setting the paper in Such-and-Such'; or 'It's about time there was a question on the royal prerogative: we haven't had one for the last two years'. Spotting the winners was obviously part of the game.

The Cambridge history syllabus looked fairly comprehensive in print. In practice it turned out to be rather scrappy. I concentrated on the Tudor and Stuart period of English (not yet British) history, which I had already studied at school. There was very little interest in anything after the mid-nineteenth century. I also took papers in medieval and economic history, and in my second year went to another supervisor for political theory. In each case we concentrated on certain topics rather than trying to read across the whole field. We were encouraged to dig deep, to know a lot about a little rather than a little about a lot. Superficiality, snap judgements, sweeping generalisations were an anathema. Scholarly exactness, intellectual rigour, and ruthless logic were the qualities most prized. 'Yes, but...', 'On the other hand', 'Do we really know...?', punctuated all our arguments. The Cambridge habit of understatement, of preferring simplicity and plainness to ornateness and the baroque left its mark on me. However, we never asked basic questions about our studies. There was no course such as 'What is History?', nor any training in historical method or research. Curiously, we were expected to answer such questions in the general paper of the entrance scholarship examination. But these were limited to themes such as 'Is History an Art or Science?' or coy references to Clio in the Trevelyan *belle-lettriste* tradition.

None of this was explicitly spelled out to us. We absorbed it from the academic atmosphere. Personal contact with dons was minimal. In lectures we simply sat and listened from afar. The only historian to whom I had regular and direct access was my supervisor; though in my second year I attended Helen Cam's seminar in medieval constitutional history. We met in her rooms at Girton and she occasionally dispensed sherry. Kitson Clark, not yet a social historian, offered the only lectures on nineteenth-century history, and so I became acquainted with the constitutional niceties of Peel and the Tory Party. Another Tory lecturer was Kenneth Pickthorn, MP for the university, but I did not need to listen to him on the Tudor constitution as Perrett covered the same ground in his course. Welbourne's lectures on economic history were refreshingly different from the usual heavy fare of political and constitutional issues. He was the first historian I ever heard who suggested that subjects like the history of fish and chips could be important.

In later life people who had learned that I had been at Cambridge would remark enviously that I must have enjoyed excellent teaching and met many famous historians. When I assured them that quite the reverse was true they did not believe me. The fact was that the standard of lecturing was sometimes abysmally low, though I was too green to appreciate this at the time. I remember on one occasion being puzzled by the curious system of notes used by a man who later became well-known as a medieval historian. He appeared to be reading from an enormously long piece of lavatory paper which he kept folding and unfolding. Years later I realised that his lecture was simply a reading from the first proofs of his latest book. Like most history undergraduates I had no idea at that time who was the Regius Professor of History, or even that such a person existed. History was for me a matter of reading a lot of interesting books while at the same time jumping a series of Tripos hurdles. The immediate impact of Cambridge was as a new style of life, away from home for the first time, rather than contact with great academic minds. Nevertheless, I think now that more in the way of intellectual stimulus must have been there than we realised at the time. Three of my friends made names for themselves in the history world later: Helli Koenigsberger in early modern European, Jack Lander in late Medieval, and Jack Ravensdale in local history. I did not at this time know Asa Briggs, though I had heard about this incredible man at Sidney Sussex College who was not only set for a double First in the History Tripos but was at the same time reading for a London BSc (Econ) degree.

At the end of each term I was summoned to a short interview with the Senior Tutor, who was supposed to exercise a general and moral oversight of my progress. He had been badly wounded in the First World War, and was to be seen limping slowly with a stick across the court. His rooms were lined with books on theology, and his war medals, including an MC, were displayed in a little *passe-partout* frame on the mantelpiece. 'Well, Harrison,' he drawled down his nose while he looked at the supervisor's report, 'you seem to be doing alright. Nothing to worry about as far as I can see'. If there had been anything to worry about I cannot imagine that I should ever have taken my troubles to him. He scarcely knew my name. Perhaps he was more intimate with the theology or the rowing men. I cannot say that I was troubled by this typical Cambridge reticence and lack of emotional warmth. At the age of eighteen or nineteen, I was quite happy to take Cambridge as I found it.

One of my first problems was how to organise the working day. At school the daily routine was organised for you but at university you were left completely free to make your own decisions. There was virtually no guidance on this, with the result that some undergraduates did almost no work at all and others toiled excessively. Attendance at lectures was optional: the only compulsory commitment was the one-hour supervision per week. By dint of trial and error, and from exchanging experiences with others I came to the conclusion that about six hours of study per day was a good average. This figure included lectures, work in the library, and study in one's room. More than that and I became weary; less than that and I fell behind. My day was divided into three parts, and work was to occupy no more than two of them. As a rule the morning (9 to 1) was given over to lectures and reading in the Seeley Historical Library or in the University Library; the afternoon (2 to 5) was devoted to some form of exercise such as walking by the river or cycling round the villages of Cambridgeshire; in the evening before dinner (5 to 7) I liked to work in my rooms, and after dinner (8 to 11) I attended meetings or went to the cinema. Obviously I could not always observe this routine. On wet afternoons, for instance, I took the opportunity to get in some extra reading in the library; or if my weekly essay was going badly I would have to work on it after hall. But in general this regime served me well and it is the one I have followed ever since.

I realise now that I had been well prepared for Cambridge, and not only in history. Thanks to the English masters at the City Boys' School I had developed a love for literature, especially modern poetry. It was for a time a toss-up whether I made English or history my main subject. When I had to choose my English subject prize in 1937 I selected Michael Roberts's *Faber Book of Modern Verse*, through which I was introduced to the work of Auden, Spender, Day-Lewis and MacNeice. Above all I was attracted by T.S. Eliot. At Christmas 1936 I bought myself a copy of his *Poems, 1909–1925*. I read and re-read *Prufrock* and *The Waste Land*. I could not understand them, but they gripped me powerfully. Eliot's dictum that a great poem can communicate before it is understood was never truer than in my case. From their very first reading the imagery of the poems burned itself into my mind:

> Let us go then, you and I,
> When the evening is spread out against the sky
> Like a patient etherised upon a table;

I can still recite the pub scene and the description of the river in *The Waste Land*.

I do not think that I read many contemporary novels at this time-perhaps because I was (still am) a slow reader and there were so many other things to be read. But I do remember reading Aldous Huxley's *Brave New World* and being pleasurably shocked and titillated by the (nowadays very mild) references to sex and eroticism. D.H. Lawrence and the American writer, John Dos Passos, I borrowed from the school library, and also the poems of John Donne. It was only many years later that I discovered Virginia Woolf and E.M. Forster.

One of the English masters at the City Boys' School had been at Downing College and was a devotee of F. R. Leavis. We were exposed to the full force of *Scrutiny* and I was familiarised with the canons of Leavisian literary criticism long before I arrived in Cambridge. *Culture and Environment*, edited by Leavis and Denys Thompson, was used as a text, and from it I absorbed a strongly critical view of the effects of advertising, the popular press, and commercialism generally on modern society. I knew all about the loss of the 'organic community' and admired the rural values of George Sturt's *The Wheelwright's Shop*. This cultural critique had political overtones, though these were not, to my way of thinking, sufficiently brought out by the Leavisites. I turned elsewhere for guidance and found it in socialism, more specifically in Marxism. With Leavis I had nothing to do in Cambridge. I did not attend his lectures and can remember seeing him, always wearing an open-necked shirt, only a few times. With socialism, however, I was much more involved.

There was nothing remarkable in a young aspiring intellectual in 1939 having left-wing views. The only question was how far to the left one was prepared to go. My political apprenticeship had begun at school, where I was strongly influenced by one of the junior English masters. Eric had decided to throw in his lot with the Communist Party as the only effective means of fighting Fascism. He married a very attractive girl who was also a member of the Party and set up house in a little flat near Medway Street school. They had very little furniture, masses of books, and seemed to be supremely happy in each other and their political activities. I had never encountered anything like this before and was completely enchanted. They invited me to their flat, lent me books, and expressed views which I had never heard before. We had endless discussions about politics, poetry and the world in general. The Left Book Club had a discussion circle in Leicester which met monthly and I began to attend its meetings. Members of the LBC received a book every month, these books being specially commissioned and socialist in tendency. I could not afford to buy the monthly LBC books, so distinctive in their orange (later red) bindings. But Eric lent me his copies; and later they became easily available in second-hand bookshops. I was particularly impressed by John Strachey's popular exposition of Marxism in *The Theory and Practice of Socialism*, and from there I went on to read the 'classics', as he called them, of Marxism–Leninism.

For my generation the formative influence in our political development was the Spanish Civil War. Day after day, week after week, we followed the fortunes of the Republican armies in their struggle, as we saw it, against Fascism. The geography of Spain, hitherto unknown to us, assumed a familiarity which it did not attain again until the British holiday invasion of the costas in the 1960s; only for us it was not the Spain of Benidorm and Marbella but the grim battlefields of Jarama, Brunete and the Ebro. We knew nothing of the internal politics of Spain. For us the issues were simple and clear-cut: on the one side was the democratically-elected Republican government, on the other the forces of Fascism. Support for Franco came from Nazi Germany and Fascist Italy, for the Republic from Communist Russia. The Basque children, International Brigades, Guernica became symbols round which to organise our thoughts. Even when suspicions were aroused that perhaps some Republicans were guilty of atrocities and skulduggery, and when the evidence of bloody internecine feuds between rival Stalinist, anarchist and socialist groups could not be ignored, we were persuaded that, nevertheless, it was right to support Republican Spain because of the over-riding necessity of defeating Fascism. It seemed intolerable that the Republican forces should have to make do with insufficient or antiquated weapons in the face of the plentiful, modern armaments supplied by the Germans and Italians to Franco. Yet this was the effect of the one-sided policy of non-intervention. The government's support of this policy served to mobilise the left in Britain and exposed (to us) the supine attitudes of the Labour Party and trade-union leaders. Hence was born the demand for a Popular Front, a coalition of all progressive forces to deliver 'Arms for Spain' and to build a mass movement to fight 'Fascism, Reaction and War'. The LBC supported this programme and the CP worked tirelessly to achieve it. But by March 1939 the Spanish Republic was defeated; Hitler moved into Czecho-Slovakia, which had been gravely weakened by Chamberlain's Munich settlement in the previous September; and the descent into international chaos under a government we deeply mistrusted seemed inevitable.

It was with this background that I threw myself into the socialist movement in Cambridge. I found a ready welcome from the comrades in the Cambridge University Socialist Club, and was almost immediately made Secretary of the Selwyn branch of CUSC. It is not easy, some fifty years later, to recapture the atmosphere of CUSC, so different was it from later political organisations. We were not just a political society like the Labour or Conservative Clubs, both of which were relatively weak. Rather, CUSC was a particular form of Cambridge culture with which one identified in the same way as one became known as a rowing hearty or a pious member of CICCU (Cambridge Inter-Collegiate Christian Union). The membership of CUSC was very large. It was claimed that it had a thousand members—perhaps swollen by the comrades from the LSE who were evacuated to Cambridge during the war—and as such was more influential than the old-established debating society, the Cambridge Union. We met in various places: a room near the Round Church; then above MacFisheries in a passage off Petty Cury, where the smell of fish was overpowering; and later in a basement on the corner of Bene't Street. Lunches were served there, and in the evenings there were film shows as well as fierce debates. Two portraits hung on the end wall: one was Lenin, the other John Cornford, the Cambridge student leader who had been killed in Spain while fighting with the International Brigade. CUSC followed the general CP line and was in fact directed by the Party, though not openly. This provoked the usual leftist sectarian arguments, and we waxed hotly against the Trotskyites and other 'deviationists' and 'wreckers'. All this occupied my evenings; and at weekends we held demonstrations, with banners and placards, on Parker's Piece.

My commitment to the cause of socialism was at this time complete, but not without difficulties. For instance, we had for many months followed the Popular Front policy of subordinating everything to the struggle against Fascism and, when 'collective security' failed, we reluctantly accepted the inevitability of war. The Soviet-Nazi pact of non-aggression at the end of August 1939, which precipitated the German invasion of Poland and Second World War, took us by surprise. Even more surprising was the discovery that the war was an 'imperialist' war which socialists should not support. It was all very confusing; but we accepted the casuistry of explaining Soviet policy until June 1941 when Hitler attacked the USSR and the line changed again to all-out support of the war. Was this the *trahison des clercs*, as has been alleged? Certainly we accepted at face value many of the claims of Soviet Communism: all those glossy pictures in *The USSR in Construction*; the films like *Lenin in October* or Eisenstein's *The Battleship Potemkin* which we watched at the Cri (Criterion) or the Cosmo cinemas; or the testimony of Sidney and Beatrice Webb in their massive study, *Soviet Communism: a New Civilisation*. After the collapse and discrediting of Soviet-type Communism in Eastern Europe and finally in Russia itself, it is tempting to see my generation as mistaken, naïve, and self-deluding. But this is to ignore the vital element of context. We were not living in a vacuum but in a world which appeared to be disintegrating around us. Socialism offered both an understanding and an alternative which were attractive. If I were to criticise this view now I would say that it over-emphasises group loyalties at the expense of individual, personal relationships in human affairs, and encourages the danger of thinking about human beings as 'forces' or things. But its political orientation was sound enough. The policies of Non-Intervention in Spain and Appeasement of the dictators elsewhere confirmed our suspicions that the Conservative government's hatred of the USSR (after all, the British had supported efforts to crush Bolshevism by force in 1919-20) was stronger than its dislike of Fascism, and that some Conservatives wished Nazi Germany to survive as a bastion against Russia.

The 1930s have been called the Red Decade, and it is not difficult to see why. One-hundred years of capitalism (not yet disguised in the fashionable euphemism of market economy) had produced a civilisation which was vulgar, superficial and divisive. After four years of the most horrendous war ever known, a world economic slump of disastrous proportions, colonial exploitation on a vast scale, and support of Nazi and Fascist dictatorships, the 'crisis' of capitalism seemed only too believable. At home we had a class-ridden society, mass unemployment, and 30 per cent of the working population living below the poverty line. 'What do you think about England, this country of ours where nobody is well?' asked Auden in his famous lines from *The Orators*. Marx and Engels had lived through the Victorian blossoming of capitalism, and their analysis of it seemed to make a great deal of sense. Moreover they propounded a way out of the morass. Marxism was more than a philosophy: it was also a guide to action. 'Scientific socialism' provided a comprehensive world outlook which answered all doubts and queries and guaranteed a better future. It is apparent now that Marx's economic and social insights have stood the test of time much better than Lenin's theories of revolution. But fifty-or-so years ago the stirring final words of the *Communist Manifesto* were a true rallying cry: 'The workers have nothing to lose but their chains. They have a world to win. Working men of all lands, unite!' If this now sounds unbelievably romantic it has to be remembered that the 1930s were in need of a large dose of romanticism if they were to be made tolerable to young men like me.

Unlike later student radicals we did not concern ourselves very much with the state of the university itself. Our efforts were directed towards national and international issues, rather than reform of the curriculum or the examination system. Although Marxism is a most historically-oriented philosophy I never made much effort to apply it to my studies for the Tripos beyond the usual assumptions of the priority of economic forces and the role of social class. I cannot account for this intellectual compartmentalism. Perhaps I sensed that GBP would not appreciate attempts to link dialectical materialism with Tudor constitutional history; or, more likely, I could not see such links anyway.

My part in the anti-Fascist struggle had certain other, less romantic and more practical dimensions. Remarkable as were the efforts of the university to carry on as usual, the fact that the country was at war could not be totally ignored. At the back of my mind was the knowledge that in a short time I would be in the army. There was a feeling of living on borrowed time:

> But at my back I always hear
> Time's winged chariot hurrying near.

My call-up had been deferred for two years, but in the meantime I was enroled in the Cambridge University Senior Training Corps, as the old OTC was now called. One day a week we spent on drill, map reading and Bren-gun training at the rifle range beyond Grange Road. On the strength of War Certificates 'A' and 'B' and a short interview with the Joint Recruiting Board I was recommended for direct entry to a commission: 'a good type and likely to make a good officer', wrote the chairman after seeing me for all of ten minutes. Clearly I already had the Cambridge label; and the rough places would, as far as possible, be made plain. I was enlisted into the Royal Fusiliers, Territorial Army, on 4 June 1941, but was not actually 'embodied' (that is, called up for duty at an OCTU) until October. The promises of the telegram two years earlier had been largely fulfilled, though I had not managed the hoped-for First in the Historical Tripos, only a 'good' II (i). My university career appeared to have come to an end, and I said goodbye to Cambridge in June.

There was, however, a final twist to the story, and five years later I was back in Cambridge. It came about like this. Once the war with Japan was over, in August 1945, there was a rush to get back to normality and start demobilisation. Universities were allowed to apply for the early release of certain students such as scholars and exhibitioners whose studies had been interrupted by the war, 'on grounds of national importance'. Suddenly, out of the blue, I received a message from Selwyn asking if I would like them to apply for my immediate return under the Class 'B' Release scheme. I could hardly believe my eyes when I saw this second telegram of good news. Dear old Cambridge had come up trumps again. After more than three years of exile in Africa I had given up all thoughts of further university life and had decided that I should have to make do with my two-year degree which had been conferred, *in absentia*, in 1942. The war seemed to drag on interminably and it would be many months before I could hope for 'demob', which was operated on the principle of first in, first out. The only snag with a Class 'B' Release was that one forfeited one's gratuity. But that seemed a small price to pay for a return to civilian life. I wired back my acceptance immediately. From then on it was all plain sailing. By this time I had become a staff officer in Mombasa. As G.S.O.III (Ops) I was informed of all troop movements, and when my name appeared in the list of repatriates I was able to ensure that No.229758, Capt. JFCH was on the very next boat.

I arrived back in England in December 1945 and so missed the Michaelmas term at Cambridge. My status there was now a very curious one. Under the wartime regulations I had been granted my BA in 1942, and in 1946 I became an MA as well. I wore a master's gown and was referred to in official documents as 'Mag.' (Magister) JFCH. For an ex-officer the situation seemed not unsatisfactory. But for the college I existed in a sort of limbo, being neither a fellow, nor a BA doing research, nor an undergraduate. I had decided not to continue with history but to switch to law. I was planning a career in some kind of administration, perhaps as a Director of Education for an LEA, and law seemed more professionally useful than history. So I settled down to work hard for Part II of the Law Tripos. This time I had few distractions, and did not live in college. I was married, but Margaret was not with me. I enjoyed law enormously, and to my surprise in June received my third telegram of good news: HEARTY CONGRATULATIONS STOP FIRST CLASS. I had intended to stay on for another year to take an LL.B, since I had not thought that I could expect much of a result after only two terms' work. But that now seemed unnecessary. I had got my First; the college made me a Scholar. The wheel had come full circle; and to expect a fourth telegram would have been tempting fate. The label was firmly stuck.

◆ 7 ◆

Love at First Sight

———◆———

For the historian, context is everything: place, time, class and gender set the bounds of explanations; and analyses and events and personalities have to be encompassed within our chosen framework. 'There is no private life that has not been largely determined by some wider public life', wrote George Eliot. From our own experience we know this to be true. And yet we also know that this is not the whole story; that there is, lurking somewhere in the background, the unique 'I' which escapes definition by the historian. 'There is nothing truly real save that which feels, suffers, pities, loves and desires, save consciousness; all men are 'I's, wrote the Spanish philosopher, Miguel de Unamuno. Or, as the novelist Alan Sillitoe explained when describing the role of the writer in dealing with those fundamental issues that lie beyond class, race and geographical divisions, 'while place is everything it is also nothing. We are all born on ships at sea as far as our souls are concerned.'

Autobiography brings this dilemma to the surface. How, for instance, is one to deal with falling in love? It is a common enough experience and I cannot pretend that my experiences in this direction were in any way unusual; yet perhaps for that reason they are worth setting down. The problem is how to do this? On the one hand, I see myself as a social atom, one of several million youths from lower middle-class homes in the late-1930s and 1940s. On the other hand there is only one me, and there are some things that only I know about him. It is sometimes easiest to write about oneself in the third person, like a character in a novel, hoping thereby to disguise or avoid or confuse delicate and embarrassing issues. I can only rely on my memory to describe what happened to me in 1940–1 and will try to recall how I felt at the time—and later.

All societies have their rituals of courtship. Those of the respectable lower-middle classes were both well-defined and unhelpful. We no longer talked of 'walking out' or 'keeping company', but 'my fiancé(e)' (however-er defined) was still the norm in respectable circles. A formal and announced 'engagement' was expected after a couple had been 'going steady' with a view to marriage, and an engagement ring was given by the man to his fiancée. The general view was that an engagement should not be overly long, but nothing was laid down about this. However, everyone knew of cases where the engagement lasted for years. At St Philip's church one of the lady choristers, in her forties, had been engaged to another member of the choir for as long as anyone could remember. They were a comical couple: she, short and plump; he, a tall, lugubrious, beanpole of a man. Their usual excuse for not getting married was that one or other of them had to 'look after an aged parent'.

Much more serious was the weakness of the system in providing opportunities for meeting what the Victorians called one's 'partner in life'—not that in 1939–40 I was thinking of any such thing. For boys of my generation of the 1930s, who were educated separately from girls, young women seemed mysterious and inaccessible. To help us to over-come these feelings of ignorance and non-availability the Headmaster at the City Boys' School even organised get-togethers with girls from the Collegiate Girls' School. Whatever romances blossomed from this source none came my way. There must have been plenty of attractive girls about, and presumably some of them took part in the various social activities at St Philip's church. But I never seemed to meet them, perhaps because I did not like dancing nor did I belong to that archetypal 1930s youth gath-ering, the tennis club. At Cambridge the situation was no better. With only two women's colleges, the men far outnumbered the women, and I was no Don Juan. I did get as far as inviting a woman from Homerton Teachers' Training College to tea in my rooms. She was the college sec-retary of CUSC; but I did not find her very interesting, and nothing came of the meeting. My knowledge of sex at this time was minimal. I suppose my views about women are best described as romantic, and I was con-scious of my awkwardness and ignorance in approaching them. My stud-ies occupied virtually all my time and thoughts, and the general view in the family was, 'Oh, John's not interested in girls.'

In the early summer of 1940, however, all this was changed when I suddenly fell in love. This phrase is of course inadequate to describe my feelings; but I fear that any attempt to elaborate would only result in clichés and banalities. Better therefore to explain how this joyful event came about and how it affected my little world.

My cousin, Barbara, was a student at the Domestic Science College in

Leicester and from time to time she used to visit us at Byway Road. One Sunday afternoon in late May she came round for tea and brought with her a college friend. Now it so happened that I was at home that weekend, having left Cambridge ten days before the end of term because of a 'flu epidemic in the college. In the afternoon I went for a walk with a friend, and on our return we found the two visitors. I was introduced to Miss Margaret Marsh and was immediately bowled over. She was, to use a rather vulgar expression of the time 'a real smasher'. Her hair was fair and worn in a pageboy bob. She had blue eyes and wore a close-fitting, princess-style dress. I thought she was lovely; and was impressed by her lively, intelligent concern for all the things I was interested in. She also seemed so much more mature than me, and therefore, I feared, beyond my reach. However, I decided to try my luck. At the end of the evening I walked the two girls back to the Domestic Science College and hinted that I would like to see Margaret again. The next day I telephoned the college and asked for Miss Marsh. After some hesitation she agreed to meet me for tea in the town; and from there our friendship grew, though at first only slowly. I pressed her for more frequent meetings; but she was reluctant to come out with me as often as I wanted, saying that she could not spare the time from her college work. This was true; though at the time I thought she was only making excuses, and that perhaps there was 'someone else'. Later she told me that she feared I was too young or too serious and that she was not ready to 'go steady' with anyone. When the college term ended she returned home to Stourbridge and this put an end to our meetings.

I thought about her all summer and even called at her parents' house in Stourbridge when I 'happened' to be passing on my bicycle *en route* to the Cotswolds, but she was out. However, in the autumn I renewed the pursuit and this time met with decreasing resistance. I can still recall those wonderful moments of first love, when I was conscious of her every movement. A refusal to meet me plunged me into despair, and when she relented and we met again the sight of her made my heart leap. As the Cambridge terms were shorter than the Domestic Science College's there was a convenient period at the beginning and end of term when we were both in Leicester. We met for tea at Kunzle's, held hands in the cinema, and I stole my first kiss while we walked across the golf links. She came frequently to Byway Road and I delighted in walking her home across Victoria Park, only just arriving at the college as the doors were locked. It was a great grievance of the Domestic Science students that they had to be 'in' so much earlier than the Leicester University undergraduates next door. She visited me at Cambridge and was duly impressed, and I was introduced to her parents at Stourbridge. By the time of her twenty-first birthday on 28 June 1941 we were able to have a party at Byway Road, and my mother contrived to bake a birthday cake from the meagre, wartime rations. My present to Margaret was a copy of *The Oxford Book of Modern Verse*, bound in blue leather. Throughout the early summer of 1941 we were both working hard, she for her Finals and I for Part I of the Tripos. After that we felt gloriously free: the weather was marvellous, and we met up, together with Barbara, for a cycling holiday, staying at youth hostels in Stratford and Gloucestershire.

Margaret's family was similar in background to my own, although her father was more successful. Thomas Marsh (1892–1967) was the eldest of seven children born to Peggy and Simeon Marsh, a coalminer and cottager from Lower Gornal in Staffordshire. Thomas left school at thirteen and began work in the drawing office of Gibbons Bros., a local firm of retort and furnace builders. He attended night school, became a qualified draughtsman and, by the time I met him, had risen to become manager in charge of all outside work and later a director. He was a small, round, generous, friendly man; of a sociable and energetic disposition, liable to bursts of temper which erupted suddenly and died down just as quickly and for which he was sorry afterwards. He lived for his work: even on holiday he could not bear to be away from it for more than two or three days, and would invent an excuse to leave the family while he visited some job in South Wales or the Potteries. In 1916 he had married Florence Hemmings, also from Gornal. She was twenty-two years old, with long, reddish-gold hair, and worked as a milliner in her mother's haberdashery shop in the village. Her grandfather, Richard Hemmings (1842–1916) had come to Gornal from Gospel End with his father in 1860, and for over forty years was a pillar of Zoar Methodist Church: trustee, Sunday-school teacher, choirmaster. For fifteen years he worked as a colliery manager and then became manager of the local Cooperative Store. He was also active in the Friendly Society movement, being Secretary of the Pride of England Free Gardeners' Lodge. His son, Thomas Hemmings (1871–1923) was a retort builder and continued in the same tradition of service at Zoar church. After their marriage Margaret's parents lived in Gornal and later in Sedgley and retained their connection with Zoar, though when they moved to Stourbridge in 1933 the family preferred the local New Road Methodist Church. Family social life revolved round the chapel, and Margaret's accounts of Sunday-school anniversaries, choir practices, and arguments about ministers and finance (her father was a chapel trustee and treasurer) reminded me of similar happenings at St Philip's. Her education too was parallel to mine: Red Hall infants' school, scholarship entry examination to Dudley Girls' High School, transfer to Stourbridge County High School for Girls (Head Girl, 1937–8), Higher School Certificate in four subjects, Leicester Domestic Science College (1938–41). Our memories of family holidays, confirmed in photograph albums, are almost identical: 'On the sands at Weston' could just as well have been 'John and Mother at Skegness'.

The progress of our courtship was played out against the background—indeed was part of—wartime Britain. The war involved everyone in some way or other. My sister Eileen, after passing the scholarship examination from Medway Street Junior School, had gone to the Collegiate Girls' School, and from there to Leicester College of Art and Technology, where she qualified as a dress designer. But by this time it was 1943 and she was soon enroled in the WRNS and posted to the Fleet Air Arm. There she met a handsome young CPO, Paul Pickersgill, to whom she became engaged and, in 1948, married. The war affected us all the time, not only in obvious ways as when one was directed into the forces or industry but also in the minutiae of daily living. It coloured our thinking, it set bounds to our expectations, and perhaps marked us for life as 'the wartime generation'. For instance, 'make do and mend' became second nature. We became used to 'saving every scrap' whether it was paper, food, or string. Years later in America it astonished me to hear a colleague, when describing someone he did not like, say, 'he was so mean he'd even save pieces of string'. My father kept a tin box of just such string in the garage. Many of these wartime habits were already familiar to working people. We scarcely needed urging to 'Dig for Victory': my father had had an allotment for years. But we were surprised to learn how wise we had been all these years in eating carrots which enabled one to see in the blackout. Even better would be the day when the blackout ended (*When the Lights Come on Again*), for nothing added more to the gloom of daily life than the utter darkness which impeded all movement outside during the winter months. For five long years cars had to navigate by the light of a narrow slit from masked headlights. Hand torches had to be dimmed with thick white tissue paper. Trains and buses crawled along with blinds pulled down and illuminated by pinpoints of blue light. Doorsteps and kerbs were painted white to avoid accidents in the dark.

Many of the things described as important or significant in histories of the war—for example, the evacuation of the school children—made no impact on us at all. We heard a great deal about propaganda. The word was usually used in a pejorative sense to denigrate a German version of events; but it did not escape notice that we too engaged in similar activities. The number of enemy planes shot down as announced daily during the Battle of Britain in 1940 was not to be taken literally; after all, we had a very busy Ministry of Information. The reality of an event like Dunkirk was brought home not by the official news or even by pictures in the papers, but by the account of one of Margaret's friends who was there. As the immortal Mr Dooley once remarked, 'there are some things we know that ain't so'. Years later it requires much greater effort to recall the sequence of national and international events than the happenings in Leicester, Cambridge and Stourbridge. None of these towns, for instance, was blitzed, though bombs were dropped on or near them from time to time. On the night of 14 November 1940 when Coventry was so heavily bombed I was in Cambridge; but Margaret and the family in Leicester recounted how they listened to wave after wave of bombers going over and knew that 'someone was copping it'. We felt involved even when we were not hit, knowing that the next time it could be our turn.

As I dreamed my love dreams through the summer of 1940 I became increasingly caught up in the after-effects of much wider events. After Dunkirk there was fear of an imminent invasion and I was swept into the Home Guard for duty in Leicester during the vacations. At first we were called the Local Defence Volunteers and issued with an armband marked LDV, later changed to HG. Once a week I took my turn at patrolling the reservoir at Evington, not for the purpose of defending the water supply but to keep a lookout for German parachutists. Armed with sandwiches and Thermos flasks we spent the night in two-hour shifts, alternately gazing into the night sky and dozing on a camp bed. At dusk and dawn we all 'stood to'. There were not enough rifles for everyone and ammunition was also short; so we had to share weapons and hand over the clip of cartridges to the next man on duty. We were fully aware of our military deficiencies, both personal and material, and the later caricature of *Dad's Army* was sometimes not too wide of the mark. I cannot remember what we were supposed to do if we did 'encounter the enemy' apart from passing on the 'info' to 'HQ'. We were hardly the guerilla army envisioned by the Leftists in *Picture Post*; and the 'Armada Spirit' and DIY defence methods encouraged by official posters would have been somewhat inadequate for confronting paratroopers. My most vivid memories are of how early the first cocks began to crow and the dawn chorus to twitter, and how ghastly I felt as I trudged home in the early morning after a sleepless night.

By the summer of 1941 events were closing in on me. I had completed two years at Cambridge, had been enlisted into the army, and was awaiting call-up. In October I was posted to Sandhurst and emerged six months later with a commission. Margaret, having successfully passed her Finals, started teaching at Bournville. She lived at home in Stourbridge

Separation: *During the long ordeal of separation, lovers found consolation in a favourite photograph of the beloved, carried in a wallet or framed on a dressing-table. These two did duty for over three years*

Wartime weddings: *Weddings in wartime tended to be either hurried or over–delayed. Ours was the latter. (above) My mother and father, June 1915 (below) Our wedding group, Stourbridge, 12 December 1945*

and had to make a difficult and tiring journey to Selly Oak each day. The happy routine of the previous months was now rudely broken and we were able to meet less frequently. Then in May 1942 I was given embarkation leave, with destination of course unknown. The war news was bleak: the Russians were fighting for their very existence; it was touch and go whether Rommel would triumph in North Africa and break through into Egypt; the Dieppe raid had been a dismal and bloody failure; the second front was as far off as ever. With no end in sight, the war seemed destined to continue for ever. However, we decided to become engaged. I went through the formality of asking Margaret's father for his daughter's hand, though both he and I secretly regarded the thing as a bit of a joke. It was perfectly obvious that Margaret and I were hopelessly in love, and that I was fully acceptable to the family. Nevertheless, from a prospective father-in-law's point of view there could have been safer candidates than a penniless infantry subaltern about to disappear to no one knew where. I had to borrow the money for an engagement ring from my mother. And then I was swallowed up into the great embarkation process and finally decanted onto the shores of East Africa. We entered the long, dark tunnel of our separation: it was three years and eight months before we saw each other again. I wrote to Margaret several times a week and she wrote to me almost daily. It was difficult to think of fresh things to say, especially as the censorship prohibited most of what would have been of interest. But that didn't matter. The sight of the familiar writing on the envelope was itself a tonic. The letters arrived in bunches, so we took to numbering them. There must have been several hundred altogether.

When at long last the light appeared at the end of the tunnel I managed to telephone Margaret and told her to expect my return. We wanted to get married with the least possible delay and so she obtained a special licence. Our reunion on Leicester station repeated for me the overwhelming sensation I had felt when I saw her first, five years earlier in the sitting room at Byway Road. I was standing on the platform as she got out of the carriage. Ten days later, on 12 December 1945, we were married in New Road Methodist Church, Stourbridge. And so began what Shelley called 'the longest journey'.

Part II

SOLDIERING ON

◆

IN 1941, LIKE SOME five-and-a-quarter million of my fellow countrymen and women, I was recruited into the armed forces; and for the next four-and-a half years experienced the privileges, perils, and boredom of soldiering. I was ridiculously young (only twenty): it is hard to believe that the young man with smooth face, short hair, and trim uniform who gazes from the sepia photographs was really me.

After Cambridge I went to Sandhurst and six months later was commissioned as 2nd Lieutenant in the Leicestershire Regiment. I joined the 7th Battalion, at that time stationed in the North East, but remained there only a few weeks before being posted to the 17th (Uganda) Battalion, King's African Rifles, in East Africa. I was soon made Battalion Intelligence Officer; and in April 1943 was promoted Captain and appointed Adjutant. The battalion served in various parts of Kenya and Uganda, and in November 1943 was sent to garrison Mauritius for a year, and then returned to Kenya for jungle training on the slopes of Kilimanjaro. A few weeks later I was posted to HQ Mombasa and remained there for the rest of the war. I enjoyed being a Staff Captain and applied for the Staff College at Haifa in Palestine, but was declared ineligible unless I signed up for a 'temporary' (as distinct from my 'emergency') commission, which I was not prepared to do. I was fortunate to get an early (Class 'B') release from military service in December 1945, though I remained on the reserve until July 1959.

I think now that in some ways the war was harder for our parents to bear than it was for us. During the First World War my mother had seen her husband, brother, cousins, and friends sent to the bloody Armageddon of the Western Front; and now her son, daughter, nephews and nieces were again being sent to far-away places on unknown assignments. I realise that I had quite a good war compared with some of my contemporaries, even though it was not the way in which one would have chosen to see the world. I learned a lot of things about which I would otherwise have been ignorant; such as how to propose the King's health on guest night in the mess ('Mr Vice, the Loyal Toast—Gentlemen, the King'), or how to recognise the mauve-and-white ribbon of the Military Cross. More useful was the advice of an experienced major who was GSO II at Mombasa. Noticing my punctiliousness in answering instructions from higher up, he took me aside one day and said: 'I don't want to discourage your keenness, Harrison, but take my advice and save yourself some work—never act on the order, always wait for the amendment.' The man who came back at the end of 1945 had learned many lessons. But in December 1945 I just wanted to forget all about the army and get on with living my life.

◆ 8 ◆

KAR

◆

THE CAMP was astir long before dawn. It was cold. Over the fires in the open-air cookhouse, cauldrons of boiling water were being prepared for the early-morning tea. Askaris in various states of undress strolled along with mess tins to collect their tea, and then squatted on their haunches, laughing and chattering. They were big, brawny men; all were black, with the strongly-marked features of the Luo and Acholi tribes of Uganda. Although the official language of the KAR was Swahili, they spoke in the vernacular amongst their friends. When as young recruits they had joined the KAR, one of the first things they had to do was learn Swahili, which was the language of the coastal Africans but which the Arabs and Europeans had quickly used as a *lingua franca*.

My boy, Mate, padded silently on bare feet into my tent. *'Jambo, Bwana'*, he said quietly as he put the mug of tea on the ground by the side of my camp bed. He lit the hurricane lamp and hung it from the tent pole. I stirred inside the mosquito net and looked at the watch. It was 5.15 am, just time to get on parade by 6 o'clock. Mate returned with a jug of hot water which he put on the tin box which served as a table. Reluctantly I got out of bed, tucked my *kikoi* round my waist, and looked at myself in the shaving mirror suspended from the tent pole. The tea was half-cold but welcome nevertheless as I gulped it down between strokes of the razor. I poured the remainder of the water into my canvas camp basin and washed my face and hands. Refreshed, or rather awakened, I put on the clothes which Mate had laid out on the camp chair, with my bush jacket hanging from the ridge pole. The slowest part of dressing was winding one's puttees, and if they were not started in exactly the right place they finished up either too high or too low. I looked out of the tent. The dawn was already near, and the stars had almost disappeared from the velvety African darkness.

I went across to the mess, a long, palm-roofed hut which sheltered lizards and snakes in its rafters, especially in wet weather. There was no one else there. My companions had either breakfasted earlier or decided to forgo the ritual. Ali, the mess steward, greeted me—'*Jambo, Bwana*'—as I sat down at the table. I told him to hurry up, and he scurried off, returning suspiciously quickly with food. The bacon was thick and fat and congealed to the cold plate. The egg was swimming in grease. I decided to limit myself to the limp toast and stewed tea. One began to sympathise with the derogatory remarks which my brother officers threw at the mess cook. Good cooks were notoriously scarce; when found they were seldom allowed to remain at battalion level but were whisked off to brigade or divisional HQ.

On the way back to my tent I called in at the '*cho*' (latrine), a primitive affair, fumigated daily by lighting a fire which blew across the cesspit. Earlier in my army career I had been sent on a week's hygiene course, especially to learn about such things, and so I appreciated the principles, if not the mechanics, of latrine construction in the African bush. Back in the tent I buckled on my belt and revolver, put on my bush hat with its red flash and ostrich feathers, and snatched up my short, swagger cane.

The company was already drawn up on the parade ground, platoon by platoon, with the subalterns standing together at one side. As I approached, the African CSM called the troops to attention with a piercing screech, stamped his foot fiercely, about-turned, and brought his hand up in a quivering salute. I returned the salute and he reported the numbers sick, AWOL and otherwise occupied—'All present and correct, SIR'. I gave the order to stand at ease; and we relaxed for a few moments before moving off.

Two years earlier I should have felt nervous when standing alone in front of a-hundred-and-twenty men on parade. Despite six months of daily square-bashing at Sandhurst, when the Guards drill-sergeants had done their best to teach us how to bawl across the parade ground, I found it difficult to overcome my self-consciousness and lack of confidence. But two years of life in an infantry battalion had taught me many things, not least the habit of authority. The daily routine was one of giving (and receiving) orders, of making immediate decisions, and seeing that they were carried out. This was undoubtedly good for my ego; my self-esteem grew rapidly and I lost many of my earlier doubts and hesitations. Cambridge had not completely dispelled my temperamental diffidence and lower middle-class inhibitions but, in my role as an army officer, I had learned to overcome or, rather, suppress them for the time being. I came to realise that others relied on me and sometimes (since I was the adjutant of the battalion and therefore close to the CO) asked my advice. There was satisfaction in doing a job competently, even though at times it seemed to be leading nowhere. Like virtually all officers in the British army I fancied that I understood 'man management' and 'how to get things done'. Moreover, my experiences as adjutant, and later as a staff officer, convinced me that I was a born administrator, and that my future career should be in that direction—so much so that I seriously thought of joining the Colonial Service and becoming a District Commissioner when the war was over.

All this was far from the mind of the young 2nd Lieutenant who had landed in Mombasa in the summer of 1942. At that time I was still bewildered, though not unduly dismayed, by the rapidity of the changes in my fortunes. It is one of effects of war that one soon comes to accept the most unlikely turn of events; and the army accustoms one to adapt to new conditions unquestioningly. In such circumstances a cheerful fatalism is the only sensible philosophy and I can only marvel at the magnitude and pace of change.

After two idyllic years at Cambridge, during which time I had fallen in love, I had landed up in Sandhurst. Although the compulsory weekly drills and weapon training in the Cambridge University Senior Training Corps had hardly prepared me for the shock of army life, the Royal Military College was in one sense not unfamiliar. Like Cambridge, it was a highly-privileged, ruling-class institution, though devoted to the military arts rather than scholarship. Officially it was an OCTU (Officer Cadet Training Unit) like others; in fact we were not allowed to forget that we were the RMC. We still (1941) had a room of our own and a personal servant (not a batman) rather like a college 'gyp'. All the NCOs and most of the officers were Guardsmen, and many of my fellow-cadets were Guards candidates from aristocratic or affluent backgrounds. One cadet, whom we knew as Freddie Mutesa, was actually a king, the Kabaka of Buganda, Mutesa II. On the parade ground we were sworn at and treated as dirt, and immediately afterwards addressed as 'Sir'. There was an enormous amount of spit and polish. We 'boned' the toe caps of our boots by rubbing in black boot polish with the handle of a toothbrush in order to make them shine like patent leather. The white bands on our forage caps and epaulettes had to be spotless; and the brass on our belt buckles and on our buttons had to shine like gold. The officers on parade wore the most immaculate uniforms and Sam Browne belts. All of this bullshit reached a weekly climax in the Sunday morning church parade, when we marched with a band to the college chapel for morning prayer. The most difficult thing was to sit down because there was no room for one's side

The disruption caused by ten years of war was the greatest external intruding event in the lives of two generations of ordinary people. First World War: Father, Staff Sergeant, Royal Engineers

Second World War: Son, Captain, Leicestershire Regiment

arms (bayonet) which hung over the left buttock. But there we sat, row by row, gazing at the names of our predecessors engraved on the columns, hundreds of young, 2nd Lieutenants killed in the First World War. Sunday afternoons were free, unless one was on guard duty; but there was little to do except walk into Camberley, where everything was closed, or lie on one's bed for a snooze—which was probably just as well, because our pay of 2s 6d. a day, which with the weekly stoppage for 'barrack damages' left us with exactly 15s a week, did not allow for much outside entertainment.

Weekday mornings began with drill on the parade ground; then breakfast; and a morning spent on weapon training, vehicle driving, camp maintenance, mines, explosives, etc. In the afternoons and evenings we had lectures and exercises on map reading, tactics, how to care for one's men, and regimental history. Some days we spent in the surrounding countryside on TEWTs (tactical exercise without troops), when we were split up into small groups under an officer and given carefully-planned problems of tactics at platoon, company and battalion level. The emphasis was on making immediate decisions, acting on them decisively, and issuing orders authoritatively. He who hesitates, we were assured, is lost—and certainly would not gain his commission. All this was quite contrary to my natural caution and scholarly training at Cambridge, where we had been taught to weigh up carefully all sides of a question and avoid snap judgements. We learned that 'there are no bad units, only bad officers'; and that a wrong order is better than no order or a hesitant one. So although I 'passed out' of Sandhurst eventually, it was hardly surprising that my final grade was only C ('satisfactory').

There was a strange fascination about the extraordinary ritualistic behaviour and insider-language of the Guards. For instance, if on parade the inspecting officer noticed a dirty mark on one's white cap band or belt, he would say to the accompanying NCO 'Take his name, Sergeant Major'. To which the CSM would reply 'Got 'im Sir'. The charge on which one would appear before the CO the next morning would be announced by the CSM (with much stamping, about-turning, and saluting) as 'Mr 'Arrison, Sir, extremely idle on parade, Sir'. The parade ground was dominated by the huge and awesome figure of the RSM (Regimental Sergeant Major), who strutted about with his pace-stick under his arm. 'Shagger' Brand was the senior NCO in the British army and his voice was reputed to carry for unbelievable distances. Like everything else at Sandhurst he was in a class of his own, and we were not allowed to forget it.

At the end of our course came the passing-out parade, when we marched up the steps and into the Old Building, followed by the adjutant on his grey horse. Weapons were in such short supply that when we went on night exercises, crawling across fields and hiding in ditches, we each took a dummy Bren gun made of wood because damage to the real light machine guns could not be risked. Some weeks before the end of the course I visited one of the military tailors in Camberley to order my uniform, for which there was an (inadequate) grant. I had already learned the intricate differences in style (number of buttons, cut of pockets) and material (whipcord or barathea) between the various regiments; and the Guards officers had been shining examples of sartorial excellence. The obsequiousness and high degree of craftsmanship of the tailors was traditional; and they made me the best-fitting garments I had ever worn.

After Sandhurst there had been a short leave before joining the battalion to which I had been posted, the 7th Leicesters. This was a territorial battalion which had seen action in Norway, where the previous commander of my platoon had been killed. Battalion HQ was at Yarm in North Yorkshire but my platoon was on detachment on the Durham coast at Seaham Harbour, where we carried out nightly patrols looking for German invaders. However, I had been with the unit only a few weeks when the battalion was ordered to find officers for an overseas draft. And so on the principle of 'last in, first out' I was soon on embarkation leave.

Although Margaret was teaching full-time at Bourneville we did manage to see each other, and we spent a last sad weekend while I was at the transit camp in Central London. I think this was the most miserable time in my life. I had no idea where I was going, though I had been issued with tropical kit—which could have meant something or nothing. We did not know when or indeed whether we should ever see each other again. The war at this stage (June 1942) seemed interminable, with no significant progress towards the defeat of Germany or Japan, and no end in sight. After our tearful farewells I went back to the transit camp; and that night entrained (as they said), along with other young 2nd Lieutenants and several drafts of troops, for Scotland. After a long night's journey (a tedious ordeal in the blackout) we arrived at Greenock and embarked in the Firth of Clyde. The *Warwick Castle*, a peacetime liner on the South Africa run, had been converted into a troopship. It was comfortable enough for the officers (four to a two-berth cabin) but pretty horrific for the ORs who had to sleep in hammocks on the mess decks. Everyone was resigned but cheerful and (underneath) rather excited. The full extent of the convoy was not evident until we put to sea; and then we began to appreciate the size of the operation. A long line of troopships stretched as far as the eye could see, flanked on either side by warships. Occasionally a plane flew over us. The convoy steamed slowly, the pace set by the slowest ship.

Life on board was tolerable enough. I teamed up with another young 2nd Lieutenant from the Leicestershire Regiment and we shared the same cabin. The food seemed wonderful after the restrictions of rationing at home. But despite constant drills, alerts, and spells of guard duty, the time lagged. The OC Troops was an unbelievably Colonel Blimpish character who gave us lectures about Africa and 'native' troops. We were by no means convinced that we were in fact destined for Africa at all; the whole thing might be just an elaborate security plot. However, when the convoy rounded the Cape of Good Hope and half of it sailed on to India and the other half docked in South Africa, we began to suspect that we were indeed destined for the 'Dark Continent'. We disembarked at Durban; and after a few days of sightseeing and patriotic welcoming I found myself once more aboard, this time bound for East Africa. The weather grew hotter and hotter, and I was glad of that tropical kit (ill-fitting as it was) when we arrived in the steamy heat of Mombasa.

Now for the first time I felt very much alone: an insignificant young 2nd Lieutenant, belonging to no unit, with nothing but my tin kit box and bedding roll, in the utterly soulless surroundings of a transit camp, set in the midst of what seemed to me then a steaming jungle. In the army one could not normally travel from one unit to another (unless on a very simple journey) but had to be handed on from transit camp to transit camp. Their function was to check, arrange and coordinate the non-operational movement of troops; and everything about these camps was impersonal, impermanent, and bedeviled by red tape. They were usually commanded by a Lt.-Colonel or Major past the age for active service, assisted by a skeleton staff of second-in-command, quartermaster, and NCOs—a cushy billet, in which the staff, but not the inmates, made themselves comfortable. The main problem, having got in, was how to get out, as the system generated interminable paperwork for the simplest operations. After about a week of routine duties such as 'officer of the day', I was informed that I had been posted to the 17th (Uganda) Battalion, King's African Rifles, then stationed at Eldoret in the White Highlands of Kenya. I was issued with the usual first-class (being an officer and gentleman as well as a white man) rail pass, and took myself off the next afternoon to the terminus of the Kenya and Uganda Railway.

The journey from Mombasa to Nairobi, which I was later to make several times, was always an adventure. The train left in the early evening and arrived in the capital about mid-morning of the following day, so one had to book a sleeping berth and take meals in the dining car. To climb the escarpment between the coast and the plateau the railway had been constructed with many steep gradients and cork-screw bends. In one place the head of the train was actually above the tail, so tight was the curve. The gauge was narrower than the standard British gauge, but the carriages were of normal width, so that they overhung the track on either side. Despite the huge double-ended locomotive, the train chugged only slowly, belching clouds of wood smoke. It soon grew dark; and when one awoke the next morning the landscape had changed from the lush tropical green of the coastal plain to the brown African bush and grasslands.

The train crawled on, often at no more than walking speed, climbing the Kikuyu escarpment and crossing the Great Rift Valley before struggling up to the Uasin Gishu plateau. From the carriage window I had my first glimpses of the Africa with which I was soon to become familiar: the dry brown bush, the blue haze over distant mountains, scattered settlements of mud huts and maize patches, African children standing by the side of the track, waving, the Indian officials in the wayside stations. At Eldoret I was met by an African driver with a truck. Arriving at the camp I reported to the adjutant, a cheerful conscript like myself, who explained the set-up before marching me into the CO's office. It appeared that I had joined one of the newly formed KAR battalions, part of that vast expansion of colonial infantry which the War Office had decided should be the Empire's contribution to Second World War. The battalion was responsible for guarding a camp of Italian officer POWs (prisoners of war); but the main concern was training for service somewhere in the Far East, probably Burma. The CO and Second-in-Command were regular officers; the rest of us were a motley crew of Kenya settlers, colonial expatriates from various parts of the world, and people from Britain like myself. There was a friendly atmosphere in the battalion, an easy tolerance of each other's tastes and preferences, and respect for our very different experiences and backgrounds. The CO, Lt.-Col. Edmund Fell Whitehead (nicknamed Fido), who set the tone of the battalion, was an abstemious, puritanical, and somewhat impatient man. He had been commissioned in the East Surreys and had served in India as well as East Africa. Now, at the age of thirty-two, he had got his first command, and he was anxious to make the 17th KAR an efficient, first-line battalion which might be selected for action in the near future. Like several of the senior officers in the battalion, he had served with the KAR in the Abyssinian campaign, and at night in the mess we heard much about it: the names of Gondar, Keren, Moyale, Juba, Jigjiga, Asmara, 'Addis' (Ababa), 'Mog' (Mogadishu), Diredawa became so familiar to me that I almost felt at times that I had been to them.

I was soon taken aside by the old Kenya settlers, who were greatly concerned that newcomers from England should appreciate the need to maintain 'correct' relationships between Africans and Europeans. Kenyan society was regulated by a rigid colour bar: no Africans, for instance, were allowed on the streets of Nairobi after dark, nor could they enter the whites' bars or clubs. The settlers' attitudes were completely patriarchal: the Africans were children who had to be treated as such. All African household and personal servants were called 'boys', even when they were old men. There could be no question of equality or fraternisation between the races; but nor should the white man ever forget that he had responsibilities and obligations to look after 'his' Africans and especially to treat them fairly but firmly. These attitudes were replicated in the KAR, where they harmonised conveniently with army dogmas of hierarchy, responsibility, and looking after the ORs. Insofar as the tone of a KAR battalion was influenced by its Kenya officers, it was an extension of life on the coffee, sisal and pyrethrum farms of the White Highlands. It was a style of life with which I was later to become familiar, for my closest friend in the battalion turned out to be a young settler of German background. Through him I was made welcome in the farm houses of Gilgil and Naivasha, where I spent my infrequent leaves, enjoying the non-military comfort of 'home'. And home it seemed in those stone-and-timber houses, with their beams and mullioned windows and log fires on an open hearth. Only the verandah and the exotic climbing plants, like morning glory, reminded one that this was the Equator, not the Cotswolds. In the high altitude the air felt clean and fresh, and there was dew on the grass in the mornings. It was not the Happy Valley society of the 1920s and 1930s lotus eaters; though the famous trial of Sir Delves Broughton for the murder of his wife's lover, Lord Erroll, in 1941, was still a subject for speculation over a sundowner.

The language of communication in the KAR was 'kitchen' (as opposed to 'safi', or pure) Swahili, and I was assured that I should soon 'pick it up'. However, since one was virtually useless without a certain level of fluency and since no arrangements for teaching Swahili were made by the battalion, I persuaded the English-speaking education sergeant, Moses (a softly-spoken Baganda) to coach me in after-duty hours. This he was delighted to do, partly I think because he gained kudos by it being known that he was teaching a *bwana* something he (the *bwana*) did not know, and also because he simply appreciated being with a European in a relaxed atmosphere. Later on I acquired a Swahili grammar and dictionary, and even attempted to learn Acholi, the language of many of our askaris from the West Nile district of Uganda, but without much success.

These things were not consciously in my mind on that early morning route march. My East-African experiences could only be fully understood later on. At the time it was impossible to separate the important from the trivial. Only much later, when, as Marcel Proust would have said, experience through memory impinges on the mind, can we comprehend its significance or reality. I sensed dimly that great changes were going on in the society around me, but did not realise at that time that I was in fact living in the last days of colonialism: the 'end of empire' was not then in sight. Nor did I appreciate how these experiences in the KAR would come to affect my own attitudes and thinking.

It was getting light by the time we left the parade ground and headed for the dusty red road leading out of the camp. But it was still cool enough to be enjoyable. The idea was to do as much as we could before the heat of the day, so a dawn start was imperative. The route march, apart from accustoming us to a twenty-mile hike, was intended as an exercise in march discipline: how to take cover from strafing by hostile aircraft; what to do when pinned down by enemy fire; how to deploy the sections and platoons 'winkling out' isolated machine-gun posts, and so on. At first we marched to attention with rifles at the slope; but once clear of the camp I gave the order to march at ease, with rifles slung. The askaris were in full marching order, with packs, water bottles, rifles and side arms. They swung along easily, platoon by platoon, and soon broke into song, starting with *Amri ya KAR*. This was one of those interminable marching songs, consisting of an improvised solo by one of the bolder spirits and an answering refrain by the rest of the company. I strode along with the sergeant major at the head of the column.

Looking back, from time to time, I saw the familiar faces and thought of those who had come to me with problems during the previous week. Was Oburu's wife looking after the chickens properly? Was Sezare's brother taking advantage of Sezare's absence to usurp his position in the family? What was the rumour that one of Chirilo's cows had died? Why had not Ogiki's wife received the money he had sent her? The resolution of these domestic affairs was vital for morale; a worried askari was unlikely to be an efficient soldier, so each case had to be painstakingly unravelled. The matter usually started with a letter from a friend or relative in the village, or perhaps by a report from an askari who had just returned from leave. First, one had to establish the exact nature of the problem, which was by no means easy, as tribal customs and African ways of thinking were far different from European patterns. I usually called in the man's NCO or another askari from the same village to explain the parts of the story which were unclear. Then, having grasped the essence of the complaint or wrong, I tried to assess the reliability of the evidence: was it mere rumour or were there witnesses to attest its likely authenticity? Most of the askaris were illiterate, and belonged to an oral culture. When they received a letter, written by a friend or the village letter writer, they had to ask the education sergeant or another NCO to read it to them. A reply similarly had to be written by someone else. The poor askari thus felt both worried and helpless, the more so as his natural mode of communication was in the vernacular, not Swahili. If the problem seemed *prima facie* genuine the only thing to do was to write to the DC (District Commissioner) and ask him to investigate. He, in turn, handed on the problem to the chief or headman of the village concerned, who reported back to the DC, and thence we received an answer. This was what the Askari wanted. He felt reassured when the *bwana* promised to write a letter, even though he knew that it would take several weeks to get a reply, as the West Nile District lay beyond the railhead and there were few roads. The great distances and poor communications in East Africa created many difficulties for us. The askaris were deeply rooted in their villages, where they were regarded as an elite among the young men. They had joined the KAR to save money to pay their poll tax or accumulate a bride price. While they subscribed to a sort of professional loyalty to the KAR (and Kingi Georgi) their hearts were in their villages 6–800 miles away. Care of one's men was a good deal more complicated and interesting than the Sandhurst injunction to inspect their feet after a route march.

The sun rose. Faintly in the distance a bugle call died away. I pictured the scene outside the orderly room, the guard presenting arms as the flag was slowly raised to the tune of the *Long* (Turkish) *Reveille*. Sunrise and sundown have a special quality in Kenya. For one thing the sun rises (and sets) very quickly, so that there is almost no twilight; and at night the insects begin to bite. In the KAR the ceremony of raising and lowering the flag at sunrise and sundown to the accompaniment of *Reveille* and the *Last Post* marked the progress of the military day. The final dying notes of the *Last Post* always seemed symbolic.

The road out of town had the usual red, earth surface, deeply corrugated by army trucks. The platoons marched by sections on alternate sides of the road, which was bordered by a thin line of trees for about half-a-mile. I fell into conversation with the sergeant major and for some time did not notice anything untoward. Then suddenly I sensed that something was wrong. The men stopped singing. The only sound was the beat of their footsteps. Somewhat annoyed, I told the sergeant major to tell them to continue singing, and he dropped back to instruct the platoon sergeants accordingly. However, nothing happened; and the sergeant major reappeared to say that the men didn't want to sing. They weren't in a singing mood, he said, but did not know why. Oh well, I thought, if they don't want to sing that's their lookout. And we continued the march.

It was the army custom to take a brief rest every hour in order to loosen one's pack and have a quick smoke. So, fifty minutes later I gave the order to halt and fall out. Walking back down the column I noticed that the askaris seemed rather lackadaisical and quiet, but thought nothing of it. However, as the day wore on and we engaged in various exercises it became more and more noticeable that they were reluctant to cooperate. The same was observed by the platoon commanders. We debated among ourselves whether the men's lassitude and lack of interest could be due to the weather, or to boredom, or to some type of infection, but decided against all of these. I called the three platoon sergeants and the sergeant major together and asked them what was the matter. At first they denied anything was amiss; but under repeated questioning they said that today was not a suitable day for a route march. I asked them what they meant by that, but they said nothing and looked at one another uneasily. By now thoroughly angry, I demanded to know what they were hiding from me. One of them then said that it was an unlucky day. I pressed him to say exactly why that was so and how he knew it. He refused to be more specific. However, the true nature of the problem gradually emerged.

It appeared that as we had set out we had passed under a tree whose branches overhung the road, and on one of those branches sat a bird of ill omen. When the askaris saw this bird they were afraid; they believed it had cast an evil spell over them. This meant that all endeavours that day would not prosper. Without appreciating the cultural differences between Africans and Europeans, I insensitively pooh-poohed this and told them that such things were powerless to hurt human beings and that I and the other *bwanas* took no notice of such rubbish. Maybe, they said; but that is because you are white men and black men's magic cannot harm you; but we are black men and our magic is potent for us. I told them that in the KAR we were all subject to white man's magic and that they had to obey Kingi Georgi's orders. They agreed that this was so, but insisted that they could not escape from the power of the spell. They thought, but did not dare say, that we should abandon our march and go home. But that was impossible. I could just imagine the reception I should get from the CO if we returned to camp halfway through the morning and I told him that we had cancelled the exercise because it was an unlucky day. It troubled me even more that such an occurrence might take place, not on a train-ing exercise, but when we were in action against the Japanese. What price then a refusal to fight because the omen's were unpropitious? 'No,' I said to the NCOs, 'we shall continue as planned and you must set an example to your men.' They went back to their platoons and we carried on for the rest of the day. But we might just as well have gone back to camp for all the good we achieved. None of the askaris showed any interest in what they were supposed to be doing; they were slow to obey even the simplest orders; and their attitude towards their officers bordered on what the army called 'dumb insolence'.

When we returned to camp I told the CO what had happened; and that evening in the mess I discussed it with the Kenya settlers, who showed no serious desire to consider the matter from an African point of view. They said they had encountered such 'superstition' many times among Africans and it merely confirmed what they had always known: that the askaris were childlike in many ways and needed firm leadership. There was even the implied hint that because of their superior knowledge of the natives they (the old settlers) would have been able to handle the business without undue fuss. But what exactly they would have done they were reluctant to say. That night I prayed that there would be no birds of ill omen in Burma.

♦ 9 ♦

The Mutiny

———————◄♦►———————

THE RELIABILITY of memory intrigues me when I try to recall the events of fifty years ago. There are some things which I think I remember, sometimes quite vividly, but for which I can find no confirmation. Have I just imagined the whole episode?—or, more likely, have I embroidered details on to something which actually occurred but not in quite the way I have chosen to remember it? From one angle of course such musings are irrelevant. That my memories might not be strictly 'true' is itself an interesting or significant fact—about me or the conditions of the time. If I remember an experience in a certain way it is for me a valid truth, whether objectively accurate or not. This is especially so in the case of childhood memories, which are sometimes widely different from adult perceptions. As a literary form autobiography is not necessarily bound by the rules of archival evidence: experience can be expressed and truth apprehended in different ways, some of which I find attractive. For historians, however, there is something uncomfortable about this position. We cannot escape from the longing for verification, the impulse to check sources, to try to describe things 'as they actually were at the time', even while we know that we can never really do so.

Such thoughts are prompted by my memories of the mysterious affair of the mutiny of the Mauritius Regiment. Details of the facts surrounding mutinies are always obscure, if only for the obvious reason that noone in authority wants to admit that they happened. References to them are carefully expunged from official histories, and contemporary references are hushed up, or mysteriously missing. Not that this particular mutiny was ever very important. It was a small affair in an out-of-the-way corner of the world, no more than a footnote to an already obscure part of the Second World War. The official history of the KAR does not even mention that the 17th KAR went to Mauritius, let alone that there was a mutiny of the Mauritius Regiment. Yet perhaps for that very reason it is worth recording: a part of the history of that great majority of people who have no history. When writing history the crucial question to be asked is: whose history? For those of us who were there, or in my case on the edge of it, this was our history.

In November 1943 the battalion received orders to go to Mauritius. Earlier in the previous year Japanese submarines had appeared in the Mozambique Channel. The Vichy French government in Madagascar was hostile, and in September the 22nd East African Brigade, consisting of Nyasaland, Tanganyika and Kenya battalions of the KAR had landed in Majunga as part of the invading force and fought their way to the capital, Tananarive. To strengthen the defence of this part of the East African Command the 17th KAR was to garrison Mauritius, a destination quite unknown to us, but which turned out to be one of a group of sugar islands in the middle of the Indian Ocean. I suppose it had once been (perhaps still was) an important calling station on the route from India to South Africa. At any rate it was now important that it should not fall into Japanese hands. We began preparations for the move with growing excitement and (for me) some apprehension as to how the askaris would react. There was a story going the rounds of one African unit which had refused to embark after being shown the security film, *One of our Ships is Missing*. The War Office had issued an order that all troops going overseas should see the film, in which loose talk in a pub causes the loss of the ship, shown vividly as it sinks with all hands. The askaris, who had never been to sea, nor even seen an ocean-going ship, were terrified when told to board, fearing the same fate as they had just been shown in the film. However, by the time our turn came for embarkation this piece of bureaucratic ineptitude must have been cancelled, as I do not remember that we showed the film. We embarked at Mombasa without incident and set sail.

The troopship was quite small—an old boat from the China seas—and the askaris were all as sick as dogs. We were escorted by a naval frigate, very low in the water, which ploughed through the waves ahead of us. After calling at Diego Suarez, Madagascar, and the Seychelles, the battalion arrived in Mauritius and disembarked, weary, ragged, and thankful that the journey was over. Our reception was something less than enthusiastic. The big, fierce-looking askaris struck terror into the hearts of the islanders, who feared for their goods and women. We were immediately dubbed savages and Zulus. When it was discovered that few askaris spoke English and none French, dismay deepened. Only later did the upper echelons of Mauritian society come to appreciate the gentlemanly qualities of my brother officers of the 17th KAR, two of whom married Mauritian girls while we were there.

It was the intention of the East Africa Command that the KAR should replace the Mauritius Regiment, who were to embark in the same ship that had brought us. The Mauritius Regiment was another of the colonial infantry battalions raised during the war. Its troops were French-speaking coloured creoles and the officers were a mixture of upper-class (French) white Mauritians and Anglo-Mauritians from the UK. Mauritius is a tiny volcanic island, some 38-miles long and 29-miles wide, taken from the French under the Treaty of Vienna in 1815. Most of the troops had never been away from the island, and the EA Command therefore ordered that they should be sent to northern Madagascar for battle training and toughening up. They were smartly turned out, with plenty of spit and polish, which put us to shame, so that we defensively said to ourselves that, unlike us, they were only parade-ground soldiers. We had no grounds for this judgement; but it subsequently appeared that we were probably right. Our first surprise was the emotional nature of their embarkation. As the Mauritius Regiment marched down to the quay, the sidewalks, balconies, and windows were crowded with people to see them off, amidst much waving and shouting. I could not make out whether the crowds were protesting or encouraging the embarkation. There were tearful scenes as women, children, parents and friends tried to kiss, embrace and hold on to the marching soldiers, some of whom seemed to me to be reluctant to go. Our askaris were amazed and amused by what they saw and wondered what kind of people were these. I remember thinking at the time that we should be lucky to get them all aboard without trouble. But embark they all did; and we watched with a great sigh of relief as the ship sailed away.

For some time we thought no more about the Mauritius Regiment. The business of settling in and finding out what we were supposed to be doing occupied all our energies. Mauritius was a comfortable change after the African bush, provided always that the Japanese did not arrive. We were housed in permanent barracks, not tents, in the village of Curepipe, situated on a central plateau about 2000 feet high, bordered by small mountains. The climate was pleasantly sub-tropical, though not free from heavy rains and terrifying cyclones as we were to discover later on. Mauritian society was dominated by a handful of old French families, the majority of the population being coloured creoles with some Chinese shopkeepers, Indians and others. The British presence was represented by the governor and his staff—and of course by the armed forces.

Unfortunately the first task we were given only increased the hostility with which the general populace had greeted our arrival. The economy of Mauritius was based on sugar, and when the time came for cutting the cane the sugar workers—poorly-paid Tamils from southern India—struck for a small increase in wages. This was resisted by the Mauritian estate owners, who requested the governor to use troops to suppress the strike. To my horror I found that we were to be used as strikebreakers. There is nothing that regular soldiers like less than being called out 'in aid of the civil power', and the CO protested strongly; but to no avail. 'C' Company was sent to a village to quell what was designated a riot. When we arrived, in full battle order and with fixed bayonets, we found a small crowd of miserable-looking Tamils who shook their fists at us and threw a few stones. The Riot Act was read in Creole French and the order given to disperse. The CSM ordered the company to present arms, which they did with much banging of rifles and stamping of feet. Faced by this show of strength, the strikers drifted away and we returned to barracks. Two weeks later we were ordered to march round the whole island in full battle kit to 'show the flag', in other words to intimidate the strikers. But we saw none. All that we learned was that our askaris were sadly out of practice, and the CO ordered a rigorous course of fitness training.

I cannot remember exactly when news of the Mauritius Regiment filtered through. The story that we heard was that shortly after their arrival in Madagascar they mutinied, whereupon the EA Command decided that they were useless as infantry, disbanded the battalion and shipped them all off to the Middle East to be employed as pioneers, loading and unloading ships in the docks. It was however impossible to get confirmation of this news. For the time being I thought no more about it. There were more immediate matters to attend to, such as the strange affair of Mahomed bin Sultani.

Before we left Mombasa, Mahomed (one of our askaris) reported sick with a paralysed arm. The doctor examined him but could find nothing wrong and, suspecting that he was malingering, sent him away. A week later his company commander sent him to the doctor again, with a note explaining that Mahomed had been quite unable to take part in exercises during the past week. This time the doctor examined him closely and, after sticking needles under his nails and performing other crude tests, concluded that his arm was indeed quite numb and without feeling, but he could not diagnose what was wrong. There were no symptoms of any kind and Mahomed could offer no explanation beyond saying that he was sick and his arm had died. At this time the doctor and I shared a tent and, one evening while we sipped our sundowner, he told me about this strange case. He was well aware of the difficulty of diagnosing illness in Africans whose ideas of what was wrong with themselves were different

110

from European notions. We wondered if this could be some disease or psychological state, perhaps even a case of witchcraft. The doctor concluded that all he could do was keep Mahomed under observation. In the meantime he was to remain with his company. Two weeks later Mahomed's arm was still paralysed and he said that he was dying. By now, thoroughly alarmed we decided to seek non-medical advice. Mahomed had a brother in another company and I called him in and asked him what he thought was wrong. He said he did not know since apparently Mahomed refused to discuss the matter with anyone. But by dint of hard questioning of the brother we gradually pieced together the story of what had happened.

One day Mahomed's company had been on a route march and they had taken a path through a field of Indian corn (maize) which was shoulder high and almost ripe for harvesting. As they passed through the field, Mahomed had plucked an ear of corn and put it in his knapsack. Subsequently he came to believe that the owner of the field had put a spell on the corn to protect it from thieves. It was the magic of this spell that had paralysed the arm which he had stretched out to steal the corn. I asked Mahomed's brother what we could do about this, and he replied that only if the spell were lifted would his brother recover. How could this be done? I asked. He said he did not know; but he knew that the magic was very powerful and that his brother would eventually die. Although somewhat sceptical of this, I realised that the affair was serious and could not be wished away by talk of white man's magic. As Mahomed was a Moslem I decided that the best thing to do would be to try to bring some religious pressure to bear. I called in the local imam who was very understanding and helpful. He said that we should try to locate the owner of the maize field and ask him to remove the spell (if there were one) and thus reassure Mahomed that he had nothing to fear any longer. After some enquiries we found the owner of the field and explained the situation. With an eye to the main chance he assured us that there was indeed a spell on the corn, but that it would be difficult to remove it quickly. However these things could always be taken care of between friends. I asked, how much? He named his price, and I accepted. He agreed before witnesses, including Mahomed's brother, that Mahomed was forgiven and that the spell was lifted. Well, that's that, I thought; and turned thankfully to preparing for the move to Mauritius.

I assumed that once Mahomed had been reassured that the spell was lifted all would be well; but this was not so. Shortly after we arrived in Mauritius the doctor reported that Mahomed's arm was still paralysed and that moreover he appeared to be wasting away. Oh Lord, I thought, this is really too much. As we were now out of touch with the owner of the field, and all our arguments, reassurances and threats were of no avail, I tried once again to enlist the support of a local imam. But his spiritual authority was no match for the strength of African magic. Mahomed continued to waste away. The doctor advised that unless this decline could be arrested he would eventually die. This was something we could not allow to happen but which we appeared to be impotent to prevent. I could already envisage the form to be filled out, the report to be written, and explanations by telephone that such a death would involve: 'Cause of Death: Evil Spell'. No, no, that would never be acceptable to the higher-ups in Command HQ. The poor man must be sent back to his village, and perhaps there he might recover. He was granted sick leave and arrangements were made for his transfer to a hospital in Mombasa *en route* to Uganda. The last I saw of him was in an ambulance about to leave for the docks. We never heard what happened to him; but he did not return to the KAR.

Matters such as this fully occupied my attention during our stay in Mauritius; and I thought no more about the Mauritius Regiment. Army life in wartime is intensely local and does not encourage speculation or enquiry beyond what is required for the immediate task in hand. Nor did the affair surface in my mind in the years after the ending of the war. Once I was safely demobbed, married, and happily working, I tried to forget about the 'wasted' years in the army. I could not completely forget about the KAR of course; and there were reminders of army life in my old boots (used for gardening), my khaki tunic which I wore about the house (clothing was still on coupons), and the greatcoat which I wore in the car on winter nights. But these were private thoughts only. Nobody was interested in listening to yarns from old soldiers: there were too many of us, and war experiences at the ordinary level have a tedious similarity.

For many years these memories slumbered peacefully at the back of my mind. Then one day when I was teaching a seminar on the 1930s and 1940s to my American students I happened to say something which indicated that I was actually alive at the time. The students were fascinated and pressed me to say more: 'Why', they said admiringly, 'you're a resource person'. I was not sure that this was quite the compliment I would have sought; but it made me realise that I was now not only a teacher of history but (to those students at least) part of history itself. From then on I began to try to remember details of my past.

One afternoon about three years ago I was waiting in the reading room of the Royal Commonwealth Society in Northumberland Avenue while the librarian was fetching me a book I had ordered. I had gone there in the hope that they might have some material on the KAR in the Second World War with which to refresh my memory. While waiting for the book to arrive I idly glanced through a rack of new books and noticed one entitled *Mutiny in the British and Commonwealth Forces, 1797–1956*. I picked it out and, like most academics, looked first through the index. To my amazement there was an entry under 'Orangea, Madagascar'. Excitedly I turned to the page and there in a few sentences was a brief reference to the mutiny of the 1st Battalion, Mauritius Regiment in December 1943. Apparently there had been a mass refusal to do PT. The men were said to be 'browned off' and angered about their removal from Mauritius. Four ring-leaders were found guilty by court martial and two death sentences passed but later annulled. I wrote immediately to the author of the book to see if he had any further details, but he replied saying that he had found no more than this one reference in an official document. This was disappointing; but it did confirm that I had not dreamt the whole episode. I determined to pursue the matter: but how?

After fifty years I had completely lost contact with members of the battalion but I thought that the CO might possibly still be alive. I wrote to the War Office (now Ministry of Defence) asking if they could tell me the whereabouts of Colonel E.F. Whitehead; but they said that they could not disclose any information without the written consent of the next of kin. The Regimental Association however were more helpful and from them I learned that he had died in 1984. So that avenue was definitely closed. I wrote to out-of-date addressees, searched library lists for items about Mauritius, and talked to historians of the Commonwealth; but all to no avail. Then one evening at a dinner party in Brighton the conversation touched upon the subject of holidays in the islands of the Seychelles, and I mentioned casually that a long time ago I had been in Mauritius and would like to get in touch with anyone who was there during the war. Our host, who was a doctor, said that he had an old colleague at the Maudsley Hospital who was a Mauritian and that perhaps he might be helpful. Shortly afterwards I wrote to him.

Dr Joseph Henri Rey, now retired and living in France, came to England in 1939 to study medicine and was, therefore, not in Mauritius during the war. However he was able to make enquiries from a friend and also put me in touch with his brother, René Rey, now living in Durban, South Africa and formerly a captain in the artillery. From him I received an account of what happened in 1943.

The Mauritius Regiment was commanded by Lt.-Col. Yates, a regular officer who was, I suspect, anxious to fashion his battalion into a first-class fighting force. Perhaps with English troops he would have been more successful. As it was, he found himself in charge of poorly-educated black creoles who hardly understood or spoke English. The officers were a heterogeneous mixture of French-speaking white Mauritians who could also speak English and creole, and Anglo-Mauritians from the UK. The latter despised the creoles and many of them equally the young, white Mauritian officers. The NCOs were a higher class of creoles who resented the attitudes of the English officers towards them and their men. When the KAR arrived there was great fear that the askaris, who looked like savages to them, would molest the Mauritian womenfolk and rumours soon spread. Hence the reluctance of the Mauritius Regiment to embark. On the week-long voyage to Madagascar most of the creoles were very seasick and spent their time in the bowels of the ship, vomiting and unable to eat. They landed on the quay in Diego Suarez late in the morning, when the sun was at its hottest, and had to parade there in full kit for over an hour. Some fell down from sheer exhaustion and were insulted by their Anglo-Mauritian officers. The local commander had thought fit to send lorries to transport the troops to their camp at Orangea, some miles away along the bay. However, Col. Yates decided that his men should march to the camp, and ordered the lorries to go back. The march was a disaster, as the troops were in no fit state and kept falling down on the road or in the ditch. Witnesses said later that at least one Anglo-Mauritian officer kicked the men while ordering them to get up. At the end of this ordeal the Mauritians found that Orangea was a camp under canvas in the middle of a jungle. Weeds and bush were the height of the tents, which were infested with snakes, lizards, scorpions, ten-inch long centipedes, and huge black cockroaches. There were no such horrors in Mauritius and the creoles thought it was something like a preview of hell. They panicked. One of them set a match to the jungle which caught fire like tinder. Half the camp was destroyed before the fire could be brought under control. Then the men really mutinied and refused to obey orders. They were surrounded by a local contingent, made prisoners, and later court martialled. At their trial the men were defended by one of their own Mauritian officers, a distinguished barrister, who pleaded the extenuating circumstances outlined above. The mutineers received prison sentences of varying lengths. The Mauritius Regiment was then disbanded and the men sent to join the Mauritian Pioneers in the Middle East.

And there the story ends. The Mauritian version does not differ substantially from the official account, but the detail adds life and credibility to the events. From a combination of memory and detective work a little bit of history emerges. There was indeed a mutiny. I suspect there were more; but we do not at present know much about them.

Part III

LEARNING AND LIVING

♦

WITH THE WAR over, happily married, and Cambridge behind me, I began my teaching career in 1946. We lived for a year in Leicester and then moved to Yorkshire, living first in the village of Copmanthorpe and then Gate Helmsley. Richard was born in August 1949 and Elizabeth in September 1950, both in the Purey Cust Nursing Home, beneath the shadow of York Minster whose regular chimes drove Margaret to distraction while she was in labour. In 1955 we moved to Harrogate, much to the envy of the local farmers who regarded the town as ideal for holidays or retirement. We remained there until 1961 when we emigrated (as we thought) to America; but returned to live in Sussex in 1970. This pattern of movement was the result of my activities as schoolmaster in Leicester (1946–7), adult educationist at Leeds (1947–61), Professor of History at the University of Wisconsin (1961–70), and Professor of History at Sussex University (1970–82). The interweaving of family and professional affairs forms the backdrop to the incidents and personalities in Chapters 10–15 in this book. A record of the busy comings-and-goings of family and friends, trips to distant parts of the world, and name-dropping references to prominent people are hardly called for in a work of this kind. Rather I have tried to select incidents which illuminate a greater theme. Thus, the problem of written work is used as a way into adult education as a whole. America in the 1950s and 1960s appears through the experiences of a householder and teacher, not from the impressions of a tourist. And the curious way in which history gets written is traced in a personal odyssey.

♦ 10 ♦

Written Work

———◄◆►———

I T WAS GETTING dark when I climbed into COP and set off for the class. The car, so-called from its registration number COP 970, was a 1937 Standard 'Flying Nine' and had been found for us by my father-in-law, who came to the rescue when I needed a car for my journey to work. Wartime shortages and rationing were continued long after the end of hostilities, in fact throughout the five-year life of the Attlee Labour government, and cars of all kinds were in very short supply. COP was an unloved wreck of a works' car when my father-in-law rescued it and had it 'done up' in his firm's garage. After much body welding, new piston rings and brakes, and a re-spray, COP looked quite presentable, even smart; though if one looked under the back seat the ground was visible, since part of the floor was missing. It had no heater, of course, and there was only one windscreen wiper. Mounted on the front bumper bracket was a huge, elliptical foglight, which was supposed to cast a yellow 'batswing' beam below the thick fog which plagued so many of my nightly journeys. Wrapped in my army greatcoat, now dyed blue, and a pair of RAF flying boots which I had found abandoned in an army store in Mombasa, I began the sixty-mile drive to Skipton. I was quickly through York and heading west on the Leeds road, a rare piece of 1930s dual carriageway. At Tadcaster I turned off for Boston Spa and Wharfedale.

The Skipton class was the second year of a three-year tutorial in international relations, and met on Thursdays at 7 o'clock in a local school, under the auspices of the Workers' Educational Association (WEA). It was known technically as a Joint Committee class, that is, the provision was made jointly by the WEA, which recruited the students, and Leeds University which provided the tutor. I usually lectured for about forty minutes: we then had a break for a smoke or coffee from thermos flasks before resuming for an hour's discussion. About 9.15 pm I set off on the return journey.

I had been appointed in 1947 as staff tutor in the Extra-Mural Department of Leeds University, with responsibilities for the York district. My programme consisted of four tutorial classes throughout the winter, plus a fifth night of organising in the York-Selby-Goole area. The classes were scattered across the whole of the extra-mural area, from Loftus-in-Cleveland to Skipton, and involved over 400 miles of night-driving per week. After a year or so the organising commitment was reduced as the Selby-Goole area was traded to Hull University for extra-mural territory in the North Riding. A strange pattern of work developed. The classes ran for twenty-four meetings between the end of September and March, with a short break at Christmas. Throughout the winter my daily routine was to prepare lectures in the morning, dig the garden or help with the children in the afternoon, and go off to the class after tea, returning any time between ten o'clock and midnight. The summers were gloriously free for research and writing, the only commitments being a couple of weeks of summer school and an occasional weekend lecture for the WEA. Attendance at local WEA and trade-union branch meetings was also expected.

At the bottom of Harewood Bank I was held up by road works; and as I waited I reflected on the events which had in such a short space of time projected me into the world of adult education, and Yorkshire in particular. After finishing at Cambridge I was urgently in need of a job. The headmaster of my old school offered me a post as sixth-form master at the City Boys' and so in 1946 we returned to Leicester. We set up home in Springfield Road, where we rented three spacious, but primitively equipped, rooms in a colleague's Edwardian house. Margaret took a job teaching at Narborough Road Girls' School. Each morning we set out at 8 am, to go by tram to our respective schools. At lunch time we met in town for a hot meal in the restaurant of one of the big stores. For 1s 9d. we had three courses of stodgy food while trying not to listen to a pretentious musical trio which played Palm Court tunes. We sat muffled up in our overcoats while eating because of the cold. However, when the price of the meal was raised to 2s and later even to 2s 3d. we decided to go elsewhere. The winter of 1946–7 was the coldest in living memory: the snow lay around for weeks and the plumbing in our house was frozen solid. In the evenings we ate our meagre rations shivering in front of a low-grade coal fire whose main heat came from the gas poker used to start it. To top it all I had a recurrence of malaria, which had been suppressed by mepacrine drugs while I was in the army.

It had not been my intention to stay in schoolteaching any longer than necessary, though I felt somewhat guilty when I handed in my resignation in less than a year. I had made up my mind that adult education was what I wanted to do. The union of labour and learning seemed to me an ideal to which I could happily devote myself. Unfortunately my experience in this direction was very limited, in fact little more than my duties as Battalion Education Officer and a few lectures under the ABCA (Army Bureau of Current Affairs) scheme. I therefore offered my services to Vaughan College, the adult education centre in Leicester, and also undertook lectures on Sunday mornings at an adult school. Hoping that this slim experience plus my Cambridge degree and army confidence would suffice, I applied for two staff tutorships which were advertised. As a fall-back I also applied for jobs in educational administration. One of the latter came up first. It was for an assistant to the Director of Education in the North Riding of Yorkshire. I successfully survived a preliminary interview with the Director in London, but completely ploughed the main interview with the Education Committee in Northallerton by expressing crudely authoritarian answers to questions about parental influence in schools. The two staff tutorships were in the Hull and Leeds Extra-Mural Departments and to my surprise I was called for interview in both cases. The Leeds interview was first. At this time I knew nothing about the personalities or policies of extra-mural departments. The cities of Leeds and Hull were equally strange to me. I was prepared to go wherever they offered me a job. So, in full innocence, I presented myself before the Leeds Board of Extra-Mural Studies. I sat down at one end of a long mahogany table and when I looked up who should be in the Chair but the ex-Master of Selwyn College. The Reverend G.A. Chase had left Selwyn to become Bishop of Ripon and, as such, had been persuaded to assume the Chairmanship of the Leeds Board of Extra-Mural Studies. 'Well Harrison', he said, 'you didn't expect to see me here, did you?' 'No Sir', I replied, 'nor you to see me either.' After which friendly opening the interview could hardly fail, since the committee members took their lead from the chairman. We chatted amicably and I took care to be more modest than at Northallerton. I was offered the job, to begin in September 1947, at a salary of £425—which was £30 more than I was getting as a schoolmaster. Cambridge had once again proved invaluable.

A condition of the job was that I should live in the York area. Housing, like everything else, was difficult to find and, moreover, we had little money. However, by borrowing from the family we managed to buy a little semi in Copmanthorpe, a village on the Leeds side of York. It proved to be very shoddily built and I feared that the bay window would collapse since the timbers were rotten. We decided to get out as soon as possible and put it up for sale. After dark one evening, a man came to the door, asked to see the house, and after a quick look round said he would buy it. I could hardly believe my luck in selling it without any bargaining and virtually sight unseen. Only later did I discover that he was building a new house on a plot of land a short distance away and that to get a building permit he had had to declare himself homeless and living in a caravan; but that having once got his permit he could supervise the work more conveniently and comfortably from our semi. We now bought a house in Gate Helmsley, a village on the other side of York. This was a Georgian manor house that had been converted into three smaller dwellings. Ours was the centre one, with an imposing portico, an original hall floor in black-and-white stone, and an almost total absence of heating. While the address Gate Helmsley House, Gate Helmsley, York—looked good on writing paper, in other respects the house was not what we had hoped it would be. For the next seven years it was the base from which I set out to conquer the world, or at any rate my part of it, for adult education.

I soon discovered that Leeds Extra-Mural Department was not just any old extra-mural department but the outstanding extra-mural department in the country—or so it was envisioned by its founder, Sidney Raybould. As with Cambridge and Sandhurst previously, I seemed to have landed in an institution which claimed, not without some justification, to be the finest in its particular field. S.G. Raybould had been born and bred in the Cleveland district of Yorkshire. He had taken up WEA teaching while a schoolmaster in Middlesbrough; and in 1936 was appointed a full-time staff tutor for the Joint Tutorial Classes Committee of Leeds University. When the Extra-Mural Department was created at Leeds in 1946 he became its first director. He immediately capitalised on the post-war enthusiasm for expansion in adult education and built up a large and influential department. I was one of his early appointments. Among the others was Roy Shaw who was later knighted for his services as Secretary General of the Arts Council; Edward Thompson, a handsome young revolutionary with a beautiful speaking voice, who read Shelley and Blake to his classes, and whose magnificent book, *The Making of the English Working Class* quickly established him as a guru of the Left; and John Rex, a refugee from South Africa who went on to become a distinguished professor of sociology and expert on race relations. In other adult education departments there were similar appointments, notably Richard Hoggart at Hull and Raymond Williams at Oxford. Raybould was a fanatic for adult education and he had an almost religious passion for it. As his wife, Nina, once confessed to me, 'You know, Sidney talks and eats and sleeps adult education—all the time.' He had no hobbies beyond an interest in Yorkshire cricket.

The new extra-mural department was in many ways a model. Old abuses were swept away: the employment of casual labour in the form of full-time, non-staff tutors, for instance, was stopped, and such tutors were given regular appointments on the staff of the department. The burden of organising work, which in the past had often interfered with the teaching and academic work of tutors, was strictly limited, and their main contribution confined to three-year tutorial classes. Full parity of salary and status with their internal colleagues was secured for the staff of the department, and every facility and encouragement for research and writing was given. There was a continuous flow of memoranda and meetings in which every aspect of the work was argued and discussed, providing an excellent introduction to the problems of adult education for the many young tutors who, like myself, had but recently come into the work. A general air of enthusiasm prevailed, and there was a strong sense of participating in an exciting new venture. Morale was high in the department, and the new staff combined academic excellence with a sense of vocation.

I had imagined that adult education was simply a matter of teaching classes to interesting and interested people. In fact I found myself plunged into a world of complex academic politics and personalities, which for some time I quite enjoyed, but which later I came to find increasingly frustrating and irrelevant to the things I was supposed to be doing. Raybould had a strong sense of mission, and he based the policy of the department on certain firm convictions about the nature of extra-mural work. He insisted above all that the work should be of 'university standard', and never tired of quoting the famous Headlam and Hobhouse *Report* of 1910 which found that in the pioneer tutorial classes taken by R.H. Tawney, work was done there which was equal to that produced by Oxford undergraduates. Tawney, later famous as Professor of Economic History at the London School of Economics, and national president of the WEA, was Sidney's hero. Raybould believed (and produced statistics in support of this) that there had been a falling away from the standards of the past: the number of tutorial classes relative to the number of shorter and less-demanding courses was declining, and moreover the work was not being pursued with the same intellectual rigour. He felt passionately that the work of the new Leeds Extra-Mural Department should be of the highest quality and he set about reforming the institutions and practices of adult education in Yorkshire. Like many reformers before him, he claimed to be doing no more than restoring things to the way they used to be. Raybould's yardstick for the assessment of tutorial classes was that the work should be a training in 'disinterestedness' or 'impartiality'—in the capacity to see things as they are, and not as our hopes and fears might prompt us to see them. Such a course of education entailed genuine study over a long period (three years), with regular reading and written work. Only thus could the university's participation in extra-mural work be justified.

Forty years on it is difficult to appreciate the passion with which we debated the issue of objectivity in our teaching. But in the Cold War atmosphere of the time there were genuine fears on both sides: the Right suspected Communist infiltration; the Left complained of discrimination and harassment. Raybould was very much aware of the need to tread carefully and to avoid anything that would make us vulnerable to charges of taking sides or, even worse, proselytising. It was essential to avoid fuelling the suspicions of critics of the WEA that 'education for social purpose' meant socialist purpose. Within the department we had both Marxist and Roman Catholic tutors; and to Raybould, who was a middle-of-the-road Labour agnostic, their views appeared potentially dangerous unless firmly controlled. In theory the Marxists rejected the idea of objectivity as bourgeois ideology which served only to blunt working-class consciousness. But in practice I doubt whether there was really much danger of Communist, or for that matter Roman Catholic, bias. Few students were Marxists or Roman Catholics; if they had not liked what they heard they would have left. Tutors were respected by students not for their views but for their personal qualities as teachers. In departmental meetings, however, the arguments were fierce and prolonged.

Our difficulty was to define university standards for students who, unlike university undergraduates, were non-selected, chose their own subject of study, did not take examinations, and who (in Lenin's phrase) could 'vote with their feet'. How was one to know whether the work done in a particular class was up to university standard, and if it were not what should one do about it? We discussed and argued the matter for many months, and the issues spilled over into the adult-education movement nationally. Pamphlets and articles and conferences fuelled a great debate in the world of adult education. Most of the directors of extra-mural studies in other universities found it hard to accept Raybould's arguments in their entirety, and some fiercely resisted him. Even within the Leeds Extra-Mural Department some tutors were sceptical about the feasibility of his demands. When pressed by Raybould as to how they would define university standards they resorted to whimsical notions. One tutor, who was fond of talking about his colleagues as 'dons', gave the impression that just listening to the ruminations of a 'don' was enough to give students the kind of education that a university offered. Another man, who was staff tutor at Huddersfield, declared that he judged the success of his teaching not by students' written work but by the way people in Delph walked around with greater assurance. On one memorable occasion, when we were discussing minimum numbers in tutorial classes, he rejected Raybould's insistence that at least six students should qualify in each of the three years of the class. 'Well then, how many should there be? roared Raybould, 'Five, four, three, two, one?' But Baxandall refused to enter into a bargaining session and, sitting back, closing his eyes, and putting the tips of his fingers together, said softly (for he was rather deaf), 'If I had only one student the class would be worthwhile'. Raybould exploded.

Entwined with the controversy over university standards was the debate about the role of the WEA. The association had been founded in 1903 to cater for the needs of the 'educationally underprivileged'. Its dynamic was 'education for social emancipation' and its object was to provide opportunities for working men and women to equip themselves for service in the community through political, trade-union or other voluntary bodies. But it was never exclusive: the definition of worker was very broad, and the subjects studied were not limited to the social sciences. Between the wars the WEA developed into the main provider of liberal adult education, supported by the government and the universities. However, by the time of the WEA's jubilee in 1953 there was a widespread feeling that social changes, perhaps connected with the arrival of the Welfare State, had largely invalidated the original aims of the WEA and that it was time for a reorientation. Raybould, who was for a time vice-president of the WEA, initiated a long and thorough discussion of fundamental problems concerning its role in contemporary society. He was concerned that changes within the WEA which had taken place since 1939 threatened to 'transform it into an organization quite different from what it was founded to be'. An examination of the statistical and other material covering the years 1928-48 suggested a decline in the percentage of students in tutorial classes, a fall in the percentage of manual worker students, a shift away from classes in the social sciences, and a general lowering of standards of class work. He called for a halt to these trends and a reassertion of the association's concern for working-class students, interpreted as those whose schooling finished at the minimum school-leaving age.

I accepted this diagnosis, which seemed to me to be reasonable and based on Raybould's long experience of the movement in Yorkshire. I was prepared to try to carry out his policies, but after a time ran into

difficulties which I found unsettling. It became apparent that the contro-
versies which so exercised the minds of we adult educators did not excite
the members of the classes to anything like the same extent. The great
debate was largely carried out among the professionals, though the activists
in the WEA branches were aware of the issues which kept appearing on
district and local agendas and in *Highway*, the journal of the association.
Like all such voluntary organisations the life of the branches depended
upon a very small number of dedicated enthusiasts who took upon themselves the burden of getting together a nucleus for a class, finding out what
subject was in greatest demand, and entering into correspondence with the
district secretary about a suitable tutor. There were also day and weekend
schools and single lectures to be organised, for it was an axiom of the WEA
that the demand for adult education had to be stimulated before it could be
provided. In all this work the tutors collaborated closely. The temptation,
which Raybould argued should be resisted, was for us to take over much
of the organising, thereby weakening the self-reliance of the WEA and dis-
tracting us from our primary role as academics. The issue here was more
than a matter of who should organise classes. In the 1950s the WEA was
regarded as a shining example of that highly-esteemed institution: the voluntary body. A whole political philosophy had been built up by scholars
like A.D. Lindsay and Lord Beveridge to the effect that freedom in a
democracy was dependent on the existence of flourishing voluntary bodies such as churches, trade unions, cooperative societies, Women's
Institutes, Townswomen's Guilds, adult schools, literary and cultural institutes. Only if there were centres of power and influence other than the state
could liberty and equality (the marks of a democratic community) be pre-
served. The WEA and our work as adult educators was thus made part of
the democratic way of life. This ideological underpinning went some way
to compensating for the practical weaknesses of the movement.

The title of the association never ceased to be a bone of contention.
Regularly at the WEA's annual conference a motion to change its name
would be proposed and just as regularly defeated. Suggestions to drop the
word 'worker', or substitute something like 'People's Educational
Association' did not appeal to the majority of the delegates. But in what
sense, if any, could we claim to be a workers' organisation? Great ingenu-
ity was exercised in devising definitions of worker which would accommodate both the students who actually came to the classes and those
whom we thought should have come but did not. The social composition
and educational background of the students in the Skipton class were fairly representative of WEA classes in Yorkshire at that time: a mixture of
housewives, teachers, clerical workers and manual workers from the

woollen mills. They were not a proletarian group like my class of steel-workers at South Bank, Middlesbrough, or the trade unionists who came to the weekend schools in Scarborough which I tutored for WETUC (Workers' Educational Trade Union Committee). But neither were they the sort of people who belonged to golf clubs or the Mothers' Union. I doubt whether many of them would have said that they were motivated by a desire for social emancipation; but they could certainly be relied on to support the progressive causes of the time. The WEA was at great pains to emphasise that it was 'non-party political'; and in our teaching we tried to be scrupulously fair and objective. Nevertheless I had no doubt that most of my students voted Labour, or perhaps Liberal if the opportunity offered. The socially purposive element in the WEA was still strong in the Yorkshire North District, as evidenced by cases from my other tutorial classes: a rural postmistress from the North Riding who went on to become a well-known radical Labour MP; a young labouring man who became an organiser for the National Union of Agricultural Workers; and many students who became local councillors, trade-union branch officers, and presidents and secretaries of voluntary bodies. In a wider sense the classes helped thoughtful men and women to evaluate the society in which they found themselves; to be critical of the commercial and cultural pressures to which they were subjected by advertising, the newspapers and television; and to question what Tawney described as 'the never-ending audacity of elected persons'. These aspects of the work I found immensely satisfying. The difficulties arose from the need to meet university standards, in particular the problem of written work.

The insistence on written work made the task of recruitment to tutorial classes harder than it had been during the war years, and was resented by some WEA branch workers. 'It is difficult enough to get a sufficient number of people to sign up for three years', they grumbled, 'without going out of your way to emphasise regular reading and written work'. The tutorial class regulations were indeed quite formidable. We knew from experience that if six students were to qualify in attendance and written work throughout the three years a minimum of at least 18 was required in the first year. This number might well drop to 12 or 15 in the second year, and 6 to 8 in the third year. The problem of the marginal class, when numbers dropped below a safe minimum but were high enough to request continuation of the class, was a tutor's nightmare. Skipton was a case in point. We had started with 15 and by the second year there were only 12 on the register. Even if the majority managed to attend the required two-thirds of the meetings, it was by no means certain that they would also fulfil the written work requirement. The class needed careful nursing and I could ill afford to lose a student through tactless demands for more work. Every student who dropped out might suggest some failure on the tutor's part. Even though one knew that this was unreasonable, doubts about one's adequacy lurked in the background. I lived with these worries for several years until I began to see that there was an unbridgeable gap between Raybould's ideal and the reality on the ground.

By the mid-1950s it was clear that the WEA could not sustain a programme of tutorial classes of the size required to employ all the extra-mural staff of the department; and since Raybould adamantly refused to allow his staff to be used for less demanding work, they were switched to extension courses provided directly by the university. This led to friction with the WEA, and ultimately to a parting of the ways. I used to think that the failure of the WEA to recruit sufficient students to tutorial class-es was due to social changes of the 1950s which reduced the pool of those needing or wanting this type of class. But the subsequent success of the Open University in attracting students prepared to accept even more strin-gent demands than those of the tutorial class suggests that some other explanation is needed. The students were there: but we failed to attract them. Perhaps the ideas of the WEA were no longer relevant; or perhaps it simply fell down on the job. Whatever the cause, the reality at the time was painfully obvious, and I could see no way out. Historians are always reluctant to subscribe to anything savouring of predestination; but when I think about it now the story of Raybould and the WEA in Yorkshire seems to have all the elements of tragedy in the sense that the outcome was virtually foreordained and the participants could not escape from their assigned roles. In my weekly encounter with the Skipton class and my demands for written work I was helping to push the WEA into a role which I was increasingly aware it could not fulfil. How could this aware-ness be reconciled with my loyalty to Raybould, whom I admired? Attempts to argue with him always ended in defeat. We seemed to be hur-rying to a confrontation or dénouement with the WEA that nobody wanted. I have dwelt at some length on these matters, which today seem so antiquated, because they occupied so many of my thoughts during those fourteen years at Leeds.

The cars in front of me began to move and soon thinned out. By modern standards the traffic on the road was light. In a few minutes I was past Pool and heading for Otley. The car headlights picked out the famil-iar twists and turns, the dark gritstone houses, and the clumps of trees by the river on my right. I knew the road as well by night as by day. In fact during my first year with the Skipton class I never did see the last part of the journey by daylight until the final weeks of the session. *Yorkshire by Night* could well have been the theme of a staff tutor's saga in the 1950s. The tutor's car, like John Wesley's horse, was an indispensable part of the job, and there were many tales of my colleagues' adventures with their vehicles. One of the best stories concerned John Melling, disarmingly honest, somewhat unworldly, very impractical and a Quaker. He had a car which he called Little Ug, from its registration letters. It was an ancient Austin Seven and virtually worn out. On journeys home from his class in Cleveland Melling had to stop at the top of Sutton Bank, get into lower gear, and then stick a wooden peg behind the gear lever to prevent it jumping out of gear. Little Ug's powers were visibly failing, and Melling reluctantly decided he would have to replace her. His 'new' car was by no means new, but it was not as decrepit as Little Ug. At a staff conference soon afterwards Melling let it be known that he had a new car and would therefore be willing to sell his old one. A colleague was interested and after talking to Melling slipped out of the meeting to take a private look at the vehicle. He decided that it was probably not completely clapped out and he was therefore prepared to make an offer. He suggested that he might try it out. 'Oh,' said Melling, 'that's not the old car, that's the new one'.

For the present, however, my thoughts were of the people I was soon to be meeting. The class had been together for over a year. They were embarrassingly appreciative of the efforts of a not-very-experienced young tutor. In a time of acute rationing of just about everything—food, clothing, household goods, petrol, tobacco, you-name-it—they would bring me gifts. Joe, a wool-sorter, produced knitting wool for Margaret to make baby's clothes; the Misses Hall, who kept hens, felt I could do with a couple of eggs from time to time; and the class as a whole presented me with a book token at Christmas. It would be tempting to say that they were a typical WEA class, except that my experience has taught me that there is no such thing since every class has too many individual and distinctive characteristics to make it typical. On the other hand, a stranger coming in to our Thursday-evening meetings could not have mistaken us for anything but a WEA class: the earnestness with which the students were prepared to grapple with difficult ideas and concepts for which they had had no academic training, and for no reward other than the satisfaction of the subject itself; the discouraging atmosphere of children's desks and uncooperative caretakers; the give-and-take of argument in which the tutor was not spared. One was conscious of being part of a tradition of adult education: certain things were expected (such as freedom to raise questions outside the syllabus, comment on the week's news, friendly help with reading found to be too difficult), others not (for example, staying away from class for some trivial reason, or becoming too heated or dogmatic in discussion). Tutor and students were part of a whole in which we all had parts to play. This was immensely supportive, though I only realised how much so when I had to teach later on without it, notably in America. By the second and even more by the third year, we were well aware of our mutual enthusiasms and limitations, which we were able to tolerate and respect in a way not possible in the relatively brief encounter of a short course; though it has to be admitted that the airing of prejudices under the guise of discussion was not always avoided. On paper the people in the Skipton class were students, but I liked to think of them as my friends. 'How shall a man learn' went an old saying favoured by Albert Mansbridge, the founder of the WEA, 'except from one who is his friend?' This however presented certain problems and they were very much in my mind as I drove on through Ilkley.

The previous week I had made a plea to the Skipton class that they should all try to produce a piece of written work. I did not mind what form it was in: an essay, a review of a book, a letter giving an account of recent reading, notes for a talk to the class. The object of the exercise, I assured them, was to concentrate and deepen their understanding of the subject, not to write a literary masterpiece. It was also (though I did not mention this) an earnest example of their commitment to the tutorial class and a token of their seriousness of intent. When I had first raised the question at the beginning of the previous session and had enquired what they had done in the past, I was assured that 'Mr So-and-So (a non-staff tutor) never bothered much about it.' This was in line with the experience of other tutors. Roy Shaw recalls how when he first took a class at Filey and reminded them of the written work commitment an old WEA member said, 'Oh that's alright, Mr Shaw, we know what you mean'. After the class Roy asked him to explain, and he said that he would send Roy a Christmas card as he had done with previous tutors. After some coaxing I had persuaded several of the Skipton students to write a bit, but they did it out of regard for me rather than from conviction that it was really necessary. This year I decided that I ought to remind them of their obligation early in the session, and not leave it until halfway through or even later. They did not argue against this, but I sensed a certain reluctance, and I knew that they would have preferred me to lapse into a comfortable forgetfulness about the matter. This I did not feel I could do if I were to justify the time, cost and effort required for a tutorial class. If university standards were to mean anything, they would have to be interpreted as standards of effort rather than achievement. The tutorial class, as distinct from other forms of adult education, had to stand upon a reputation for long and disciplined study.

I was still thinking about written work as I drove on through Ilkley and Addingham and began the final stage of the journey over the moors to Skipton. The car seemed to be running smoothly and there was no fog about. Suddenly there was an almighty bang. It sounded to me (still accustomed to thinking in army terms) as if an anti-tank rifle had gone off under the bonnet. The engine cut out, and I coasted into the side of the road. The car began to fill with smoke. I leapt out, expecting it to burst into flames; but nothing happened. After a few minutes the fumes cleared, and I plucked up courage to open the bonnet. By the light of an electric torch I could see that the entire engine chamber was covered in thick black oil. And there, sticking out of the side of the engine block, was a piece of metal. One of the piston rods had snapped and had been driven right through the engine casing. COP was well and truly out of action. Captain Harrison's further advance was stymied.

The journey back was long and tedious. I managed to catch a bus to Leeds; then took the train to York. There was plenty of time for reflection before I arrived home in the early hours of the morning: what to do about COP? How to get to the meeting on Friday without the car? I tried to read a book, but was too tired, and the poor light soon made me give it up. I fell to thinking once again about the problem of written work. The wheels of the carriage beat a steady rhythm: Headlam and Hobhouse, Hobhouse and Headlam, Headlam and Hobhouse...'25 per cent of the essays examined were equal to the work done by students who gained first class honours in the final schools of modern history....', university standards, university standards, 'long and severe mental discipline', written work, written work, written work....I awoke as the train pulled into York station. It was 1.30 am when the taxi delivered me to the door of Gate Helmsley House.

◆ 11 ◆

New Horizons

————◄◆►————

BY THE MID-1950s Margaret and I felt the need for a change. The honeymoon period of our acceptance in Gate Helmsley had quickly faded and the limitations and frustrations of rural life became increasingly onerous. Our involvement and non-involvement in village affairs were equally hazardous. Gate Helmsley, like most villages, was a closed community. Newcomers were tolerated rather than welcomed. The gulf between the handful of farmers and cottagers and 'foreigners' like us was always there. I knew that this was only to be expected from listening to the way my aunts at Bentley talked about people in the village; but somehow we did not take account of this when we went to live in Gate Helmsley. Sadly almost everything we did seemed to give offence to someone sooner or later. When Margaret and our next-door neighbour, Marjory Powell, tried to organise a children's choir for the church, the idea was viewed with great suspicion and their efforts failed because of petty rivalries between the farming families. Even though Margaret might have been classed as an interfering foreigner from the Midlands, Marjory Powell was from York, only seven miles away, and her husband was a freeman of the city. Our decision not to buy milk from one of the farms in the village because we feared for the children's health caused lasting hostility (the place was reminiscent of *Cold Comfort Farm* in its primitiveness and lack of hygiene).

My non-appearance in the village pub or local branch of the British Legion were marks against me. The owner of the village shop and petrol pumps suspected that I was a communist agitator as I used petrol coupons stamped 'JTCComm' (Joint Tutorial Classes Committee). Such suspicions were confirmed by my efforts to organise WEA classes for agricultural workers (I was at this time a paid-up member of the National Union of

Agricultural Workers). Farm workers were the lowest paid workers in the country and the farmers bitterly contested any attempt by the NUAW to raise their wages. Farmers are notoriously tight-fisted and Yorkshire farmers were no exception. Laurie Dring, a farm worker and secretary of the local branch of the union in Sand Hutton, the neighbouring village where I had organised a WEA class, told me that one day his employer gave him a bottle of beer. The next day the farmer asked him if he had enjoyed the beer. 'It was alright,' said Laurie. 'What d'y mean, alright?' asked the farmer. 'Well,' said Laurie, 'if it 'ad been any better y'wouldna' gi'en it me: and if it 'ad been any warse ah couldna' supped it.' On polling day when our car appeared displaying a Labour Party poster the lady of the manor was so surprised that she almost drove her car into the ditch while craning to get a closer look at this unheard-of abomination.

We had few friends in the neighbourhood. The nearest were the Caldwells at Easingwold. Tom was WEA organising tutor in the area and later a staff tutor in the department. Roy and Gwen Shaw were far away in Leeds. The Bakers likewise were a long way off. Bill Baker was what in Yorkshire they called a lovely man: kind, considerate and knowledgeable. He had come to us from the Cambridge Delegacy for Extra-Mural Studies, being appointed Senior Staff Tutor for work in the rural areas of the North Riding. He and his wife Ruth and family lived in a splendid old farm house in Ebberston, a village between Pickering and Scarborough. They had an old table to which was fixed a small brass plate claiming that John Wesley had once stood on it to preach; but Bill was somewhat sceptical of its provenance. Bill's wise counsel helped me on many occasions and his long experience of rural life was distilled into a little book, *The English Village* (1953). Ruth doted on babies and was full of good advice about child-rearing, which we were much in need of. But Ebberston, alas, was thirty miles away and so we did not meet as often as would have been good for us. The comparative isolation of extra-mural life restricted opportunities for socialising, in addition to the exigencies of family life with small children.

The need to move became urgent when the children came of school age. Richard's first year at the all-age, two-roomed school in Sand Hutton, to which he was bussed daily, revealed the inadequacies of rural education in the North Riding. The ladder of educational opportunity from infant school to university had more than a few rungs missing. We decided to move, either into York or to Harrogate. The problem was selling the house. The market was depressed and Gate Helmsley House was a difficult sort of house to sell at the best of times. We put it on the market and several people came to look it over. But we discovered to our cost that they were mainly people who made a hobby of visiting houses for sale as a means of spending an interesting afternoon. They usually came by bus and we innocently offered them tea. After several months we were so fed up with this nonsense that we felt we must get away at all costs. So we packed the children into the back of our Ford Anglia (bought with a loan from the university when COP finally expired), put the luggage on the roof rack, and set off for Switzerland, picnicking *en route*. When we returned a month later we were greeted by the estate agent with the news that he had sold the house provided we gave possession within four weeks. The price was much lower than we had paid seven years earlier and we had nowhere to go. However, it so happened that Sidney Raybould was in a similar dilemma in Harrogate. He had bought a larger house and could not sell the one he was living in. Number 16 Norfolk Road was more than twice the price of our house in Gate Helmsley; but we agreed a deal and with the aid of a large mortgage moved there in the autumn of 1955.

Among the changes that came into our lives after the move to Harrogate was a deeper and more active involvement in the affairs of the church. By the time I went to Cambridge I felt that I had outgrown the religion of my childhood and my Marxist views were not consistent with church going. During my time in the army I lost contact with virtually any form of religion apart from the occasional regulation church parade. Such religious beliefs as I had evaporated in the alien surroundings of the army in Africa. I also had difficulty in reconciling my firm socialist beliefs with institutional religion. The Marxism of my student days no longer satisfied me either theoretically when dealing with labour and social history or practically when working with trade unionists and the labour movement. I came to see that my socialism had a moral or ethical basis, and that my desire for a more just and equal society would have to be realised through the traditional institutions of the British labour movement, which (as a cliché of the time put it), 'owed more to Methodism than to Marx'. Perhaps my thinking at this time was influenced by R.H. Tawney, who was not only a pioneer of adult education but also an Anglican and Christian socialist. However it was not until later that I found a spiritual home in Christian socialism.

After our marriage Margaret and I discovered that we were both in some sense believers, though unhappy with the forms of religion—Methodist and Church of England—in which we had been brought up. For a time we did nothing about this. I felt drawn to the Quakers and while we lived at Copmanthorpe attended the Friends' Meeting in York. But Margaret was not attracted by their silent worship; and after we moved to Gate Helmsley we needed something closer to hand, and drifted to the parish church. Margaret decided that she wished to be confirmed in the Anglican Church and in due course the children were baptised. However, we regarded our attendance at church as a duty rather than a pleasure and longed for something more positive than the rather feeble ministrations of the Vicar of Gate Helmsley. In Harrogate our local parish church was again good old C. of E., with matins at 11 am and evensong at 6.30 pm. One of the great achievements of the Church of England has been its ability to hold together very diverse, not to say contradictory elements within its fold. From Catholic dogma to Calvinist evangelicalism there is room for everyone, and in that sense it is a national church. Despite the powerful intellectual arguments of converts to Rome like Roy Shaw, who emphasised the lack of authority in Anglicanism, it always seemed to me that this very weakness suited the English temperament which has never welcomed authoritarianism, especially from overseas. Taunts about Henry VIII as founder of the Church of England fell on deaf ears; and although I could seldom refute satisfactorily many of the claims of Rome I always felt that it was somehow alien to English ways. In any case, if one could find Catholicism within the Church of England why leave it for Rome? There was also the insuperable problem of the Roman Catholic opposition to contraception which we were not prepared to accept. So we shopped around and to our great delight found what we were looking for. St Wilfred's was (and still is) a magnificent High Anglican church, with a Parish Eucharist at 9.30, High Mass at 11, and daily masses throughout the week. We soon made some good friends there, including the pioneer Anglican liturgical reformer, Fr Henry de Candole, the Suffragan Bishop of Knaresborough, who lived in the parish. The type of worship at St Wilfred's suited us more closely than anything we had enjoyed before; not just the smells and bells, but the sense of being in a place where 'prayer has been valid'. I became aware, perhaps for the first time, of the reality of sacramental worship; and I prayed with George Herbert, 'Teach me, my God and King, In all things thee to see'. To describe the complexities and social subtleties of that Anglo-Catholic parish I should need the genius of Barbara Pym. It was indeed for us a 'Glass of Blessings'.

In university circles it was traditional wisdom at this time that lecturers should, if possible, move jobs after the sabbatical seven years, perhaps stretched to ten if necessary. In default of a new appointment a change of

An adult education group: Teaching at WEA and Trade Union summer schools was part of the programme of Extra-Mural tutors. This photograph was taken at the Yorkshire Summer School, held in Madingley Hall, Cambridge, August, 1954. Second row, standing: JFCH in centre, Edward Thompson second from left

Rewards of scholarship: A Chartist Portrait. Not all historical research was conducted in libraries and archives. The tracing of this 1848 portrait of a Chartist leader (now in a Leicester museum) was the result of letters in the local press and visits to descendants living in the area

Visitors, 1957–58: *Outward bound. The Fulbright Scholarships provided travel (tourist class) to America on the Queen Mary and Queen Elizabeth*

venue at least was desirable. I certainly felt the seven-year itch and Margaret also longed for new experiences. I began to think of the possibility of spending a year in America. I wrote to a fellow labour historian in Cambridge who had recently spent a year there. Henry Pelling advised me to write to the University of Wisconsin in Madison, with the result that I was offered a visiting fellowship in their School for Workers. This was worth only $2000 and was really intended as a top-up to a full-time salary. Raybould backed my successful application for a sabbatical year with pay, which he regarded triumphantly as a demonstration of our equality of status with internal staff. A Fulbright award covered travel costs; and I was assured that I should be able to eke out our minimal income by teaching summer school. I knew nothing about Wisconsin and had to look at the map to see where Madison was. The UW had been famous for fifty years as a centre for the study of labour history and labour economics. I was fortunate later in the year to be able to meet and talk with Selig Perlman (author of *A Theory of the Labor Movement*), who was the last of the great John R. Commons school of labour historians.

The journey was our biggest family adventure so far. It took place in the last days of travel by ship and railroad, before they were displaced by the airlines in the 1960s. Like my days in Kenya, I was unknowingly witnessing the end of an epoch. Encumbered with a huge leather trunk and several suitcases, we boarded the *Queen Elizabeth* at Southampton and arrived five days later in New York. Fulbright scholars travelled economy class; but even so the cruise-like atmosphere was luxurious: magnificent food, nothing to do, and stewards always to hand. A little more luxury on the train journey, however, would not have come amiss. The cavernous proportions of Grand Central Station overawed us; but the hot dog, hamburger and coke counters reassured us. Our budget did not run to sleepers, and it seemed a long night on the Twentieth Century Limited before we arrived next morning at Union Station, Chicago, and an even longer day before the Chicago and Northwestern railroad deposited us in Madison.

My first impressions of America have remained with me ever since; they set the tone and measured my responses to all that came subsequently. As we sailed into New York harbour I felt that I had been there already, so familiar was the well-photographed skyline. As the train roared past switch (marshalling) yards the names on the freight cars read like a roll call of the Union: the Chicago, Burlington and Quincy railroad, the Chesapeake and Ohio, the Texas and Pacific, the Baltimore and Ohio, the Nashville, Chattanooga and St Louis, the Topeka and Santa Fe. I have often thought how fortunate we were that our introduction to living in

America was in Wisconsin. From the moment that we were met at the station in Madison by the Director of the School for Workers, Bob Ozanne, whose enormous station wagon swallowed us and our trunk and suitcases, I felt that this was 'our' sort of country, a place where we could make friends and expand. The stereotypes of America were of course all there; but so too were its paradoxes, its subtleties, and its underlying plain family decencies. Everyone has to discover his or her own America, remembering that America is as much an idea as a place. For me it opened up new horizons. I thought I knew something of American history and culture, for I had been lecturing about it to my classes for years. But after a month in Madison my confident generalisations evaporated, and ten years had to elapse before I dared again refer to the subject in public.

When asked to describe Wisconsin to English friends I used to say that it was the nearest thing you could get to an American version of Sweden. Southern Wisconsin is a country of rolling hills and woods; the northern part of the state is a land of lakes and birch forests. The red barns clustered round white, frame farmhouses reminded us of southern Sweden. The slogan on the Wisconsin car registration plates was 'The Dairy State', though some Wisconsinites would probably have preferred 'The Beer State', for Milwaukee (the largest and most industrial town) was the home of a great German brewing tradition. The conflict between the dairying and brewing interests was amusingly brought home in the struggle over the sale of milk versus beer in the university Students' Union. The outcome was that vending machines dispensed cartons of milk, while beer with a low alcohol content was available in the Rathskeller. Not so amusing was the state tax on margarine, which resulted in weekend forays across the state line into Illinois to load up with tax-free supplies.

Madison is one of the most 'scenic' towns in the United States, being built between and around three small lakes. Apart from the Oscar Meyer meatpacking plant and some small engineering firms there was little manufacturing industry. As the state capital, Madison had a large administrative and professional population, to which was added the main (and at that time, only) campus of a huge university, beautifully situated on the southern shore of Lake Mendota. Many universities claimed to be the Athens of the West, but the University of Wisconsin at Madison was pre-eminent. The UW had a great liberal reputation, and had successfully championed the cause of academic freedom during the previous sixty years. To my surprise and chastening I discovered that the UW had been founded in 1848, which made it older than most of the universities in England, including Leeds: so much for any notions of superiority that I might have brought with me.

The Swedish parallel extended beyond physical appearances to social and political philosophy. Wisconsin had been the home of Bob LaFollette and the Progressive movement earlier in the century. His 'Wisconsin Idea' of honest and progressive government of the people in place of patronage and corruption lingered on, notably in the assumption that the public interest should come before 'selfish interests'. By the 1950s this had resulted in a high level of social services, virtually a welfare state in all but name. I had come prepared to preach the gospel of social welfare, but the wind was taken out of my sails when I discovered that in Wisconsin the level of provision was as high, and in some areas higher, than in Britain. Only with the National Health Service were we ahead of the Badger State. Madison prided itself on being a safe, clean and incorrupt city, not like Chicago or those dreadful cities in the East.

This was put to the test almost immediately after our arrival. As a temporary measure, while arrangements could be made for renting a house, we were accommodated in a student lodging house which was vacant during the summer. Our rooms were on the top floor and it being August and terribly hot we all decided to take a shower before going out to dinner at Bob Ozanne's. When we returned from the shower room we discovered that we had locked ourselves out of our rooms, and the keys were inside. There was no one else in the building and no way of getting duplicate keys. I therefore telephoned the police and told them what had happened. A cop with a pistol prominently displayed on his hip soon appeared, appraised the situation, and offered to shoot out the lock provided the owner of the building agreed. The children, all agog, waited excitedly. I explained that this was impossible since I had no idea to whom the building belonged. So he said that in that case the only thing to do was call the fire brigade and get in through an upstairs window. Ten minutes later Langdon Street was blocked by a huge fire truck and swarms of firemen in helmets and full gear. Up went their ladder, off came the window screens, and within minutes they had entered the flat, opened the door, and departed. In the street below the neighbours had gathered and enquired where the fire was. 'No fire', said the cop, 'only a Limey locked himself out'. Disappointed, they melted away. Having been warned of the dangers of trying to bribe the police I thanked the cop profusely and asked how I might show my appreciation. 'That's alright, son', he said, 'just give a donation to the benevolent fund'. By the time Bob Ozanne returned to collect us and enquire if we were now nicely rested after the journey, Langdon Street looked as if nothing had happened.

A few days later we rented a small furnished house on the east side of town. Its owner ran a plumbing and heating business and spent at least half the year in a caravan near Biloxi, Mississippi, to escape, he said, from the Wisconsin winter. I thought this sounded extravagant, but that was before I had experienced Wisconsin in January and February. In the meantime we enjoyed almost three months of near-perfect weather: warm sunny days, cool nights, and glorious fall colours. The children enroled in the local school, and we were soon deep in the rituals of PTA, Halloween, and the Cub Scouts of America. On Sundays we dutifully attended St Luke's Episcopal Church where we were roped in for reading the lessons, helping with the altar guild, and providing dishes for potluck suppers. We acquired a car for $350—a huge green, cigar-shaped Hudson—and went shopping in the Piggly Wiggly supermarket. There were picnics in the parks, barbeques in friends' yards, fishing in the lake. From December to March the lakes were frozen hard and at Christmas the snow came in blizzards. The temperature was below zero for days at a time, and the water froze as it came out of the firemen's hoses. But the city was well equipped to deal with this climate; and the parks had lavish facilities for skating, tobogganing and skiing. Spring was short and late in Wisconsin; summer came with a rush in June, and then we were back to sunbathing by the lake and picnics in the woods. Friends and neighbours showered us with the proverbial American kindness and hospitality. I had forgotten that the oldest industry in America is welcoming the immigrants.

We found ourselves in a political and academic *milieu* not unlike that which we had been used to in England. Madison was a fiercely Democratic town and campus in an overwhelmingly Republican state. Our friends at the university were nearly all liberal Democrats, the sort of people who in England would have voted Labour; and the first public occasion we ever attended was a 'Welcome Prox' celebration in a downtown cinema. William Proxmire had just been elected as Senator for Wisconsin on the Democratic ticket and we stood and applauded as he came down the aisle, shaking hands, to the strains of *Hail to the Chief*. Only three years previously the notorious McCarthyite witchhunts had come to an end after tearing apart the political nation. McCarthy was a local Wisconsinite and from 1946 a Republican Senator for the state. Naturally we heard much about his attack on civil liberties and academic freedom in the early 1950s. The university faculty, including many of our friends, were active in the 'Joe Must Go' campaign. Strangely, even at the height of his red-baiting, McCarthy did not turn on the University of Wisconsin, perhaps because he did not want too many enemies in his own backyard. Equally strange was our inability in 1957 to find anyone who had actually voted, or would admit to having voted, for McCarthy. When we teased our friends about this they would explain at length the intricacies of state and national politics, and how in a Republican area like up-state Wisconsin, a vote for Joe did not necessarily imply support for his demagoguery. Nevertheless, the assumptions and limitations of American politics in the Cold War period were everywhere apparent.

My daily routine followed, more or less, the same pattern as at home. During the day I worked in the library, usually the State Historical Society Library, where I was allocated a carrell, or small study space. Here I met other historians: Larry Cremin, later to become President of Teachers' College, Columbia University, New York, and then on a year's research leave; Dave Shannon, an historian of twentieth-century America; and others from the History Department and the School of Education. We met for seemingly endless cups (rather, cartons) of coffee; and at lunchtime they introduced me to the delights of the American 'deli' (hot pastrami on rye), the Toddle House (hash browns), or the Brathaus on State Street, staffed by hearties from the fraternity houses, where we had brats (bratwursts) cooked over charcoal, and beer. At night I went to the School for Workers' classes or other extension classes held in various towns around the state, sometimes teaching, at others just observing. In the summer the routine changed, with daytime teaching on the campus in summer schools organised by School for Workers for trade unionists from labor unions such as the United Steelworkers of America (USA), the International Ladies Garment Workers' Union (ILGWU), the International Association of Machinists (IAM), the Communications Workers of America (CWA), or the American Federation of Teachers (AFT).

Wisconsin had (still has) a fine tradition of adult education stretching back over a hundred years—another surprise to add to my store of re-evaluations of America. The Extension Division of the University of Wisconsin had been established in 1906 with the intention of 'taking the university to the people'. This soon grew into a very big operation under the inspiring slogan: 'the boundaries of the campus are the boundaries of the state'. School for Workers, founded in 1925, was part of this outreach and catered to the needs of trade unionists throughout the state. In the 1950s the emphasis was more vocational or utilitarian than workers' education in England, concentrating on grievance handling, collective bargaining, arbitration, job evaluation, time study, and steward training. But more liberal studies were also included, especially labor history, civil rights, political action, and world affairs; and this was where I came in.

School for Workers enjoyed very friendly relations with the members of the International Association of Machinists (an engineering union equivalent to the Amalgamated Engineering Union in Britain) at Beloit, a small industrial town some forty miles south of Madison. There I was introduced to the members of the local (branch), all of whom worked at the Beloit Iron Works, making heavy machinery for the paper mills of northern Wisconsin. Throughout the winter and spring I got to know this little group of American trade unionists and enjoyed my beer and sandwiches (though not their appetite for beef tartar) which they insisted I needed to sustain me for the drive back to Madison at night. The chief officers of the local were the president, vice-president, recording secretary, financial secretary, and treasurer. There were also three trustees, a conductor, and a sentinel. All were elected annually by the membership. The bargaining committee and the grievance committee (of which the vice-president was chairman) met as and when required. These two committees were elected on a departmental basis, and were to all intents and purposes identical, being composed of the officers and shop stewards. A business representative (or 'business agent') was present at most meetings of the local. He was a full-time, paid official of the union, elected by all the locals in the district. His advice was frequently sought by the local officers, and he was the chief negotiator with the company on all matters affecting the contract, and handled the more intractable grievances. How they worked together is shown in the following account, written in the summer of 1958.

◆ 12 ◆

For the Good of the Association

———◆———

'IF IT WEREN'T for the door prize they wouldn't come at all,' confided the president of the local. The doorkeeper stood with his bowl of dimes, religiously unlocking and relocking the door as each member presented himself for admittance, reaching at the same time into his trousers' pocket for his ten cents contribution to the evening's sweepstake. Outside, the temperature was ten degrees below freezing; inside, the gas heater on the ceiling buzzed noisily. One by one, the members flopped into the vacant chairs, unzipped their padded jackets, and smoked and chewed and chatted happily. The room was pleasantly warm, the chairs uncomfortably hard, and the walls had the timeless dinginess of dark-green paint. On the dais at one end, between the narrow trestle table covered with files, dues books, and loose papers sat the four officers of the local. To one side, leaning precariously in a wobbly standard-holder, was the Flag. From the wall behind the dais, past presidents of the International and the State Federation of Labor looked down on the meeting. Between them was the charter of the local; around the other walls, in varying degrees of ornateness, were the framed charters of different locals in the town which also used the Labor Temple. A painted piano in one corner, a refrigerator and a row of coat hangers completed the furnishings. Smiling broadly, the president rose and banged his gavel on the table gently. The hubbub subsided as he began reading the historic formula for opening the meeting.

It was a scene with which I was soon to become familiar, and it seemed even then a long way removed from the stereotype of an organsation run by power-hungry labor barons depicted in the popular press. Perhaps this little group of working men, some shaved and in their clean suits, others in their working clothes, really were a bunch of hoodlums and racketeers. But at least they didn't look that way to me. Nor did they appear to be that mighty economic force which could hold the nation to ransom pictured by some enthusiastic journalists. They looked remarkably like any corresponding meeting of British trade unionists; and as I learned to know them better I found that this was indeed the case. Their goals, their triumphs, and their frustrations were very similar; they too were perplexed by the old problem of 'apathy'; they too were anxious to find out 'why they don't come to meetings'.

It was on this perplexing issue that the idea of a survey of membership attitudes seemed relevant. The officers of the local were worried that, despite all their best efforts, the response of the rank-and-file membership, at least as reflected in attendance at meetings and willingness to hold office in the union, seemed disappointingly weak. Most active members had their own explanations of why this was so, but there was little mutual agreement among them and even less as to how they could be remedied. The suggestion was therefore made that it would perhaps be worthwhile to establish what the rank-and-file membership thought about the union, particularly in relation to those topics which most worried the officers. Once the fact-finding had been carried out, the way would be clear for any appropriate action to be taken. Even if, as was quite likely, the survey were not to reveal any startlingly new facts or suggest any neat answers to problems, it would provide a valuable educational experience for those union members involved in it. Some of the facts revealed might shake the members' complacency and force them to recognise the existence of opinions other than their own; and perhaps for a short time they would be enabled to glimpse something of those social tensions which in any organisation are normally covered up. Even though the survey revealed nothing new, the old 'facts' would appear in a new light. The vital difference between knowing the facts and fully apprehending them would have been established in the minds of the participants. A heightened awareness of the issues involved would then provide a basis for future action.

Meetings of the local were held every first and third Wednesday in the month. I recorded several such meetings from notes taken down at the time. The first, held in November, began at 7.30 pm with about twenty-five members present. By 8 pm, the number had risen to forty. (In conversation afterwards the president said he thought there were 'about sixty' there.) The president, holding the gavel in his hand formally declared the meeting open, and asked the recording secretary to call the roll of officers and read the minutes of the last meeting. This was done haltingly as the secretary had some difficulty in deciphering his handwriting. Four new applications for membership were read out and approved. The reports from committees were next called for, and there was some discussion about a banquet for retired members. It was proposed that eleven old members should be invited and that each should be presented with a pen-and-pencil set, value $3.50. The president then introduced 'Brother John Harrison, a visitor from England, who will tell us something about a new survey which we are thinking of having'. I then outlined the proposals for a survey of membership attitudes which had been discussed and approved by the officers previously, and invited discussion. A number of questions of detail were asked, but only one member raised doubts about the usefulness of the scheme. There was a general attitude of interest and friendliness towards the project. The obvious enthusiasm of the officers and a tradition of cooperation with the State University in workers' education classes stretching back for several years undoubtedly smoothed the way for the acceptance of the idea. It was unanimously decided to go ahead with the survey and vote the necessary funds.

This business had taken about forty minutes and now the president called for 'anything for the good of the association?'. A renewed discussion about the retired members' banquet developed, mainly over who should be invited. There was animated argument as to whether some of the persons proposed were actually members of the union at the time of their retirement. The issue was temporarily shelved by the president announcing that there was still a lot of important business to be gone through and time was getting on. In particular, he required nominations for officers. Under the International's constitution, he explained, the officers of the local have to be nominated by the first Wednesday in November, and so he would now call for nominations. Beginning with the presidency (for which he declined to be renominated on the grounds that he had already held the office for several years) he went through each of the offices of the local union and asked for nominations to be proposed and seconded. Usually three or four nominations for each office were shouted out and, after banging his gavel three times, the president declared nominations closed. One by one, the nominated candidates rose and declined nomination, leaving only one name on the ballot. It took about half an hour to draw up this slate of candidates and at the conclusion a discussion arose as to the constitutional correctness of allowing the night men (who could not attend the regular meeting and who therefore met separately) to add nominations to the list as they would not be able to do this by the first Wednesday in the month. The business agent then jumped up from his seat on the front row and explained that the International would have no objection to waiving this point. In fact, he said, the position was even more complex, since the views of the men at a subsidiary plant (who were members of the same local) had also to be considered and the list of nominations would have to be put to their (separate) meeting. He then castigated the members roundly for refusing nomination for office and said this showed clearly the need for a survey, which he heartily supported.

By this time a general weariness in the meeting was apparent. It was already after ten o'clock. As the president appealed for 'any new business?' he had to speak loudly to make himself heard. The treasurer asked for permission to buy a rubber stamp to endorse the cheques; he was authorised to spend $5. Amidst increasing restlessness the president read out the cheques for payment, mostly officers' expenses, and reimbursements of wages for night men attending union business or educational classes. Finally he came to the much-anticipated item, the draw for the door prize. A condition of winning the prize is that the winner must be present at the meeting when his name is drawn; if he is not, the prize money is allowed to accumulate until the next draw. By this evening the prize had grown to $100, and noone cared to risk leaving the meeting before the draw. The treasurer produced the familiar cardboard shoebox containing the slips on which were written the members' names, and passed it to the president. Shaking it vigorously and chaffing his fellow officers, the president stepped down from the dais and invited me (as a visitor and therefore a neutral) to draw out a name from the box. 'Read it out' he instructed. I did so. It was the name of a non-attender and was greeted with general groans of disappointment. The meeting now broke up as the members came forward to collect their cheques from the president, who finished signing them while he declared the meeting duly closed.

At the next meeting of the local, held a fortnight later, there were about forty members present, this time somewhat cramped for space as they had to meet in a smaller room, the larger one being required for a women's meeting. The president being ill, the vice president conducted the meeting, which started at 7.45 pm. After the minutes had been read, a detailed and patient report on recent grievances was given by the chairman of the grievance committee. Questions and complaints from members followed thick and fast. There was a prolonged argument as to whether job cards were grouped or not by management. This led into a further discussion about 'down time', which the chairman of the grievance committee urged members to claim whenever they were entitled to it and assured them that if it were refused the union would take the matter up as a grievance. There was some argument, from contrary experiences, against the practicability of this procedure. One member then asserted that the contract was useless, as the workers could not even secure the rights laid down in it. He alleged that the grievance committee had not yet settled a grievance on overtime raised in the summer; and went on to complain that management in the past had taken work from the black-smiths to give to the welders who were short of work, but now the welders had plenty of overtime while the blacksmiths had only forty hours of work per week. The chairman answered this by explaining that their union was not a craft but an industrial union, and that therefore the local could not claim jurisdiction over jobs which was the preserve of manage-ment. At this point the business agent stood up to correct (or, as he put it, 'come to the rescue of') the chairman of the grievance committee. He said theirs was not a craft union, but had both craft and industrial workers in it, and reminisced at some length about his own experiences as a skilled worker and the nature of craft grievances. After this the nominations for officers were read out. No new names were added, and it was announced that the night men would make their nominations at their meeting on the following Tuesday. A report on the retired members' banquet, which had been held since the last meeting, was read, and it was decided to hold another one next year. There was some discussion about a dance for mem-bers and their wives, to be held in the New Year as part of the twenty-first anniversary celebrations of the local. The treasurer's statement was read as usual, and permission sought and obtained to buy candies and masks for the children's Christmas party. At 9.10 the meeting was closed.

The next meeting followed the same pattern as the preceding ones, except that the ballot for officers was conducted. The voting papers were locked away in a filing cabinet and were not to be counted until after the night men had voted. Discussion at this meeting ranged over two topics. The first was occasioned by the business agent who produced copies of a sales catalogue from a store in a neighbouring town which offered a dis-count rate to all members of the local on production of their dues book. Great interest was shown in this and all the copies of the catalogue were eagerly snapped up.

The second subject took more time to debate; it concerned the hold-ing of a 'stag party' in the week before Christmas. A decision to lay out $100 on beer and sandwiches, to be recouped by the sale of tickets at $1.25 apiece, was soon reached. But details of the programme proved more involved. It was reported that the chief of police whose permission had just been sought was not very enthusiastic but said it was within the law to hold it in the room at the Labor Temple. There was general enthusiasm for the idea, and much joking about the likely extent of drunkenness. Dissent was expressed by some of the quieter members, but was not voiced strongly. From conversation afterwards it appeared that they intended to absent themselves on the night in question, but had no wish to interfere with the enjoyments of others. A programme of cards and film show was agreed on, and the question then arose as to what sort of films should be shown. The president said he knew of a man who could get stag films, and it was suggested that perhaps a projector could be borrowed from the local Vocational and Adult School. A member from the floor, however, reported that he had heard of a mail carrier in the post office who had both projector and stag films, and that he would be prepared to put on a show. It was therefore resolved to investigate this, and to show, if possible, one sports and one stag film.

These descriptions could have been multiplied almost indefinitely but they sufficed to establish certain outstanding characteristics of a labor union operating at the local level. In the first place, the main burden of running the organisation fell upon a small cadre of activists, in this case probably not more than forty or fifty; from their ranks were recruited the officers, committee men, and stewards; they were the key men in the union and without them it would have fallen apart. Outside this dedicated group was a wider circle of interested, loyal, but not very active members; the exact size of this group did not emerge from the survey, but was probably not less than the number who returned the questionnaire and may well have been larger. Beyond them again lay a wider circle of members from whom little was heard, except perhaps in times of crisis. These three concentric circles of the membership represented different degrees of participation in the union. It may well have been that there were ways of participating in a democratic union other than attendance at meetings or holding office. Certainly a man could be a perfectly loyal member of his union without doing anything beyond paying his dues and going along with the majority decisions of the local. But he could hardly be said to be a very effective or responsible trade unionist. And the instinct of the local activists to judge the effectiveness of their work by its visible results was probably sounder than the tendency of some social scientists to look for intangible and largely unmeasurable benefits among the inarticulate sections of the membership.

The survey highlighted three areas of concern to members: the meetings, grievances, and the incentive system. The conduct of meetings did, understandably, worry many members. They felt that the meetings should be shorter, brisker and more business-like. Frequently the meeting got bogged down in some comparatively minor point of procedure. A good example of this was a proposal to increase the officers' honoraria. These were not in any sense salaries, but rather token payments in appreciation of the very considerable services rendered by the four chief officers, all of whom worked on the shop floor. The only full-time salaried officer of the union at this level was the business agent, whose services were not confined to this local but spread over some three or four locals in his district. The proposal came from the floor during the period allocated to 'any new business', and was sympathetically received by the meeting. There was an obvious desire to raise, there and then, the payments to the officers. But this proved to be very far from the simple matter it had first appeared to be. To increase payments the bylaws of the local had to be amended. This could only be done on recommendation from the Constitution and Bylaws Committee, about which little seemed to be known. It subsequently transpired that of the three members who constituted the Bylaws Committee, two had left the town some time ago, so that nominations for their replacement had to be called for. All this took several weeks to work itself out, with the result that a simple intention could only be effected by lengthy and cumbersome machinery.

Members were asked how they felt about the grievance procedure and invited to comment on why they thought some workers did not use it when they have a complaint. A variety of reasons was hazarded as to the reasons for this, such as that the workers don't know about it, that it is ineffective anyway, or that too many men are non-unionists. But the biggest single factor attributed to this reluctance was fear; 42 per cent of all respondents said that fear of possible consequences of filing a grievance prevented many workers from doing so. The older union members were especially emphatic on this point. It was not that they feared discharge, but rather reprisals from the foreman—'I think they don't use the grievance procedure because they think the company and foreman will hold it against them and make it rough on them', explained one member. Under the incentive system as operated in several departments of the plant it is important for the worker that he should be given jobs on which he 'can make out' (that is, earn more than the base rate by putting forth incentive effort) and in the allocation of such jobs the foreman exercises considerable discretion. As a worker succinctly put it, 'With the incentive system, the workers realise supervision is capable of making it very tough to make a livable wage by giving the rougher jobs to the men who file grievances'. It is scarcely surprising, therefore, that a minority of members expressed dissatisfaction with the company's incentive system. Not only did some of them object to it on financial grounds, but there was also a realisation that it was an effective intimidatory instrument in the hands of management.

The overall picture which emerged from the details of the survey was of a local doing a sound if unspectacular job of trade unionism. Whether (as originally hoped) the survey helped the local to do that job more effectively I do not know. For Bro. John Harrison it was an insight into American life which he would not have missed for worlds.

✦ 13 ✦

The Emigrants

———◄◆►———

OUR FIRST AMERICAN adventure came to an end in August 1958. After a series of School for Workers' summer schools which kept me busy throughout the hot weather, we regretfully said goodbye to our friends and once more boarded the train for Chicago and New York with even more baggage than when we came. A hectic three days of sightseeing in New York with the Cremins was followed by a welcome collapse into idleness on board the *Queen Mary*. As we huddled in our deckchairs sipping our luke-warm bouillon (Oxo cubes) there was time for reflection on the past year's experiences. Like all visitors who do not expect to repeat their visit, we had crammed as much as possible into our year in America. Not only did we make the most of the opportunity to travel round Wisconsin, we also undertook a tour throughout the southern states, camping in state parks where possible and staying in cheap motels where necessary. When we first announced our intention of doing this our good Wisconsin friends were politely mystified by our desire to see what they regarded as the poorest and most benighted parts of their country, and were only mollified when we explained that we had to visit Margaret's Uncle Bill (her father's youngest brother) who lived at Fort Pierce in Florida. The physical impact of Kentucky, the Great Smokies, Mississippi, New Orleans and Florida was tremendous. But of course it was a visitors' impact, whereas in Madison we had felt at times (perhaps mistakenly) that we were becoming part of the landscape. With children in school, involvement in neighbourhood activities, and a job at the university we were conscious of values and commitments hidden from the fleeting visitor. At the same time we were happy to play the visitor's role when it suited us, as if we were only on the outside looking in. For instance, a British accent was still sufficiently novel to attract attention and at times we exploited this shamelessly. One day Margaret got a parking ticket for leaving the car opposite a fire hydrant. When she went to the local police station to explain that she had not noticed the hydrant as we did not have such things in England, the cop was so fascinated by her accent that he engaged her in a long discussion about police in England and ended up by waiving the fine. On another occasion when we stopped to admire a fine ante-bellum plantation home in Natchez, Mississippi, the owner came out and when he discovered that we were from England (despite the Wisconsin plates on the car) invited us in for a mint julep.

Three aspects of America left an indelible imprint. First were the amenities of daily life. Never again could I tolerate the dirt, inefficiency, and labour of coal fires after a year of living in a centrally-heated house. Immediately on our return to Harrogate I rang up the Gas Board and asked for a quotation to install a system of ducted hot-air heating. They said they had never put in such a system before but would be happy to try. Several weeks of effort by a team of Laurel-and-Hardy-like plumbers followed, during which time the back garden was turned into a tinsmith's yard while they remade the ducts to the correct size, having miscalculated at first. At last the great day when the heat could be turned on arrived. The workmen collected their tools together for the last time and discovered that some of them were missing. After searching high and low they concluded that they must have left them under the floorboards, where presumably they remain to this day. That weekend the walls of the house ran with water as forty years of moisture oozed out. The wallpaper peeled off, the floorboards shrank, the furniture creaked, and the house shrivelled up. But we were warm. And those coal-devouring fireplaces were reduced to no more than interesting 'features'. From time-to-time during the next three years the Gas Board, who, I suspect, had greatly underestimated the cost of the job, would ring us up to ask if they might bring an interested customer to see the system. Number 16 Norfolk Road ranked as one of the wonders of Yorkshire.

Second, we discovered a society in which 'The Label' didn't matter. Nobody judged us by our accent, who our parents were, or what school we had been to. I was welcomed into the fellowship of a very great university, notably by members of the history department and the extension division. None of these people had had any knowledge of me before and yet they were prepared to take me as they found me. This was perhaps the most striking demonstration of that democratic openness of American society which I had often read about but which I had never fully appreciated. We experienced a sense of freedom during that year in Wisconsin, a freedom from all the social rigidities and limitations and snobberies so deeply ingrained in Britain. If this sounds starry-eyed (and I know now that there are ugly sides to the American dream) I can only say that it made a deep impact on me at the time—he more so as it happened not in some socialist Utopia but in the home of capitalism.

Third, we came away with an overwhelming sense of the possibility of change. I am not sure how much this was a reaction to the general torpid state of Britain in the 1950s and how much was the traditional American optimism and belief in the inevitability of progress. Whatever it was, it encouraged me to think radically and critically about my work and plans for the future. America convinced me that fundamental change could be achieved—if conditions were right. The question was whether the conditions ever would be right, at any rate for me, in Britain.

When we left America in the summer of 1958 we had no plans for a return. We felt as one does at the end of a long summer holiday, that it had been a wonderful time, but it was now, alas, over and we had to get back to real life. Yet three years later we were back in Wisconsin, and this time not as visitors but as immigrants. What had happened in that brief period of 1958–61 to lead us to such a momentous decision, to uproot ourselves so completely and to embark on a new career and a totally new way of life? Reading the few letters that remain from that period I have tried to recapture my feelings; but I am not sure that the reasons for our going sound completely convincing. We balanced all the arguments for and against the move, but found it difficult to come to a decision. It was an opportunity that had come at the right time, from the right place, and which might not come again. To overcome any lingering doubts we comforted ourselves with the thought that we should be able to return regularly to the UK, which indeed turned out to be true. The future lay all before us and we had all the confidence of forty-year-olds.

On my return to Leeds in 1958 I had taken over the position of Deputy Director of Adult Education and Extra-Mural Studies, which was a considerable promotion in salary and status. From the mid-1950s Raybould began to be away from the department more and more. He had become disillusioned by the WEA's failure, as he saw it, to uphold its traditional standards, and he turned increasingly to direct university provision through extension courses. Although his policies met with scepticism and opposition from other extra-mural heads at home, he found a new role in the international adult-education movement, where he was respected as a powerful and influential leader. He saw a chance of spreading his mission of university standards in extra-mural work worldwide, or in the first instance throughout the Commonwealth, and spent periods in West Africa, the West Indies and Canada, as well as attending congresses to meet adult educationists from Europe, the United States, and Asia. In the early days of the department he had been involved directly in all aspects of its work; but now he had to leave the day-to-day running of the classes to others. I think he secretly believed that having set up the structure of the department according to the best principles, the operation would more or less run itself, provided we followed his precepts. He had confidence that I was the man to oversee this, and I was quite happy to try. Since he was away so much I was virtually the director, and during the year 1960-1 when he was on leave in the West Indies, I was appointed Acting Head of the Department and paid accordingly.

The idea of looking after the store while Sid was away at first seemed quite acceptable, and was certainly welcomed by my colleagues, some of whom were chafing under his growing rigidities and relentless pressure for three-year tutorial classes. But after a while I began to see the drawbacks of the arrangement. Much as I admired Raybould I could not always agree that his policies were either desirable or practical. He was no longer at the coal face, and did not, I thought, fully appreciate the problems which tutors had to face in their tutorial classes. Nor did he really grasp the dimensions of the newly-emerging extension side of the department's work, so competently organised by my devoted assistant, Pamela Cobb. Raybould was still in his mid-fifties and unlikely to move elsewhere: the prospect of soldiering on for years ahead became worrying.

Moreover I became aware that I did not want to spend the rest of my days as an administrator. I had always assumed since my army days that I could take any form of administration in my stride. Being of a neat and orderly temperament I found the work congenial and unexacting. But when I found myself in the position of having to organise classes and courses only for other people instead of for myself I grew weary. I realised that I preferred teaching, research and writing. Unfortunately the senior positions in adult education were administrative, despite the title of professor which was conferred in some universities. I also wanted to move beyond adult education and its history to social history in general.

So, the offer of a professorship in history at the University of Wisconsin seemed providential. It was not entirely unexpected, as is the way with such things. During our year in Madison I had made several good friends in the history department and they were keen to get me to join them. For many years British history at Wisconsin had been taught by Paul Knaplund, an authority on Gladstone's foreign policy. When Knaplund retired his successor was Phil Curtin, a specialist in African history. Knaplund taught courses in British Empire as well as English history, mainly political. But Curtin wanted to separate the two subjects and

At home: An American newspaper idealisation of the visiting family

At work: Teaching at a School for Workers summer school

Chairman of the meeting

persuaded the department to move to separate appointments for British Empire and English history, while he set up a new area of African history. Under this rearrangement the department created a new position, tailor-made for me, in modern British history. I was to teach the social history of Britain from the eighteenth century to the present and also offer a course on European social movements. The UW History Department was one of the very best in America at this time. It was especially strong in American history but several of the Europeanists were also outstanding. I felt thrilled at being invited to join such a distinguished band of scholars. The starting salary was $10,000, which was nearly twice what I was getting at Leeds, and there were additions for summer-school teaching, research leave, and conference expenses. It was an offer you could not refuse.

The offer was made the more attractive by my gloomy assessment of the state of British society in the late 1950s. Although the austerities of post-war Britain had gone and there was much trumpeting about affluence and assurances that 'you never had it so good', too many of the old class divisions and inequalities remained for my liking. Three consecutive Conservative victories and unhappiness with 'Butskellite' policies did nothing to improve morale. It seemed that there was little prospect of change in Britain and that the elitist, hierarchic society would continue into the foreseeable future. There had been a steady growth in the size of universities but the blueprint for significant development in higher education, the Robbins' *Report* (1963) was still in the future. In light of the great expansion of British universities in the 1960s my dissatisfaction may now seem to have been premature. But as historical figures we all ride with our backs to the engine.

Our journey this time was a much more elaborate affair than the 1957 trip. We were now emigrants, or as we soon learned to call ourselves, immigrants. For this purpose we had to acquire immigrant visas, which involved the collection of a formidable array of documents, a medical examination, and an interview with the American consul in Liverpool. We also had to dispose of our house and such things as we were not taking to Madison. To keep the removal costs down we decided to take only our best and most cherished possessions with us. Even so, the resulting baggage seemed huge. Six large trunks containing all our clothes, linen, silver and small items travelled with us on the boat. The furniture, china and books were packed into a specially-made wooden crate. When I ventured some remarks about this the man from Dean and Dawson's said proudly that it would come in handy as a garage when I arrived 'out there'. Thinking he had been watching too many westerns, I dismissed this as a mere fantasy. But sure enough some years later in the Australian capital, Canberra, I saw just such a crate being used for this purpose by an immigrant pommie although in Madison it would have been a joke.

My father was seventy-nine in 1961 and in good health; but when we said goodbye I don't think he expected to see us again. He too thought of America as 'out there'. Margaret's father was sixty-nine and already showing signs of Alzheimer's disease from which he died in 1967. We knew our mothers would miss the family very much. Nevertheless when we gaily announced that we were going they never raised the smallest objection or suggested that we had any duties towards them, though in their hearts they must have felt sad and perhaps forsaken. They had always said from childhood that they wanted us to do the best we could for ourselves and that they would never stand in our way; and they never did. We tried to mitigate their sense of loss by coming back frequently and by writing regularly every week. But I now feel that there was an inevitable element of heedlessness, perhaps of selfishness, in our decision. It was a price to be paid for what I think was, in the long run, the right course of action. Another sadness was leaving our friends in Harrogate and the department. As a parting gift my colleagues presented us with an admirably chosen piece of Victorian silver.

On 20 June 1961 we sailed from Liverpool on the *Empress of Britain* bound for Montreal. We had decided to see something of Canada *en route* and pictured to ourselves the delights of sailing down the St Lawrence river. Alas, the journey from Quebec to Montreal was at night and only a few hours in Montreal elapsed before we had to board the train to Chicago. Our entry into the United States lacked something of the romantic glamour suggested by the Statue of Liberty; but then we could hardly claim to be part of the 'huddled masses yearning to be free'. At about 4.30 in the morning we crossed from Windsor, Ontario, to Detroit, where an immigration officer boarded the train, inspected our visas, stamped our passports and wished us well. And he did not even mention the large chest X-ray which I had been assured was essential for entry and which I had therefore laboriously toted separately throughout the voyage.

In Madison our life resumed from where we had left it three years before. For the first year we rented an unfurnished house in Shorewood Hills, a lovely suburb on the shores of Lake Mendota and near to the university. The children settled into the local school and the tradesmen of the area showered us with free gifts and special offers for newcomers. Neighbourhood organisations fell over themselves to welcome us into membership: 'feel at home, folks' had more substance than the ubiquitous 'have a good day'. We would have liked to stay in Shorewood Hills; but the complications of the school system made it desirable to look elsewhere if the children were to progress to West High School which we were advised they should do. We toyed with the idea of building a new house, and got as far as having an architect's plans drawn up, but the project was frustrated by difficulties over buying the lot. At the end of 1962 we bought a house on the west side of town, convenient for school and university. It was quite unlike anything we had even contemplated before. Built in 1953 by an architect influenced by Frank Lloyd Wright, it had won an award of the American Institute of Architects. It was a split-level house on a heavily-wooded, sloping site. A huge window occupied one wall of the living room which was cantilevered out beyond the ground storey. In the hot summer months it was shaded by the oak trees: in the winter it was dazzlingly bright from the reflected snow. When we moved in on 1 January 1963 the temperature was twenty degrees below zero and there was deep snow.

The routine of domestic life in Madison varied according to the seasons. Not only were there new holidays to be celebrated, such as Labor Day on the first Monday of September and Thanksgiving on the last Thursday of November, but annual chores such as 'putting on the storms' had to be carried out. Because of the extreme cold the windows of houses were protected in winter by an extra, or storm, window which was fitted from the outside. So every fall I had to struggle up a ladder and hang the heavy storms, and in the spring take them down and replace them with screens for the hot summer. Leaf raking was another autumn job which occupied many a Saturday afternoon. But it is the food which most haunts my memory of those Madison days in the 1960s. I don't know why this should be so because I am no gourmet and American cuisine is often looked down on by Europeans. The style of American eating suited our needs at that time; and I recall those special Saturday evenings when we dined out as a family at Crandall's Restaurant near Capitol Square, sipping our daiquiris, nibbling away at the *hors d'oeuvres* (a meal in themselves), before the arrival of the gigantic T-bone steak. Or there was brunch after church on Sunday mornings at the Pancake House when we gorged ourselves on streaky bacon, pancakes with maple syrup, toast and jelly, and as many refills of coffee as you wanted. Even the hamburgers were delicious to an extent quite unimaginable to someone brought up on the pale, stodgy imitation offered in England: the meat was superior, the buns warmed, and the 'fixings' lavish and varied. And for sweets I loved those open pies, especially pecan or blueberry.

The 1960s was a period of great expansion in the universities. At Wisconsin there seemed to be no limit to what we could expect. Student

Emigrants, 1961–70: *The Good Life in Madison, Wisconsin. Our house, 2802 Ridge Road, Madison, had been awarded a commendation by the Wisconsin Institute of Architects in 1953*

Research in the library

numbers grew by leaps and bounds. The Madison campus reached 31,000, including 9,000 in graduate school. There were 5,000 enrolments in history courses and about 500 in the history graduate programme for MAs and PhDs. The history department had about sixty full-time faculty members plus a small army of teaching assistants recruited from the PhD candidates. As this expansion was nation-wide and there was a consequent shortage of teachers, the top universities engaged in a continuous battle to poach each other's best faculty. At our fortnightly departmental meetings we spent much time arguing about whether we should bid for another position in American, European or Third-World history; and having come to a decision we appointed a small committee to draw up a slate of candidates whom we then invited for interview, 'to be looked over'.

We seemed to be perpetually wooing, wining and dining people from out of state, emphasising our rich library holdings, generous research funding, and the charms of life in Madison. We were not always successful. Sometimes one suspected from the start that the man was just 'telegram waving', that is, using our offer to bargain up his salary and position in his own university. And of course we played the same game ourselves. The risk was that it might backfire. If you went to the Dean with an offer which you said was very tempting but which you secretly did not intend to accept, he might say: 'Congratulations, Harrison. We're sorry to lose you, but you obviously cannot refuse such a splendid offer.' But where the offer was genuine and we did not want to lose a good man, the Chairman and the Dean tried to put together a 'package' sufficient to hold him: a reduced teaching load, an extra year of research leave, a research assistant, an increase in salary. In one famous case a distinguished Americanist had been offered practically everything we could think of to keep him. When he finally complained that the climate in North Carolina was more congenial than the rigours of Wisconsin we felt that all was lost. But as a last desperate throw the chairman appealed to the president of the university, himself an historian and previous chairman of the department; and he agreed to offer him the ultimate in UW status: a space in parking lot 90, right next to Bascom Hall, the historic centre of the university where only the bigwigs could leave their cars.

The older members of the department viewed the rapid expansion with some scepticism, asking what would happen when the euphoria (and funding) came to an end. But the Young Turks dismissed such doubts as only what you could expect from the Depression generation. I did not question that this state of affairs was anything but normal: it accorded with my expectations of America and my belief that real change was possible in American society.

One of the strongest attractions of the UW for me was its great tradition of academic freedom and defence of liberal (even socialist) values. A bronze plaque fixed to the wall of Bascom Hall commemorates a famous case of academic freedom in 1892 and affirms the dedication of the University of Wisconsin to 'that continual and fearless sifting and winnowing by which alone truth can be found'. The history department had long been imbued with the spirit of Wisconsin progressivism which encouraged radical, anti-establishment thinking. Toleration, respect for minority views, and the duty of intellectuals to serve the state were part of the Wisconsin academic inheritance. In the 1960s these principles were once more put to the test.

◆ 14 ◆

Sifting and Winnowing

————◄◆►————

IN OUR FAMILY photograph album there are several pictures of an anti-war demonstration in Madison which I took on 18 April 1970. Margaret and Elizabeth are standing on the steps of the Capitol with another student in front of the peace banner of St Francis's Church, the Episcopal chaplaincy of which we were members. The Wisconsin State Capitol, modelled on the Capitol in Washington, stands on a narrow neck of land between Lake Mendota and Lake Monona, at the very centre of the town where the main streets converge. Looking down State Street from the Capitol one can see the main buildings of the university, half a mile away. A crowd of perhaps a thousand or so, has already assembled and more are arriving in processions, with banners and flags: 'Peace Now', 'Veterans for Peace', 'Wisconsin War Resisters', 'Women's Action Movement—Out of Vietnam Now', they read. There are also CND signs, SDS (Students for a Democratic Society) placards, and the black flags of the anarchists. We stand together in our little church group: others do the same. On the opposite side of the road stands a line of Madison City policemen in riot gear. They are wearing padded jackets and helmets with plastic visors and hold long night sticks (billy clubs). We listen to speeches denouncing the war and the draft; we join in the shouts, applaud the speakers, and join in the singing of freedom songs. The police look on impassively. After a while the crowd begins to ebb away. It is cold standing there, and we decide we have done our duty and can go home. The demonstration has passed off peacefully this time. But it was not always so.

In the album there are other pictures. In one of them an angry crowd of students faces a group of riot-police holding night sticks; in another the chief of the campus police is arguing with a dense throng of students packed into the corridors of the Commerce building. Clouds of tear gas drift across the parking lot outside Bascom Hall; and a dramatic close-up of a policeman standing beside a paddy wagon is backed by the whitened face of a member of a visiting mime troupe from San Francisco peering out of the grilled window. This is the famous Dow Chemical demonstration of 18 October 1967, when 50 students and 21 policemen were injured in violent confrontation. The Dow Chemical Company were the manufacturers of napalm, which was being used with horrific results in Vietnam, and opponents of the war tried to prevent the company recruiting for staff on campus by blocking the interviews. An earlier protest against Dow in February of the same year had resulted in the arrest of seventeen students but there had been no violence.

Turning the pages of the album I come to another demonstration outside the library building in October 1969. This is the Vietnam War Moratorium, part of a national campaign which culminated in a quarter of a million people converging on Washington to protest the war. The banners and placards this time are mainly moral and religious, and the atmosphere is non-violent. Some earlier photographs, taken on 5 April 1968, mark the Martin Luther King memorial demonstration. The whole length of State Street, from Bascom Hill to the Capitol is a dense mass of people. There are no banners and no police.

These pictures do not show the whole extent of campus disruption in the last five years of the 1960s by any means. But they do help to recall the turmoil in American society at that time. We had come to America expecting life to be more exciting than in the UK, but not in quite this way. We were drawn into the issues of the day along with our friends. The most remarkable thing was the speed with which the change in the social and political climate came about. When we arrived in Madison in 1961 the only student demonstration to be noticed was a panty raid by the fraternity boys. True there was a Socialist Club and a small group of Marxists grouped round *Studies on the Left* which was published in Madison; and for a short time I was faculty adviser to the WEB DuBois Club, a group of left-wing socialist students. But such student political activism was very limited in numbers and focused mainly on education and journals. Soon however this state of affairs began to change. In the early 1960s students turned in increasing numbers to a variety of causes and forms of protest. The awakening began with the Civil Rights movement in the South. Madison had only a tiny black population and there were few black students on campus. The dramatic struggles against segregation caught the imagination of young people in the North who volunteered to go as 'freedom riders'. The university faculty was also sympathetic; and one of the members of the history department took part in the Selma march. Groups supporting SNCC (Student Non-Violent Coordinating Committee) CORE (Congress of Racial Equality) appeared on campus and linked up with sympathetic townspeople.

By the later 1960s liberalism was all-pervasive. It invaded the most unlikely institutions, including the Episcopal Church. In fact the student chaplaincies on campus—Roman Catholic, Episcopal, Lutheran, Jewish— outbid each other in unorthodox efforts to hold their students. For some years we were members of down-town Grace Church, where I was a lay reader (sub-deacon) and vestryman; but later we felt that we ought also to support St Francis House which was the Episcopal chaplaincy. Here we met the full force of the 'winds of change' as interpreted by a rather witless priest. I did not mind too much having guitar instead of organ music, and even tambourines for the happy-clappy hymns. We were also on the fringe of charismatic manifestations and people would sometimes stand up and utter gibberish (*glossolalia*, or speaking with tongues) or stand with their arms outstretched for several minutes at a time. One Sunday morning we all stood like zombies with balloons floating from cords tied to our wrists while Vietnam War scenes were projected onto a screen at the back of the altar. But the ultimate was reached when one of my colleagues discovered that the basement room in the church was being used for the production of a blasphemous and pornographic radical magazine. The priest was most put out when told that this must stop, complaining that we were being intolerant and out-of-touch with the sensitivities of young people, for whom it was vital that the church should be 'relevant'.

I always felt that the student movement was heavily infiltrated by government agents, perhaps even by *agents provocateurs*, and one day I thought that my suspicions had been confirmed. I was walking down the corridor in Bascom Hall to go to the men's room when I was accosted by a man wearing a grey mackintosh and trilby hat. 'Excuse me Sir,' he said, 'are you Mr Harrison?' I said I was; and he then said 'I am from the Federal Bureau of Investigation and I would like to have a word with you', showing me his FBI badge in the palm of his hand. It was just like a 1930s movie or a Raymond Chandler novel. 'Okay,' I said, 'I'll be with you in a moment,' and slipped into the men's room. Oh Lord, I thought, now what have I done? Has he come about my sponsorship of the DuBois club? Have they been digging into my past associations with labor unions? Shall I be deported as an undesirable alien? We went back to my office and he sat down. I waited expectantly. 'We are investigating Mr David Goldberg who has applied for a career position in government service and we understand he is one of your students. Can you tell me anything about him?' he said. 'Just a routine check-up. He has given your name as a person able to speak on his behalf.' I tried desperately to remember who David Goldberg could be. It was a common enough name. There must have been at least a dozen Goldbergs on campus. Goldberg, Goldberg; no I could not envisage any particular student of that name among the dozens who sat listening to me while I held forth on British history. But obviously he must have been there, and had been hard pressed to find a sufficient number of 'persons in authority' to complete his application form. 'Well,' I said, 'I don't know any reason why David Goldberg should not enter government employment. I'm sure he'll make a good civil servant'. 'Well thank you, Sir, that's all I needed to know', said the agent, 'I won't take up any more of your time.'

The full force of protest came in 1965 with the intensification of the war in Vietnam. From then on the Madison campus was the scene of one conflict after another. The radical members of faculty opposed the war from the beginning; but some of our liberal colleagues (confused, I thought, by long-standing anti-Communist attitudes) were for some time hesitant to come out against the war. For male students the issue was sharpened by the draft. Under the Selective Service System college students were granted deferment, provided they attained satisfactory grades. This meant that if one gave a student a failure mark one might be jeopardising his deferment status, in fact sentencing him to go to Vietnam. Those who graduated were faced with the choice of either being drafted and subsequently deserting if posted to Vietnam, or evading the draft altogether by not responding to the call-up notice. I had students in both categories who fled to Canada, where they tried to get jobs or continued their postgraduate education. Some of them were reluctant exiles for several years and kept in touch with me by letter and later by visits to England. Not until 21 January 1977, the day after the Presidential inauguration, were pardons granted for most of the 10,000 Vietnam War draft evaders by Jimmy Carter. In May 1966 the Madison protestors organised a sit-in against the draft, occupying the administration building for several days. After the Dow Chemical demonstrations in 1967, organised mainly by SDS, the campus unrest broadened to include other issues, notably questions of student power such as participation in departmental meetings and the planning of courses. These issues came to a head in the first week of the spring semester in February 1969.

On the Monday morning I went to my 11 o'clock class as usual. 'History 364 (*Society and Politics in England, 1780–1960*)', as it appeared in the University Catalogue, met three times a week. On Mondays and Wednesdays I lectured for an hour to the undergraduate third and fourth years, and on Friday met the graduates while the undergraduates had a quiz session with the teaching assistants. Outside the humanities building where the lecture was held, a large picket of students was gathered. 'Support the strike', 'End racism', they shouted. I then remembered receiving a leaflet outlining a week-long conference on 'The Black Revolution: to what ends?' which had been held the previous week; but I had not attended any of the events. The pickets asked me not to go in. I said that I supported their demands but that I could not see how failing to meet my students would help anyone. So I pushed past and went to the lecture room. The attendance was less than usual, perhaps two-thirds of normal. Before I began the lecture a member of the strike committee asked if he could address the class. I said I would allow him five minutes. He asked the class to support the demands of black students for a Black Studies Department and the elimination of institutionalised racism by boycotting classes and holding 'talk-ins' instead. The students listened: he left and I got on with the lecture. I sensed that most of them were sympathetic to what he said but were not prepared to get up and leave. But the next day things hotted up. The picket lines were denser and there were noisy disruptions in classrooms which were 'liberated'. I did not go into the university that day; but the *Capital Times* reported 'Police on Campus, but Leave Quickly' and showed pictures of students chanting 'On strike, shut it down'. The third day of the strike, Wednesday, the students were out in force, blocking entrances, halting buses, and invading classrooms. Riot police were everywhere on campus, surrounding the main buildings and pushing back the pickets. I made my way to the class, but only a handful was present, and so we had a discussion about the current situation. That evening the *Capital Times* carried banner headlines: 'Hit-run Blockades are begun at UW' above a picture of a long line of grim-looking riot police facing white student protestors in front of Bascom Hall. There were also reports that enraged Republican state senators were demanding a full investigation of 'everything going on at the university' and threatening to fire the university president. 'You can't sift and winnow in a sewer of crime and corruption', roared one of the senators. 'These kids are against our whole system and they want to tear it down. They want to tear down our society by filth and corruption'. He contended that the university's student newspaper, the *Daily Cardinal*, was run by 'dirty little minds'. 'They use four-letter words that aren't fit to write on out-house walls', he said. 'And one of the biggest four-letter words in their vocabulary is M-A-R-X. This is all part of a national conspiracy.' The faculty response to this kind of attack was to close ranks; and the arrival next day of 900 soldiers of the National Guard (reservists) provoked a strong reaction from the students. Guardsmen with rifles and fixed bayonets stood outside main buildings and tear gas was used to break up the crowds. That night a torchlight procession, estimated at 10,000 students, marched from the university to the Capitol. On Friday another 1,200 Guardsmen were called to keep classes open, and there were clashes between strikers and police. Over the weekend the Guard was withdrawn from the campus and stationed nearby; and the number of militant strikers dwindled. After a week of marches, rallies, confrontations, and skipping classes the level of general student activity fell. On Monday classes resumed and History 364 met as usual. Sporadic violence and confrontations continued throughout the week, but the strike was effectively over.

However, the issues raised by the strike had now to be dealt with. The Legislature was calling for a full 'investigation'; and the university faculty began its own postmortem. We now entered a period of intense and, as it seemed, continuous meetings, reports and resolutions. Unlike some other universities the top administrators were drawn from the ranks of academics. The President of the University, Fred Harvey Harrington, was a historian and former chairman of the history department. The chancellors, vice chancellors and deans had all been professors with widely-recognised academic reputations. They were our colleagues and neighbours. We met in each other's houses and were on first-name terms. Hiring, promotion, tenure, and salary, as well as courses, degrees and student discipline were controlled by faculty committees. Deans of students, registrars, admissions officers, and suchlike acted as agents of faculty policy. In practice faculty government was limited by various constraints, some of which became very apparent during the strike. As a state university the UW is funded and ultimately controlled by the Legislature through a nine-member Board of Regents appointed by the governor. The UW is therefore subject to political pressures. Wisconsin is not a wealthy state and it has always been something of an enigma that it should have supported such a large and prestigious university. The reasons for its greatness however were not always apparent to the legislators, some of whom judged the institution by the record of its football team rather than its graduate school. The UW was highly visible. In a small town like Madison, with a population of 200,000, anything to do with the university was news and reverberated throughout the state. Issues like student power, minority rights, and draft resistance were strange aberrations to many Wisconsinites and were but imperfectly understood: outside agitators, especially New York reds, were responsible, and the university authorities were to blame for not cracking down on these undesirable out-of-state elements.

It would be tedious to recount our long-drawn-out faculty meetings following the strike, even if I could remember the details. We had gone through much the same sort of exercise after the Dow Chemical confrontation in October 1967 and were to do so again in May 1970. The general impression that remains with me is the division between liberals and radicals. Some of the younger faculty sided with the students, but the older and more senior people took a conservative line. The majority view was probably nearer to the traditional liberalism of the UW: a desire to uphold high academic standards while tolerating the exuberant and sometimes impossible demands of youth. In the history department we had several faculty who were men of the Left in the European sense, notably Harvey Goldberg, George Mosse, and William Appleman Williams. To radical students of the New Left, as the 1960s radicalism was dubbed, they were guru figures. I counted myself close to them; but to my students I think I must have appeared no more than a pink liberal. In a strongly research-oriented university like the UW most faculty wanted to be left alone to get on with their research and publications, and some even resented having to spend much time on teaching. When the performance of the multiversities (academic supermarkets) in the 1960s came to be analysed later, this attitude of the profession came in for much criticism. The history department was unusual in that some of our most distinguished faculty devoted much time and effort to undergraduate as well as graduate teaching, and their courses were hugely popular. But this did not save us from student demands.

After the February 1969 strike the protests died down, but an underlying sense of grievance lingered on. In May this erupted in the Miflin Street riots. Miflin Street, a few blocks from the Capitol, was an area of student lodgings, mostly old frame houses. A request to hold a block (street) party was refused by the city authorities, but the students held the party all the same, and the police moved in to break it up. For three days and nights, clashes between police and youths (not all of whom were students) went on, with incidents of fire-bombing, street barricades, brick throwing, tear gassing and arrests. Although these disturbances were off campus and did not involve the university authorities directly, the town–gown hostility was evident. The youth culture, or perhaps counterculture, which expressed itself in unorthodox dress and hair styles, the use of drugs, loud music, and easy sexual relations, was anathema to many citizens who believed that the student unrest was reinforced by 'street people'.

The next crisis came in May 1970. This time the scenario was set by a combination of anti-war protest and labor unionism. The graduate students employed as teaching assistants had organised themselves into a Teaching Assistants Association (TAA) in May 1966, and had joined the

Campus confrontation: *Demonstrations against the Vietnam War and the draft flared up on university campuses across America. These pictures were taken when a recruiting team from the Dow Chemical Company (manufacturers of napalm, used in Vietnam) visited the University of Wisconsin, Madison, in October 1967. Tear gas floats across the parking lot at Bascom Hall*

A member of an anti-war visiting mime troop in the paddy wagon

Outside the Commerce Building

Dow Chemical protest in October 1967. From their original concern with the effects of the draft, the TAA developed into a full-scale labor union and pressed for recognition as the bargaining agent on issues of wages and hours. The TAs also felt that they were a link between the students and regular faculty, and should have some share in the shaping of courses and curricula. The university, to the dismay of some liberal faculty members, was prepared to enter into discussions with the TAA. But the slow progress of the bargaining sessions finally exasperated the TAA and in March 1970 they called a strike, which lasted for three weeks. Again, pickets were out, campus buses halted, and demonstrators paraded round the campus. While I sympathised with the TAs in their struggle to improve conditions I was not very happy when they turned to the Teamsters, of all unions, for support. It was hard for me to see the university as an industry, though in one sense I suppose it was. Like all academics I was jealous of any challenge to my authority in the classroom where I was king; and I found it easiest to assume a master-apprentice relationship with my students. So I carried on with my teaching but the atmosphere was soured. And then we were hit by the invasion of Cambodia and the killing of four anti-war demonstrators by National Guardsmen at Kent State University, Ohio, in May. An all-out student strike was called and many faculty members supported the anti-war protest.

The situation was similar to previous strikes and boycotts, but this time the numbers involved were greater and confrontations more violent. The object of the strikers was to close the university; the determination of the administration and the governor was to keep it open. The National Guard were called out and city police in riot gear were again on campus. The students' usual tactic was to march on a war-related building such as ROTC (Reserve Officers' Training Corps) or AMRC (Army Mathematics Research Centre) and the police responded with tear gas and clubbings. At night the police helicopters hovered over the campus with searchlights, dispersing any groups of students with tear gas. Shop windows in the business area were 'trashed' (that is, smashed) to the extent that parts of State Street looked like a battlefield. The smell of tear gas was everywhere, including in the heating and ventilation systems. For a week, classes had to be cancelled; and in fact for the last six weeks of the semester the academic programme was disrupted. The university did not officially close; but special arrangements for grading had to be made to take account of student absences and work not done. The final act in the drama came after we had left Madison. In the early hours of the morning of 24 August 1970 a bomb exploded which demolished the AMRC and killed a research physicist who was working late.

From this account it might sound as if the UW during the 1960s was in a state of continuous disruption. This was not so. For most of the time we functioned quite normally, apart from the three peak times of protest in October 1967, February 1969 and May 1970. The leaders of student radicalism in Madison until the mid-1960s looked for an intellectual base in Marxism and European thought. But the dynamism of the later mass movement was almost entirely pragmatic and American. The constituents of student unrest were demands for civil rights, student power, and the Vietnam war. This was an explosive mixture; but the most potent element in it was the anti-war protest. As the war escalated, the American involvement in Vietnam appeared more and more unsuccessful, unnecessary, and grotesque. In all, 58,000 Americans died or were missing in Vietnam before the United States withdrew its forces in 1972.

As we stood with our peace banners on the steps of the Capitol we had no illusions about the effectiveness of what we were doing: we simply felt that we had to add our mite of testimony against the futility and obscenity of the war. The years of turmoil had not made me disillusioned with America: quite the contrary, for I was conscious that this was the society in which the important decisions affecting the rest of the world were being made, and it was therefore all the more necessary to get those decisions right. But as I watched the black flags of the anarchist contingent marching up State Street I felt that we still had some way to go before the ideals of sifting and winnowing could be made to prevail.

◆ 15 ◆

The Quest for Robert Owen

————◄◆►————

I CANNOT REMEMBER exactly when I became aware that I wanted to be a historian as distinct from a teacher of history. At Cambridge I had listened to lecturers who were also writers of history—and to some who were not. But the distinction between the two was but dimly perceived at the undergraduate level. Moreover the Cambridge system, as I remarked earlier, did nothing to make explicit the nature and methods of history. We were simply left to absorb or infer such things. As a result during my first few years at Leeds I was quite content to spend my time preparing for what was a fairly heavy teaching load in international relations and English social history. I had to read widely in areas such as American and Russian history as well as social history which were new to me. Like all young university lecturers in their first appointment the immediate task was to accumulate sufficient scholarly capital to see me through the session.

It was when I began to work for a PhD degree at Leeds that the attractions of research and writing became apparent. In his desire to raise the academic standards of the Department, Raybould encouraged his staff to publish and undertake research. A PhD was not at that time regarded as a prerequisite for a university lectureship and most of my contemporaries were appointed without such a qualification, though in the USA it was already necessary as a teaching ticket. Enrolment for a PhD, however, was taken as evidence of a serious commitment to research and was useful in securing a reduced teaching load and such minimal financial support as was available. Two supervisors, Raybould and the Professor of Theology, were appointed to oversee my work; but since I was a member of the faculty they were only nominal. Neither of them was a historian nor had any knowledge of research methods and techniques. I was left entirely on my own to collect material and write a thesis, which was eventually presented in 1955 under the title *Social and Religious Influences in Adult Education in Yorkshire between 1830 and 1870*. Working at weekends and during the summers I completed the thesis in four years, and was proudly presented for the degree by Raybould at the summer Congregation in July 1955. My mother was very proud of me, though secretly confused as to how I could be a doctor and know nothing about medicine. The hierarchical distinctions of academia were beyond her, whereas a doctor of medicine ranked high in her social estimation. The only memento of the occasion that I have, apart from the degree certificate, is a sad-looking black-and-white snap of me, sitting in the garden at Gate Helmsley, attired in my hired gown and fancy hat. Fortunately this was before the popularisation of colour photography, so that the true, olive-green horror of a Leeds PhD gown is decently obscured.

I would have completed my doctorate earlier had it not been for a temporary diversion of my energies. In the autumn of 1952 Raybould was asked by the Working Men's College in London if he could recommend someone to write their centenary history to be published in 1954 and he suggested that I might be interested. The WMC was founded by F.D. Maurice and a group of Christian Socialists in 1854 and had a continuous history thereafter. Such a project, calling for both a knowledge of nineteenth-century social history and experience of adult education, seemed an opportunity which I should not refuse, despite the tight deadline and my existing PhD commitment. I therefore accepted the invitation of the Principal of the College, Sir Wilfrid Eady, to stay with him at his house in London and discuss the matter over dinner. Eady was Second Secretary to the Treasury, friendly, sympathetic, tolerant, and formidably wise. This was my first introduction to the high intellectualism of the top civil service, set amidst the faded Edwardian comfort of Hampstead, London NW3. The college was a curious relic of Victorian middle-class philanthropy and evangelical social concern combined with the moral earnestness and passion for self-improvement of radical working men. The teachers were still mostly unpaid volunteers drawn from the ranks of middle-class professional and business men. I discovered that the College had an excellent library and muniment room containing virtually all the material necessary for the history. It also had valuable letters and documents relating to the Christian Socialists, Owenites, Pre-Raphaelites, and various great Victorians associated with the college in its early days. For me it was a real bibliographical feast. Throughout 1953 I dashed up to London to spend weekends working in the archives and talking to older members of the College. I completed the manuscript by the end of the year. The college paid me a fee of £350 for the book which was published by Routledge and Kegan Paul, whose directors were members of the Franklin family and closely connected with the WMC. A specially bound copy was presented to the Queen when she attended the centenary celebrations. My mother was again impressed.

My main task after finishing my PhD thesis was to turn it into a book, and for this some more research was necessary. However, my immediate plans were once again derailed by a more pressing demand. The new Professor of Modern History at Leeds, Asa Briggs, was keen to publish a volume of essays on Chartism, the great social and political movement of the working classes between 1837 and 1854, and I was invited to contribute along with several other historians. We met in Asa's room and quickly drew up a list of topics and likely contributors. The main thrust was towards local studies and this was reflected in the chapters we agreed. Other aspects of Chartism were assigned to a subsequent volume, but this never materialised. I volunteered to write two chapters about Chartism in Leeds and Leicester, which I completed during the next two years. For the Leeds chapter I had to rely heavily on the local press of the 1830s and 1840s; but for Leicester I was also able to draw upon local memories. One of these incidents is worth recalling because it is the sort of thing that makes history come alive and delights the heart of all romantic historians.

One afternoon in the summer of 1955 I was sitting on a bench outside the Town Hall near the Central Reference Library in Leicester, relaxing for half-an-hour from my labours on the Chartist materials in the library. So far the sources had proved meagre. My secret hopes of discovering some unsuspected cache of old Chartist letters and manuscripts had gradually evaporated, and I was driven back to the only considerable untapped source—the local newspapers. These had not been unrewarding. At least they had enabled me to reconstruct the activities and shadowy personality of the leader of the Loughborough Chartists, John Skevington. His name was now forgotten but in the 'Hungry Forties' it had been a household word, linked invariably with that of his acknowledged master, Feargus O'Connor. I had often wondered what he must have looked like, this much-abused, much-worshipped Methodist preacher who, after the disappointments of the Reform Bill in 1832, had turned wholeheartedly to championing the People's Cause. A police spy had sneeringly described him as a beer-house keeper and a worthless character; but from snippets in his own and others' speeches I had gleaned that he was in fact a small tradesman of some kind, and had originally been a handloom weaver. I remembered seeing somewhere a report of a meeting at which his portrait had been presented to him by his admirers, but I had not thought any more about it. I already had several files bulging with references to unimportant little meetings. Then as I sat watching the pigeons strutting about the square the idea suddenly flashed across my mind: what if the portrait were still in existence?

From then on I could think of nothing else. The difficulty was to know where and how to begin to look for it. On several previous occasions I had been helped in my incursions into local history by a friendly journalist on the local daily. He was by temperament something of an antiquary and was always on the look-out for something to fill his daily column of local gossip. He now came valiantly to my aid in the centre page of the *Leicester Mercury*. Beneath an out-of-date snapshot of myself ('local boy makes good') he appealed for anyone who knew anything about Chartists to write to me. The response at first was not encouraging. A publican wrote to say that his great uncle had been 'an important Chartist' and had once been in a clash with the police. An old lady sent a note in a very shaky hand describing how she had heard the old Chartist, Thomas Cooper, preach at a local chapel in the 1880s. From a spiritualist came a letter reminding me that many of the older generation of spiritualists had been ex-Chartists.

Then, three weeks later, I received a short note from a man named Fergus Stevens who ran a drapery and clothing business. It appeared that the writer was a great-great-grandson of the Chartist leader, who had named his son after his political idol, and the name had since become a family one, though the spelling had been modified. I had seen in the *Northern Star* periodical lists of Young Patriots who had been named after democratic heroes, Chartist and European, but I had not suspected that the tradition might be continued through several generations. Fergus Stevens however knew little about his ancestor beyond the fact that he had been 'a famous Chartist' who had suffered imprisonment. He suggested that I should talk to his mother, and hinted darkly that she might know about 'the papers'. I found her, a frail old lady dressed in black, living in a home for the blind in Leicester. Like most old ladies she was delighted to tell what she could remember of her youth and family. Not that it amounted to very much beyond establishing genealogical details. Yet she definitely remembered the portrait. Indeed, she once had a photograph of it; but a prolonged hunt through albums and a variety of little ornamented boxes failed to bring it to light. Where was it now? Perhaps, she suggested, I should have a talk with her brother. In any case he had all 'the papers'.

He turned out to be a retired yarn agent, living with his housekeeper in a Victorian villa in a large village a few miles away. It was clear that he had not a single idea about Chartists, but if he had would have strongly disapproved of them. Nevertheless he felt a vague pride in having an ancestor sufficiently important to have his portrait painted. The papers? Oh yes, he'd burnt all that stuff during the war; but there wasn't anything of interest, otherwise he would have saved it. My heart sank. What of the portrait? His niece had it now—and he gave me an address in one of the suburbs of Leicester.

It wasn't clear to me just why the portrait was at his niece's house; she certainly did not want it there. As she said, what could you do with an old-fashioned thing like that? It had already fallen down twice, and when it was up it seemed to fill one side of the little dining room in the semi-detached. At present it was in the outhouse. If I could call back on Saturday she would in the meantime ask her husband to get it out for me. A few days later, dusted and propped against the dining-room table, I saw it. From a murky background a firm, thin-lipped face looked out proudly. His hair was light and wavy, and in his hand he held a scroll of paper labelled conspicuously 'People's Charter'. There was no doubt that this was the portrait presented in 1848 by the 'Patriots and Democrats' of Loughborough 'for his great services to the cause of liberty'. I felt a vague sense of awe and, more strongly, triumph.

Some months later, it being a wet, bank-holiday Monday, I strolled into the new city folk museum in Newarke House. There in a place of honour on the staircase was the portrait. The canvas had been cleaned, the frame regilded, and underneath was a short inscription. A father and two children paused at the turn of the stairs to look at the portrait. The elder child read out the inscription slowly. 'What's a Chartist, Dad? he inquired. 'Oh, never mind no,' was the reply. And they hurried on to look at the arms and armour in the next room.

By the time *Chartist Studies* was published in 1959 I was well into the writing of *Learning and Living, 1790-1960*, a study in the history of the adult education movement based on Yorkshire materials. The thesis had dealt only with the early and mid-Victorian period and to this I now added the results of my researches into the early history of the WEA and other adult education and social reform movements down to the present. Yorkshire in the 1950s was a veritable gold mine for nineteenth- and early twentieth-century social history, and my travels to classes all over the North and West Ridings enabled me to comb the libraries, mechanics' institutes, and bookshops of the area for material. I soon succumbed to the dreadful yet delightful disease of bibliomania. The smell of the basement of Symington's bookshop in Harrogate or the temptations of Ken Spelman's ordered shelves in York were too powerful for me to resist. When I think now of all those volumes of Cobbett's *Register* mouldering away in Symington's basement, which I could have bought for 2s 6d. but for which I refused to pay more than 2s, I could weep. In those days when such treasures were still available I had no money; and when later I had more to spend the books had all gone. Even so, I managed to build a fine collection of nineteenth-century social history, spurred on by competition with Edward and Dorothy Thompson. Actually our respective book forays somehow did not clash, and we exchanged Chartist and Owenite pamphlets from time to time. I always felt envious of the Thompsons because I imagined that they had more money to spend on books than I had.

On one memorable afternoon in May 1960, Edward rang to say that he had just heard that the library of Bradford Mechanics' Institute was about to be sent to the municipal destructor and could I do anything about it as he had to go out to a class. Fortunately I was free that day and so I jumped in the car and rushed off to Bradford. Sure enough, when I got to the Mechanics' Institute I found a huge mound of books piled ten-feet high in the middle of the reading room, awaiting the arrival of the dustmen. I asked the librarian what was going on and she explained that the members had complained that the library stock was out of date and should be replaced. The second-hand booksellers apparently did not want any of it, so it was being sent for pulp. A quick glance showed me that in addition to the unwanted 1930s light fiction there were also items of solid Victorian history, biography and science; and, horror of horrors, sticking out on one side were the manuscript minute books of the Bradford Mechanics' Institute from 1832 which I had worked on some years previously. My request to be allowed to rescue some of the books was reluctantly granted, with the strict proviso that I should not upset the pile as 'the men will be here any minute now'. I was only able to pick out a few Victorian books for myself, but collected all the minute books which I later deposited in the reference section of Bradford City Library.

The pursuit of material relating to nineteenth-century social movements introduced me to many fascinating local characters. I found that my self-educated, working-class Victorians had left a rich legacy and a tradition that was still alive, though only just. It was a revelation to talk to Ben Carter in his little terraced house in Halifax, stuffed with furniture, books, ornaments and mementos picked up for virtually nothing. Ben, a widower, was a packer in a woollen mill. At the weekends he travelled all over Yorkshire and the Midlands to give addresses in spiritualist churches. He talked about Ernest Jones, the Halifax Chartist leader, as if he had died but yesterday, instead of in 1869. He gave me a ceramic bust which he said was Ernest Jones but which I suspect was more likely W.E. Forster (of the

1870 Education Act). From time to time Ben would let me have out-of-the-way pamphlets and books; but for this privilege I had to endure having a meal with him and his penchant was for half-cooked, rancid bacon and stewed tea. Then there was George Almond, also of Halifax. He lived over his second-hand furniture shop and had attics full of nineteenth-century books, newspapers and pamphlets, which he lent (and occasionally gave) me. I also found journalists on the local papers extremely helpful, both for their knowledge of local history and their readiness to suggest the names of others who might help. At Loftus in Cleveland in 1955 when I enquired about Joseph Toyn and the Cleveland Miners' Association, founded in the 1870s, one of the members of my tutorial class immediately put me in touch with two old miners, both aged 82, who had been members of the executive committee of the union.

I was also fortunate to be able to talk to George Thompson, the legendary first District Secretary of the WEA in Yorkshire. Born in Halifax in 1878, the son of a radical master joiner, he followed his father's trade. He attended his first tutorial class in Halifax in 1909 and became WEA organiser in 1913. Talking to him during the summer of 1951 about the early days of the WEA made me realise the limitations of written records. When I put to him the received wisdom from official publications he robustly rejected some of it and made me see that the nature of the early Tutorial Class movement arose out of the necessity of solving immediate practical problems rather than ideology. For me this was a training in historical method more valuable than any course on *The Nature and Methodology of History* which I was required to inflict on my students later. In the mythology of the early tutorial classes, attributed to R.H. Tawney and others (though rejected by Thompson as 'slosh'), it was claimed that the tutor learned as much from his students as they from him. I cannot say that this was quite how it was for me in the 1950s, but it is apparent to me now that without the experiences, friendships, and contacts arising out of my classes, *Learning and Living* would have been a much poorer book.

The other strong influence in my work came from H.L. Beales, Reader in Social History at the London School of Economics. I always felt that I came away with more ideas after half-an-hour's conversation with Lance than days of discussion with anyone else. He had a most prodigious grasp of nineteenth-century social history, derived from omnivorous reading in his huge collection of books. When I mentioned any Victorian topic, no matter how obscure, he would immediately draw upon his vast bibliographic knowledge and say 'Ah, you must look at so-and-so', naming some book or pamphlet which had no obvious connection with what I was seeking but which turned out to be a brilliant insight. He read my thesis and advised me how to turn it into a book. 'Shake it out,' he said, meaning 'get away from the institutional approach, and write it as social and intellectual history.' This I tried to do; and thereafter I always remembered Beales's precepts. He was also for me the model bibliophile. Beales's style of lecturing was quite unusual. He would arrive in the lecture room with an armful of books, perhaps as many as twenty, all marked with slips of paper, and immediately begin talking. He spoke without any notes, and picking up a book he would read a passage and comment on it. This he would contrast with a reading from another volume, and so on for an hour. Each lecture was thus original and was never repeated in exactly the same form. Sadly his great talents were never officially recognised in his own university. He was not given the chair he so richly deserved, mainly I think because of his failure to publish, though he attributed it to academic enemies who disliked his radical and secularist ideas. His memorial lies in the numerous acknowledgements in the introductions and prefaces to the books of his students and friends like me.

Another social historian who helped me at this time was G.D.H. Cole. As with Beales he had a background involvement in the adult education movement and the WEA, but unlike Lance was a most prolific writer. He was also an avid book collector, as evidenced by the Cole Collection, now in Nuffield College, Oxford. He was the foremost labour historian of his generation and was the acknowledged expert on Robert Owen and the early English socialists. I wrote to him about my interests, in particular my discovery of James Hole, a Leeds Owenite socialist who had been Secretary of the Yorkshire Union of Mechanics' Institutes in the 1840s and 1850s. Cole invited me to meet him in All Souls' College and over lunch encouraged me to think of writing a monograph on Hole. I followed his advice and the results were published in 1954 as *Social Reform in Victorian Leeds: the work of James Hole, 1820–1895*. The publication was made possible by a grant to the Leeds Thoresby Society from the Passfield Trust on Cole's recommendation. I mention this incident as a testimony to the kindness with which the enquiries of an unknown tyro were met by established historians of the calibre of Cole and Beales.

James Hole became a family joke ('Where's Dad?' 'In his hole again.' Ha, ha). But for me he was the stepping-stone from the history of adult education to my next piece of work which was a study of Robert Owen and the early socialist movement. I had long wanted to do something along these lines; my studies of Chartism and educational movements had provided the necessary base from which to start; the way forward seemed clear. Then in the summer of 1961 we emigrated to America and my plans were temporarily checked. But not for long. One of the main attractions of the University of Wisconsin was the support for research and writing which I could expect. Within a year I was back on track with revised and even more ambitious ideas. Every book is in some degree an intellectual or spiritual biography, and *Robert Owen and the Owenites in Britain and America* was no exception. It was also the centre round which our family life largely revolved for the next six years.

The 1960s in America was a truly golden age for academic research and my project blossomed into a cottage industry. There was money from the Graduate School for a succession of research assistants: Eileen Yeo (née Janes), Bob Storch, Barbara Frankle (née Stein), Bob Orrill, and David de Giustino. Fellowships and grants from outside bodies like the Social Science Research Council and the American Philosophical Society relieved me of teaching duties and subsidised my travel. The department provided secretarial help with correspondence. Wisconsin was famous for the fine collections of American material in the State Historical Society Library. But I also discovered in the basement stacks of the university library a tremendously rich assortment of books and pamphlets relating to the early European and British socialist and labour movements. For instance, there was a complete run of Owen's periodical, the *New Moral World*, as well as first editions of many of his pamphlets. On one occasion I found a German pamphlet with Engels's signature on it and took it delightedly to the Rare Book Room for safekeeping—only to be deflated by the young librarian who asked, 'Who was Engels?' Most of this material had never been used. I think it was part of the Schlüter collection, brought to Milwaukee by one of the old German socialists after the 1848 revolutions. The university library had a generous budget and was always ready to buy anything I requested, including collections of nineteenth-century pamphlets when they came on the market. Sometimes at the end of the financial year when he had not spent all his budget and so was in danger of being penalised the next year, the librarian would ask me if I knew of any collections which we could buy to absorb the surplus. In this way we increased the already impressive holdings in British social history. Working in this heady atmosphere—so different from the restrictions and petty economies to which I had become accustomed in the UK—I felt I was a very lucky man. Much has been said about the pressures of publish or perish in the academic market place. I was never conscious of any pressure, perhaps because I needed no spur to pursue my scholarly inclinations. The exigencies of academia harmonised with an interesting Anglo-American family life, for the career of Robert Owen conveniently spanned both sides of the Atlantic.

In 1963 we returned to the UK for a year while I worked on the sources. We rented a house in Islington; the children enrolled in the American School in London; and I burrowed deeply into the magnificent Goldsmiths' Library of early economic literature in the University of London. The Goldsmiths' collection had been assembled by H.S. Foxwell, a Fellow of St John's College, Cambridge, and later Professor of Political Economy at London. He was a great bibliophile; and to work through his collection of rare early nineteenth-century books and pamphlets, all beautifully bound in half morocco and arranged chronologically, was a daily treat. Like Beales and Cole, he was for me an inspiration in book collecting. The pursuit of Owen and the Owenites was not confined to libraries. At Easter 1964 I visited New Lanark, where Owen established his fame as a successful cotton spinner and pioneer social reformer. The mills and village were decayed and neglected, not yet restored to their former glory by the New Lanark Association; though the grim, granite buildings, set in wild beauty below the Falls of Clyde, were impressive enough. There were trips to Owen's birthplace at Newtown, Montgomeryshire, to the National Library of Scotland in Edinburgh, and to the International Institute of Social History in Amsterdam.

Back in the United States the hunt continued. In 1824 Owen had founded his most ambitious experiment in community socialism at New Harmony, Indiana. To my surprise I discovered that his descendants had remained there ever since, and that Jane Blaffer Owen, the wife of Kenneth Dale Owen, had begun a restoration of the settlement which has gone on ever since. In the summer of 1965 I made the first of several visits to New Harmony where I was warmly welcomed by the Owens and the Elliotts who were descended from pioneer settlers in Owen's community. The archives of the community and the Owen family papers were of course invaluable; but equally eloquent for me was the little Indiana town itself on the banks of the Wabash river, basically unchanged from the day in December 1824 when Owen first saw it and made up his mind to acquire it for his community. It seemed to me, like New Lanark, a monument to the Owenite past, a quiet, sleepy backwater which time had passed by.

When I began my study the standard life of Owen was Frank Podmore's, which could be usefully supplemented by the biographies of G.D.H. Cole and Margaret Cole. In the 1930s and 1940s the general interpretation of Owen and his followers was to see them as part of the history of the British working-class movement. Owen was accorded a niche in the standard histories of British labour and socialism, and Owenism was regarded as a link in the continuous chain which stretched from 1789 to the contemporary Labour movement. There was an older but still vigorous tradition which revered Owen as the Father of Cooperation and the inspirer of secularism and other late nineteenth-century reform movements. In America the emphasis was different. There Owenism was treated as part of the communitarian tradition by historians from John Humphrey Noyes to Professor Arthur Eugene Bestor. The standard accounts presented it as an episode in the quest for Utopia or an aspect of 'freedom's ferment'. New Harmony exercised a continuing fascination for essayists, novelists and writers of semi-serious history. For historians of American labour Owenism was a warning example of what could happen to working men if they allowed themselves to be misled by intellectual reformers instead of concentrating on job-conscious trade unionism.

As I read deeper into the sources I came to the conclusion that all of these interpretations were valid facets of the Owenite story, but each was only partial. None of them was adequate to comprehend the whole of the Owenite record, putting the British and American material together, and seeking the relationship of Owenism to the two different societies. The most widespread interpretations, which presented Owen and his work as part of the consumers' cooperative or working-class movement syndrome, seemed particularly unsatisfactory. They did not accord with the tone or feel of much of what Owen wrote and said and did; they largely ignored the significance of Owenism and the Owenites except in so far as they were theoretical socialists; and they distorted the chronology of Owenism by over-concentration on a few selected years. It seemed to me that the working-class movement approach to Owenism was too constricting to make full use of the sources, and was based on certain narrow assumptions about the nature of social history, the relation of ideas to society and the process of social change. If we were to set aside the various partial interpretations (that is, Owenism as an aspect of this or that social or intellectual development in one particular country) the central feature of Owenism was the dual nature of its role in two such different societies as early nineteenth-century Britain and America. That contemporaries should have considered Owenite ideas and institutions relevant in these two very different contexts could be the starting point for new questions and new approaches. Instead of asking what Owenism contributed to the making of the English working class, or how it related to American frontier conditions and westward expansion, we should have to examine the points of contact or similarity in British and American social experience which made Owenism acceptable in certain situations. I was greatly helped in working out an interpretation along these lines by my colleagues in the Madison History Department, where Merle Curti's work in intellectual and comparative history inspired a whole generation of young scholars. In order to break new ground I decided to try to use some of the techniques from intellectual history and also to experiment with a comparative approach.

Speculation on the pedigree of Owen's ideas was not new. Whether he borrowed his ideas from Rousseau, Bentham and Godwin, or was influenced by contemporaries in Manchester, has been discussed in his biographies with somewhat inconclusive results. Perhaps a more profitable approach, I thought, would be to consider Owenism as part of the whole complex of ideas of the late-eighteenth and early-nineteenth centuries. The hypothesis underlying this was that the ideas of the period are contained within a framework and have a certain unity based on common assumptions and attitudes. Owenism thus becomes a cluster of social ideas drawn from several sources united within an overall intellectual boundary. In this context both the originality and limitations of Owen's ideas would become apparent.

The second method—comparative study—had long been familiar in other social sciences and in literature, but was still rare in history. Although historians sometimes made allusions to parallel developments outside their particular topic of study, these were usually incidental insights, bright ideas thrown off in passing, and not followed up very far. Again, historians frequently made judgements (as for instance on the uniqueness or otherwise of an institution) which implied comparative knowledge, without being aware of, or making fully explicit the assumptions of their statements. In the analysis of the Owenite movement three types of comparative treatment seemed likely to be fruitful. First and most obvious was the transnational comparison between Britain and America, and to a lesser extent between England and Scotland. Area studies of Owenism in the different regions of Britain also invited this approach. Second was the technique of comparable personalities. In order to establish the uniqueness or ordinariness of Owen and his followers it was necessary to compare them with contemporary figures who were in a similar situation. Given two philanthropists with basically the same social position and ideology, why did one become an Owenite and the other not? Third, and most difficult was the use of comparative concepts and techniques from other social sciences. In establishing the role of Owenism in the new industrial civilisation of the early-nineteenth century I hoped that some help might be obtained from sociological concepts and from the comparative study of ideological systems. None of these three methods was without its weaknesses and difficulties, but it is in the nature of experiment that risks have to be taken. Moreover it seemed to me then that the general plight of academic history was such as to justify the historian in seeking help wherever he could find it, for history is no less than the study of man and society in the dimension of time.

The possibilities and limitations of this kind of study only became fully apparent as the project developed. It is in the nature of historical research that one's original plans have to be modified as one goes along. I decided to cast my net widely, to include not only Robert Owen himself but all those who could be called, in some sense or other, Owenites. The story was also extended in time: backward into the eighteenth-century Enlightenment, and forward into the post-1848 period. Nevertheless the life and thought of Owen seemed to be the central thread running throughout the material, and this provided a natural structure for the book which eventually emerged.

Of course there were some parts of the search for Robert Owen which were less exciting than others, which indeed bordered on drudgery. Owen's works do not make for easy reading. He was very repetitious and often verbose and tedious. At times I almost sympathised with Leslie Stephen's characterisation of Owen as 'one of those intolerable bores who are the salt of the earth'. Only Owen's autobiography has a freshness and charm quite different from his other writings. I always regretted that Owenites did not produce creative works of high literary quality, nor make any distinctive contributions in other art forms. There was nothing like the work of William Morris and the artistic socialists of the 1880s, nor anything resembling the communitarian architecture and furniture of the Shakers.

By 1969 my search for Robert Owen appeared to be at an end. The book was published—in good time for the bi-centennial celebrations in 1971, which gave an added impetus to Owen studies. But just as *Robert Owen and the Owenites* had developed out of my studies in the history of adult education, so another theme now emerged from its chrysalis. I had observed that many Owenites and other social reformers in the nineteenth century used ideas and vocabulary which were millenarian, that is, derived from a belief in a sudden change which would usher in a new and perfect society, the millennium. Although I devoted a chapter in the book to millennialism there was not room to explore the topic fully. But my curiosity was whetted; and ten years later the offspring saw the light of day as *The Second Coming: Popular Millenarianism, 1780–1850.*

Part IV
EPILOGUE

♦

A S WE GROW older
The world becomes stranger, the pattern more complicated
Of dead and living.

T.S. ELIOT, 'East Coker', *Four Quartets*

◆ 16 ◆

The Return of the Native

———————◆———————

WHEN WE WENT to live in the United States in 1961 we had thought that we should not be returning to the UK except for holidays and research leave. Yet a decade later we were back permanently in Sussex. So how and why had this great change come about? To our family and friends the move was unexpected and largely inexplicable. We ourselves had doubts and, in many ways the decision to return made little sense. Why give up a lovely home, a full professorship at a top university, and a host of good friends for a job at a lower salary? Even today I am not sure that I know the answer, though I remember the agonies of indecision and our subsequent rationalisations only too well. Had we not been so fortunately placed or had the family been unhappy the decision might have been easier. But Margaret had a large circle of friends among the weavers and craftspeople of Madison; we were well ensconced in Episcopal church circles at downtown Grace Church and at the campus chaplaincy of St Francis House; Richard was completing Part II of the Archaeology and Anthropology Tripos at Cambridge; and Elizabeth was halfway through her degree course at the University of Wisconsin. Why rock the boat by uprooting ourselves once again?

Until 1969 I had not thought seriously of leaving the University of Wisconsin. I had toyed with an offer from a Canadian university but decided that any possible gain was not worth the upset. Still less was I attracted by discreet enquiries from the UK as to whether I would like to return. In 1968 we spent a semester at the Australian National University in Canberra, returning early in 1969 via Tahiti and Mexico in time for the second semester at Wisconsin. That summer we left Madison again, this time for London, where we rented an elegant flat in Holland Park. The object of the visit was further research in the Goldsmiths' Library at the

University of London. But I was also excited by the opportunity of finding out more about an enquiry from the University of Sussex.

The first Professor of History at Sussex, Asa Briggs, had become Vice Chancellor and the university was looking for another professor to carry on the work Asa had begun. The post had been advertised and enquiries made, but no suitable candidate had been agreed upon. Would I be interested? At first I was inclined to treat this enquiry in the same way as I had dismissed other offers. However, as we were going to be in England that summer I agreed to visit Sussex and discuss the matter. I was already familiar with the university and some of the faculty and was much impressed by the whole venture. Sussex was the first of the new (1960s) universities and had already acquired a reputation as 'Balliol by the Sea' in the Sunday supplements. The campus, on a beautiful Downland site, had originally been part of the park belonging to Stanmer House, an eighteenth-century seat of the Pelham family, Earls of Chichester. The architecture, by Sir Basil Spence, was designed to meet the educational ideas which informed the new university. Teaching was to be mainly in small groups (tutorials and seminars) rather than in large lectures; subject boundaries were to be transcended by grouping studies together in schools instead of separate departments; a large graduate school was being built up; and a friendly, informal atmosphere was to be encouraged. A new 'map of learning' (to use a favourite Sussex phrase of Asa's) was to be drawn; the best elements of the British university tradition were to be combined with the most impressive achievements of American universities. It seemed to be a happy marriage between the Cambridge and Wisconsin systems. The Sussex history group under Asa's leadership was particularly strong in nineteenth-century social history; and one of my former Wisconsin graduate students and research assistant, Eileen Yeo, was now at Sussex. It was clear after I had talked to Barry Supple (at that time Dean and Professor of Economic History), Asa, and others at Sussex that they would like me to join them, and that I had only to say the word and they would make me a formal offer.

I came away flattered and tempted, but hesitant. That summer we debated the matter exhaustively with inconclusive results, since the contra arguments seemed to balance the pros. On the one hand we were perfectly happy in Madison and felt completely at home there, to the extent that, had we stayed, I should have had no objection to taking out citizenship, though Margaret might have been more hesitant. The UW was very 'supportive', as they say, and I felt a strong loyalty to the history department. On the other hand the offer of what was at that time arguably the most desirable chair in history in England after Oxford and Cambridge was highly attractive. The idea of developing a strong faculty and graduate school in nineteenth century social history appealed to me enormously. We also liked the notion of living in Sussex. At night we dreamed of the comparative merits of Regency terraces, leafy suburbs, and gentrified villages—and London within an hour's train journey on the *Brighton Belle*.

At the end of the summer we had still not made up our minds, and we returned to Madison hoping to put off the dreaded decision a bit longer. By October, Sussex was pressing me for a reply one way or the other. Still unsure, and fearful that I was being a fool to take a job at a much lower salary, I cabled my acceptance. In the last resort two factors tipped the balance. First, we asked ourselves whether we wanted to spend an indefinite time in Madison, and we said no. Attractive as the city was, the old ten-year itch was upon us. It was time for a change. The second factor which weighed with me was that I had come reluctantly to the conclusion that there was no great future for British history in the USA. The old emphasis on Britain and the British Empire as a major field of historical study had melted away, replaced by separate histories of the Third World. The special position of British history as the basis of American civilisation was lost, and the UK was increasingly subsumed under general European history. From an American point-of-view this was perfectly understandable. The decline of Britain's role in the world was naturally mirrored by a decline of interest in British history and a reduced demand for specialists in that field. The old Anglophilia of the Ivy League universities was no longer the potent force it had once been. This was likely to be a limiting factor for me in the future.

Our American friends and colleagues were surprised and hurt by our decision. 'But you belong here', they said, 'and we want you to stay. What can we do to persuade you?' Unfortunately there was nothing they could do, given the limitations of the American system. Normally an offer of this sort was met by a small increase in salary, an extra semester of research leave, and professions of comradely affection. Perhaps if Wisconsin had come up with some fabulous offer of a special professorship I might have stayed, at least for a time. But given the state of regard for British history this could not be. Even so, to our Madison friends the move was distinctly odd. To some of them it seemed as if we were leaving the human race. It looked as if we were rejecting America, which was far from the case. In fact two years later we were back in the States for a year at Harvard; and in 1977–8 we spent the academic year in Madison, where I was a visiting Research Professor in the Institute for Research in the Humanities.

Nevertheless, 1970 marked the end of a definite period in our family saga. We put the Madison house on the market and soon found a buyer.

He did not try to bargain on the price but requested that we should include three items that took his fancy. One was a large copper cauldron in which was growing a huge monstera plant. The others were two of Margaret's oil paintings, one of a leaping footballer, the other a landscape inspired by the cooling towers of an electric power station. We agreed to let him have these, though I now regret that we no longer have the paintings which were the products of Margaret's attendance at art classes during the Madison years and earlier. The house made $33,000, which was an increase of $7,000 over the purchase price, providing us with sufficient money to buy a home (with mortgage) in the UK. By June 1970 we were in Brighton, busily house hunting, while all our books and furniture were on the high seas, eventually arriving via Hamburg because of a dock strike in the UK.

But there for the time being, the story must end. This was how the fifty years of the mid-twentieth century appeared from the perspective of one of the lucky ones. Historians are very fond of labelling periods the 'Age of This' or the 'Age of That'. Yet we know that was not how it was for everybody at the time. In the 'Age of Elegance' there was a great deal of squalor; in the 'Age of Improvement' many people were untouched by the ethic of getting on; in the 'Age of Anxiety' some affluent people had few worries. Moreover a person's life span does not always coincide with the historian's neat periodisation by decades or single generations. So it has been for me. My life was not untouched by the events and attitudes of the Depression Years, the Second World War, and the 'Age of Welfare'; and I am only too conscious of the extent to which I am the product of my Age. But which Age? For me those fifty years are perhaps best labelled the 'Age of Opportunity'.

On the whole they were good years for the lower-middle classes, who were able, but only just, to preserve their distinctiveness from the manual wage-earners and to cling to the hope of 'getting on' in the world. The Second World War has been regarded by some historians as marking a decisive break in social history. For me it widened and deepened the break which had already occurred when I left home and went to Cambridge. But when the war was over it was apparent that not as much had changed as had been anticipated. True there had been a certain breaking down of social and gender barriers, educational opportunity had been widened, and the lower-middle classes were soon to benefit enormously from the provisions of the Welfare State. But in the 1950s the pattern of middle-class life was still much the same as earlier. However, when we returned from America in 1970 it was apparent that much had changed, and not only ourselves. The days of ill-fitting de-mob suits and underwear made out of parachute nylon were already distinct memories. Thirty years of virtually full employment had provided the basis for a new prosperity among ordinary people; and consumerism (a new name for the standard of living) produced impressive statistics of the ownership of homes, refrigerators, television sets, washing machines, central heating, cars, and holidays abroad. The cultural hegemony of middle-class England was undermined by the onset of mass affluence; or, to put the matter another way, there was a wider diffusion of the middle-class way of life. The 1960s also saw a spread of progressive ideas which undercut lower middle-class conceptions of respectability, especially among middle-class youth; the end of empire, already threatened during the war, reached its logical conclusion; and the ideology of self weakened old beliefs in class and nation.

I had hoped that the scholarship boy would also be a thing of the past, that in future there would be no need for such an imperfect and haphazard system of selection. For a time after our return it was possible to believe that such was indeed the case. The extension of government grants for higher education made the university scholarship system redundant. The number of university students from working- and lower middle-class backgrounds increased. But from the later 1970s there was a drastic reduction in the public funding of universities, which soon meant that students were back in the same position of having to borrow money as I was in 1939. Nevertheless, significant gains had been made. My parents (who were still alive) were in no doubt that they were better off than they had ever been. When I looked back to my childhood I agreed with them. But when I remembered my hopes and certainties as a young man in the 1950s I was reluctant to agree that anything more than a modest beginning had been made towards the realisation of that more just and equal society which it was my ambition to promote.

Index

INDEX

INDEX